Myers-Briggs Typology vs Jungian Individuation

In *Myers-Briggs Typology vs Jungian Individuation: Overcoming One-Sidedness in Self and Society*, Steve Myers unravels the century-long misinterpretation of Jung's seminal text, *Psychological Types*, to show how Jung's thinking offers solutions to the conflicts that have torn apart our societies. By challenging the popular interpretation of the *Myers-Briggs Type Indicator®* and similar instruments, Myers argues that we have not only missed Jung's main proposition, but our contemporary interpretation runs counter to it.

Myers aims to rediscover the overlooked argument of Jung's *Psychological Types* and make it of practical relevance to contemporary issues. He intends to refocus rather than discard Myers-Briggs typology, showing that there are further stages of development after becoming a type and that typological principles have a much broader application. Raising queries about the way typology is used in contemporary society, Myers uses literary examples, such as *Romeo and Juliet* and Carl Spitteler's *Prometheus and Epimetheus*, to show how one-sidedness leads to conflict and to illustrate Jung's solution to the problem of opposites. He also applies this to real-life political crises by examining the decision-making of key political figures, such as Nelson Mandela, Robert Mugabe, and those involved in Brexit or the Northern Ireland peace process. The latter part of the book relates Jung's process of typological development to his later writings on alchemy, notably the axiom of Maria, to show how they all have a common goal, the transformation of attitude. The book concludes by analysing the implications of the divergence of Myers-Briggs typology and Jungian individuation for the communities who use those ideas.

This book puts Jungian individuation back at the forefront of debate and will be essential reading for intermediate and advanced users of Myers-Briggs typology. Due to its political relevance, it will also be of interest to Jungian analysts and their clients, and to academics and students of Jungian and post-Jungian ideas and political science.

Steve Myers (no relation to Isabel Briggs Myers) holds a Masters in Jungian and Post-Jungian Studies and PhD in Psychoanalytic Studies, and was the first winner of the David Holt Prize at the University of Essex. He has published several academic papers, including in the *Journal of Analytical Psychology*, and has used Myers-Briggs typology in his commercial consultancy for over 20 years.

'Imaginative, captivating, and thoughtful, Myers provides a useful look into the malaise of contemporary culture and psychology. Through the lens of how a popular psychological tool (the MBTI) magnifies one sidedness in individuals, Myers explores the question of whether we can use Jung's real purpose of psychological types to identify and maximize the energy of opposites to build a healthier world.'

Roger R. Pearman, Past President, International Association for Psychological Type; recipient of the Isabel Myers Research Award and the Association for Psychological Type Lifetime Contribution Award; researcher, coach, and consultant

'The central thesis of the book, Jung's explanation of human one-sidedness, came as a revelation to me. Myers sets out to unravel a very complex story, and he does it with panache. He lays out what is meant by the transcendent function in such a fashion that it can seem like a realisable thing. He works through examples in our recent history of how transcendent results occur (and don't occur) because of attitudes major players have.'

Wynn Rees, former President, British Association of Psychological Type

'In a beautifully readable style, Steve Myers clarifies the connection between Myers-Briggs typology and Jungian individuation. He goes much further though by applying typological theory, spiced with contemporary psychological developments, to a conflicted political arena. Myers uses copious examples to illustrate, such as Nelson Mandela, the "Chuckle Brothers" (Paisley and McGuinness from Northern Ireland), as well as more contemporary examples such as Trump and Brexit. This is undoubtedly an important book for our times.'

Mathew Mather, author of The Alchemical Mercurius; *director of the Certificate in Jungian Psychology with Art Therapy and lecturer at Limerick School of Art and Design, Ireland*

'Susan Sontag once said, "The only interesting answers are those which destroy the questions." In a sense, that's what this book sets out to do – to reframe the way Jung's type theory has been understood, thus to provide answers that are larger than the questions that are usually asked. By accomplishing this, the book stands as an application of its thesis: that the transcendent function, which Jung intended as the beating heart of psychological type, moves one outside oppositions that cannot be cognitively reconciled – not just opposing type functions, but opposing models, opposing political standpoints, imagination vs common sense, adaptation vs individuation. I learned a great deal from this book and would recommend it to anyone interested in Jung, psychological types, the MBTI, and a practical understanding of one-sidedness – its contribution to the moral problems of our time and what can be done to solve them.'

Lenore Thomson, M.Div., author of Personality Type: An Owner's Manual *and former managing editor of* Quadrant: The Journal of Contemporary Jungian Thought

'*Myers-Briggs Typology vs Jungian Individuation* raises fundamental issues and challenges current practices that concern all type/MBTI practitioners. If we are to truly tap into the potential of Jung's theory of psychological types, Steve Myers' book is a must read.'

Danielle Poirier, MBTI qualifying faculty member, trainer, and author of The Magnificent 16

'By challenging us to think beyond the limits of typologies, Steve skilfully guides us through an understanding of Jung's problem of opposites. Using artful metaphors and insights drawn from contemporary global events, this insightful book calls us to confront and transcend one-sidedness in ourselves and the institutions we are part of.'

Ray Linder, leadership development consultant and trainer

'Steve Myers has written an important and timely book. Not only does he do a masterful job of explaining Carl Jung's concept of the problem of one-sidedness in Western society, he also corrects the widespread misunderstanding of Jung's seminal work, *Psychological Types*. While doing so, Myers also provides powerful examples of how moving beyond one-sidedness in our individual and collective development offers a better way to be and relate to each other. Given the polarized nature of much of contemporary discourse, this is a timely message indeed.'

Scott Campbell, international speaker, consultant, and author

Myers-Briggs Typology vs Jungian Individuation

Overcoming One-Sidedness in Self and Society

Steve Myers

LONDON AND NEW YORK

First published 2019
by Routledge
2 Park Square, Milton Park, Abingdon, Oxon OX14 4RN

and by Routledge
52 Vanderbilt Avenue, New York, NY 10017

Routledge is an imprint of the Taylor & Francis Group, an informa business

© 2019 Steve Myers

The right of Steve Myers to be identified as author of this work has been asserted by him in accordance with sections 77 and 78 of the Copyright, Designs and Patents Act 1988.

All rights reserved. No part of this book may be reprinted or reproduced or utilised in any form or by any electronic, mechanical, or other means, now known or hereafter invented, including photocopying and recording, or in any information storage or retrieval system, without permission in writing from the publishers.

Trademark notice: Myers-Briggs Type Indicator, Myers-Briggs, MBTI and MBTI Logo are trademarks or registered trademarks of the MBTI® Trust, Inc., in the United States and other countries. Product or corporate names may be trademarks or registered trademarks, and are used only for identification and explanation without intent to infringe.

British Library Cataloguing-in-Publication Data
A catalogue record for this book is available from the British Library

Library of Congress Cataloging-in-Publication Data
A catalog record for this book has been requested

ISBN: 978-1-138-23083-5 (hbk)
ISBN: 978-1-138-23085-9 (pbk)

Typeset in Times New Roman
by Wearset Ltd, Boldon, Tyne and Wear

Contents

List of figures	ix
Acknowledgements	x
List of abbreviations	xi
Foreword	xiii
Preface	xvi

1	Introduction	1
2	The type problem	14
3	The solution	31
4	The transcendent function	48
5	Many forms of opposite	60
6	Individuals, relationships, groups, society	72
7	The caduceus	92
8	Two movements	106
9	Axiom of Maria	122
10	Four perspectives	139
11	One-sidedness and analytical psychology	150
12	The future of reconciliation	175

Appendix A: *Prometheus and Epimetheus*	191
Appendix B: *Psychological Types*	201
Index	224

Figures

P.1	The psyche or self	xx
2.1	Capulet's projection of aggression	16
2.2	Four types of art	21
2.3	*Weltanschauung* draws on a range of attitudes	26
3.1	The caduceus	40
5.1	Psychological vs visionary sources	62
6.1	Raising awareness of personal vs collective unconscious	75
6.2	Interpersonal relations	77
6.3	Split group projections	80
6.4	The spread of complexes	84
7.1	The caduceus	92
7.2	Psychological and visionary modes of creation and analysis	104
8.1	Projection of unconscious and fused typological functions	110
8.2	Two types of differentiation	111
9.1	The axiom of Maria	127
9.2	Ego development vs Jungian individuation	134
11.1	One-sidedness score by age – East vs West	152
11.2	Different views of the spine of the personality	155
11.3	The colour green in *esse in anima*	169
11.4	The flag of Dominica	169
11.5	The checkershadow	170
11.6	Creating the reality of others' personalities	171
12.1	How Western one-sidedness spreads out in later life	183

Acknowledgements

Figure 2.2 contains a public domain version of Duccio's *The Calling of the Apostles Peter and Andrew* which is in the collection of the *National Gallery of Art*, Washington, DC. A public domain version can be found at https://commons.wikimedia.org/wiki/File:Duccio_di_Buoninsegna_-_Calling_of_Peter_and_Andrew_-_WGA06774.jpg.

Figure 8.2 includes photographs of the author completing a jigsaw entitled 'The Queen of Scots', which is made by Handley Printers Ltd, Stockport, SK6 2BR, England.

Figure 11.4 contains the flag of Dominica which has been adapted from the version at https://openclipart.org.

Figure 11.5, the checkershadow proof, is reproduced by permission of Edward H. Adelson from http://persci.mit.edu/gallery/checkershadow/proof.

This book is based on the author's PhD research (Myers 2017). Some of the arguments in this book have previously been published in a peer-reviewed journal for Jungian analysts (Myers 2016a; Myers 2016b).

All quotations are reproduced under fair use principles for the purposes of academic commentary and criticism.

References

Myers, S. (2016a). 'The five functions of psychological type'. *Journal of Analytical Psychology* 61(2): 183–202.

Myers, S. (2016b). 'Myers-Briggs typology and Jungian individuation'. *Journal of Analytical Psychology* 61(3): 289–308.

Myers, S. (2017). *Mythology for Christians: An Investigation and Empirical Test of C.G. Jung's Proposal that Protestant Theologians and Adherents Should Think of God as a Mythologem.* Colchester: University of Essex Research Repository. Online at: http://repository.essex.ac.uk/20065/1/mythology%20for%20christians%20-%20author%20final.pdf, accessed 13-Mar-18.

Abbreviations

CW3   Jung, C.G. (1960). *The Psychogenesis of Mental Disease*, trans. R.F.C. Hull. London: Routledge, 1991.

CW4   Jung, C.G. (1961). *Freud and Psychoanalysis*, trans. R.F.C. Hull. Princeton, NJ: Bollingen Paperbacks, 1985.

CW5   Jung, C.G. (1956). *Symbols of Transformation: An Analysis of the Prelude to a Case of Schizophrenia*, second edition, trans. R.F.C. Hull. Princeton, NJ: Bollingen Paperbacks, 1967.

CW6   Jung, C.G. (1971). *Psychological Types*, a revision by R.F.C. Hull of the translation by H.G. Baynes. London: Routledge, 1991.

CW7   Jung, C.G. (1953). *Two Essays on Analytical Psychology*, second edition, trans. R.F.C. Hull. Princeton, NJ: Bollingen Paperbacks, 1972.

CW8   Jung, C.G. (1960). *The Structure and Dynamics of the Psyche*, second edition, trans. R.F.C. Hull. London: Routledge, 1969.

CW9i   Jung, C.G. (1959). *The Archetypes of the Collective Unconscious*, second edition, trans. R.F.C. Hull. London: Routledge, 1991.

CW9ii   Jung, C.G. (1959). *Aion: Researches into the Phenomenology of the Self*, second edition, trans. R.F.C. Hull. London: Routledge, 1991.

CW10   Jung, C.G. (1964). *Civilization in Transition*, second edition, trans. R.F.C. Hull. London and Henley: Routledge & Kegan Paul, 1970.

CW11   Jung, C.G. (1958). *Psychology and Religion: West and East*, second edition, trans. R.F.C. Hull. London and Hove: Routledge & Kegan Paul, 1969.

CW12   Jung, C.G. (1953). *Psychology and Alchemy*, second edition, trans. R.F.C. Hull. London: Routledge, 1980.

CW13   Jung, C.G. (1967). *Alchemical Studies*, trans. R.F.C. Hull. Princeton, NJ: Bollingen Paperbacks, 1983.

CW14   Jung, C.G. (1963). *Mysterium Coniunctionis: An Inquiry into the Separation and Synthesis of Psychic Opposites in Alchemy*, second edition, trans. R.F.C. Hull. Princeton, NJ: Bollingen Paperbacks, 1970.

CW15   Jung, C.G. (1967). *The Spirit in Man, Art and Literature*, trans. R.F.C. Hull. London: Routledge Classics, 2003.

xii   Abbreviations

CW16   Jung, C.G. (1954). *The Practice of Psychotherapy: Essays on the Psychology of the Transference and Other Subjects*, second edition, trans. R.F.C. Hull. London: Routledge, 1993.

CW17   Jung, C.G. (1954). *The Development of Personality: Papers on Child Psychology, Education, and Related Subjects*, trans. R.F.C. Hull. Princeton, NJ: Bollingen Paperbacks, 1981.

CW18   Jung, C.G. (1977). *The Symbolic Life: Miscellaneous Writings*, trans. R.F.C. Hull. Hove: Routledge, 2004.

Letters 1   Jung, C.G. (1973). *C.G. Jung Letters Volume 1: 1906–1950*, selected and edited by Gerhard Adler in collaboration with Aniela Jaffé, trans. R.F.C. Hull. London: Routledge, 1992.

Letters 2   Jung, C.G. (1976). *C.G. Jung Letters Volume 2: 1951–1961*, selected and edited by Gerhard Adler in collaboration with Aniela Jaffé, trans. R.F.C. Hull. London: Routledge, 1990.

Foreword

I studied psychology in the early 1970s. It is with disappointment that I was exposed to Skinner and not to Jung. I first experienced Myers-Briggs typology on a qualifying workshop with Gordon Lawrence in the early 1980s. I subsequently became the first person to run *MBTI®* qualifying workshops in the United Kingdom (UK) – and by qualifying I mean ones that were recognised by the UK's guiding body the *British Psychological Society*. The wonderful thing about being the first to do this in the UK meant that I had a lot of scope to put my own stamp on the training. And all these years later, I find that Steve's book articulates the issues that faced me back then – the dilemma between a measurement process that appears to classify people that was derived out of a philosophy based on the exact opposite. So there we have a great example of the dynamic tension of opposites!

But winding back, let me say that it is with great pleasure that I write this foreword. I first met Steve when he attended one of my courses on 17 February 1993. I remember an enthusiastic and highly questioning young man with bright eyes and a sharp intellect. But I also remember wondering if, with his background in information technology (IT), he would get beyond the need for 'intellectual understanding, scientific rigour and theoretical modelling'. I am reminded of Jung's disarmingly wise quote:

> Learn your theories as well as you can, but put them aside when you touch the miracle of the living soul.
>
> (Jung 1928, p. 361)

Steve may not have heard me use it then, but few people I know have embodied that message as well as Steve. It is deeply satisfying to know that I have contributed, in some small measure, to his journey of exploration and understanding. And I now see that culminated in his PhD and in this book.

I pride myself that I know a thing or two about typology and Jung. My years of teaching people about the *MBTI* instrument, and then about the *Type Mapping* system, was always founded on the hope that it would ignite an interest into the nature of the human condition – and of course into Jung's ideas because he is one of the few psychologists who truly made that the focus of enquiry.

xiv Foreword

Today I continue to communicate and educate people using Jung as one of the ways of appreciating self and others, of healing divisions and building relationships. For those introduced to psychological type it requires a much better understanding of how type is a dynamic process of change and not a static process of identification of tendency. Communicating this idea has not always been easy or successful – and questionnaires that label in this way can sometimes be counterproductive. Hence, on reading Steve's book, I am delighted to say that it has helped me in more ways than I could have imagined. After years of hearing a certain comment second-hand, I have now learnt it first-hand – *that there are few things more satisfying than when the pupil surpasses the master.* Of course I hesitate because it is grandiose of me to cast myself as the master. However, I do not hesitate to say that Steve's appreciation and understanding of Jung now surpasses mine and that he is now teaching me.

The wonder of this book is severalfold. First of all, anyone who has tried to read Jung will know that his writings are not always easy – and at times they are downright confusing. However, Steve has been digging for gold and has brought to the surface numerous nuggets. But more than that, he has crafted them together to tell the story – the story of what was most important and profound in Jung's work; the story of how Jung's ideas evolved. What Steve has managed to do is to illustrate those ideas with clear and meaningful examples, analogies, and metaphors, many of which I will use myself.

I regard this as an important work. It is especially important for those who have grasped the limitations of psychological type – at least as it is commonly practised. It will appeal to people who wish to engage with the full depth of Jung's ideas. If you have been seduced into the simplistic view of type, if you have become locked into a one-sided view of type that focuses, if you have bought into the Isabel Briggs Myers view that you can only hope to develop your dominant and auxiliary functions, and the best you can do is to manage your inferior, then this book is your wake-up call or your antidote. One other highly significant achievement is the way Steve illustrates the parallels between the inner and the outer, the personal and the communal, and how the conscious and the unconscious are relevant for understanding and overcoming large scale international problems as well as those of the individual psyche. As such it gives a tool (and it gives hope) for addressing the big issues of the day.

One fundamental reorientation, that better use of Jung's ideas requires, is to become less focused on the past and more focused on the future. This parallels Jung's intense relationship with Freud. Freud can be characterised as focused on the past – 'how I became what I am'. In contrast Jung should be characterised as focused on the future – 'how I will become the person I was meant to be'. These are different worldviews and philosophies. This book will help you sort out where you stand and, if you desire, it will help you focus on the future, on the process of becoming, of being an agent in your own (or your client's) evolution. Yes, this is Jung's big idea which he called individuation. This book gives you both the intellectual tools for embracing this philosophy and the practical illustrations to make them real. There are few books where I would say that they can open the door and set you free – but this is one of them.

Roy Childs
Chartered Occupational Psychologist
Associate Fellow of the British Psychological Society
April 2018

Reference

Jung, C.G. (1928). 'Analytical psychology and education'. In *Contributions to Analytical Psychology*, trans. H.G. and Cary F. Baynes. London: Kegan Paul, Trench, Trubner.

Preface

This book is a spin-off from PhD research completed in 2017, but its roots go back 25 years. The journey has felt like being in the film *The Matrix* (1999). Morpheus gives Neo a choice. The blue pill keeps him in a familiar world, but it is only a virtual reality. The red pill takes him down into the strange world of the matrix which is a true and genuine reality. I have never faced such a choice but, over the last quarter of a century, have found myself slipping inadvertently down the rabbit hole. In my view, Morpheus didn't get it quite right because both worlds are real, though they are different kinds of reality.

The story begins with being trained and qualified to use the *Myers-Briggs Type Indicator*® (*MBTI*®) for use in team building. This is a popular questionnaire, developed by the mother-daughter pair of Katharine Cook Briggs and Isabel Briggs Myers (no relation to me) during the middle part of the twentieth century. It helps identify the different preferences people have for thinking and behaving. Along with other training in counselling and psychology, it helped me begin the process of developing better self-knowledge. However, when running a workshop with an IT team, I tried to use the *MBTI* instrument alongside a team role model (Belbin 1981). The aim was to discuss the differences between what people would prefer to do and the roles they were performing in the team. The exercise did not work because the team were more interested in trying to resolve the theoretical conflicts between the two models.

The obvious solution, it seemed to me, was to develop a new team role questionnaire that is based on the same theory and could therefore be used alongside the *MBTI*. The theory is described in *Gifts Differing* (Myers 1980), which is based on *Psychological Types* (Jung 1921). Using the former as my guide, I encountered various statistical anomalies in the new team role questionnaire that were difficult to resolve. This triggered a period of informal and formal research that has lasted more than two decades.

In my initial investigations, I found an intriguing statement in another book – *Jung's Function-Attitudes Explained* – that said: 'Scattered throughout Jung's writings are vague references to the functional operating modes: active and passive; concrete and abstract' (Thompson 1996, p. 40). This prompted me to read *Psychological Types* which at first seemed incomprehensible. However, when I eventually fathomed what these modes were, and changed the new team role questionnaire to take account of them, the statistical problems disappeared.

Developing the questionnaire was a powerful personal experience. I learned how to 'flex' outside my personality type in order to adapt better to each situation. The positive experience with the statistics – in which insights from *Psychological Types* improved psychometric performance – prompted further reading of Jung's work. One book that had a significant impact was *Answer to Job* (Jung 1952) in which he presented some controversial and radical ideas. To my reading, he reconciled the conflicts between science, psychology, and religion, using mythology.

In late 2006, I suffered a serious health problem that gave me more time to read work by Jung. The recovery was an enforced period of greater reflection, and my attention turned more to the meanings of dreams and films for my own personality and development. Thereafter, my interest in commercial activities waned significantly and the story takes a couple of different directions – one into greater introspection and the other into deeper analysis of the theory. Also, in October 2007, my research entered a more academic phase when I embarked on a part-time Masters in *Jungian and Post-Jungian Studies* at the University of Essex. My long-term goal was to undertake doctoral research to examine Jung's view of the relationship between consciousness and mythology. The present book is a spin-off from that research; it looks at the relationship between consciousness and the unconscious.

In arriving at this book, there have been many people who helped in the journey down the rabbit hole, too many to mention them all. Roy Childs was my first introduction to this area of psychology. He qualified me to use the *MBTI* and other psychometric instruments and has since become a collaborator and friend. Lenore Thomson, Danielle Poirier, and many others helped to develop my understanding of Jung through extensive discussions in internet groups and at conferences.

Several people supported my work through financial sponsorship to discuss my research and development at various overseas type events. These included Linda Berens, Kris Kiler, Dario Nardi, Jeanne Marlowe, Margareta Lycken, Dick Otter, Delia Homan/Jan van Rooyen, and Carolyn Barnes. I found these to be as much a learning experience as the opportunity to share ideas. Stephen Mathews has provided valuable friendship and support, particularly during my prolonged illness when he undertook much of my client work. My commercial work has also informed my research, and I am grateful to those clients who enthusiastically embraced type – particularly Rosie Sherry who promoted it widely for 20 years in each organisation that she worked for.

Andrew Samuels, a Jungian analyst and professor at the University of Essex, was my first tutor who encouraged a critical approach to Jung's writings. He also prompted me to publish papers at an early stage of my academic studies and provided the introduction to Routledge that led to this book. Roderick Main, another professor at Essex, supervised my MA dissertation

xviii Preface

and PhD research, and provided a great deal of expert and wise guidance. Other staff at Essex also played important roles. For example, during the empirical stage of the doctoral research, Jochem Willemsen took over the role of supervision and taught me a lot about the use of various statistical techniques. Also, my first academic paper was submitted to the *Journal of Analytical Psychology (JoAP)* and, because it was controversial, the editors wanted it to make a stronger case. Matt Ffytche gave valuable guidance on the extra research and revision needed to get the paper accepted (Myers 2009). Although the peer review and editorial process at *JoAP* is tough and rigorous, I believe my writings have benefited greatly from it.

Some of the above people have also helped by reading draft material – Roderick, Roy, Stephen, Lenore, Danielle, and Dario. Other readers include James Alan Anslow, Mathew Mather, Wynn Rees, Ray Linder, Scott Campbell, and Roger Pearman. All work within the field of either Jungian psychology or Myers-Briggs typology. There are four friends, with no direct connection to either field, who have looked at this work with a fresh pair of eyes to assess how accessible and relevant it is to a broader audience – Ben Green, Tim Swettenham, Alan Hunt, and Lou Holliday. I am very grateful for everyone's time, thoughts, and feedback, even though it did lead to a lot of rewriting!

Finally, I would like to thank Ann for her friendship and support over the past four decades. In particular, she looked after me during my illness, and has lightened the load during the last decade by taking on additional responsibilities and accommodating the extra demands that extended research and writing involves.

Terminology primer

There are four themes in the present book where it may be helpful to clarify the terminology. Many of Jung's words can have multiple meanings but, for this introduction, we will focus on the most relevant.

The first theme is how to overcome the problem of **one-sidedness** in self and society. One-sidedness describes an attitude that does not see things in a balanced way. For example, some politicians only ever emphasise the good aspects of their political party and the bad aspects of the opposing one. This is not a case of them being able to see both sides and putting the counter-argument for the purpose of good debate. The problem is that some politicians, and their supporters, do not understand why the other party have such different priorities or why they are against very sensible policies. Their reactions can lead to debates degenerating into verbal slanging matches, believing the other side to be stubborn, prejudiced, or pursuing impractical ideological agendas. This prevents us having a good political debate, which is what leads to better policies. Therefore, our biggest political problem is not our policies; it is the one-sidedness that prevents us from producing better policies.

One of the goals of this book is to overcome one-sidedness and reconcile opposites by developing a new, dialectical **attitude**, in ourselves and in our public debates. Attitude is a central concept in *Psychological Types*. It describes the tendency to see certain things or react in certain ways, and not see alternatives. Developing a dialectical attitude does not mean getting everyone to agree on the same view, nor does it mean that we have to impose rules of civilised discourse. It means that we become less tendentious and bring the opposing points of view into a constructive dialogue, even when some views seem to be offensive or irrational. In the political example, opposing politicians might still hold their different views, but they see a new purpose to the debate. They are no longer concerned with winning the argument and defeating the opposition, but using the discussion to find a solution that meets the differing needs or aspirations of both sides.

The use of the word 'attitude' in this context may be unexpected for some readers. For those familiar with Myers-Briggs typology, the term usually denotes the difference between extraversion and introversion. For those familiar with Jungian theory, the concept of attitude is not usually given such a central role. However, Jung made extensive use of it in *Psychological Types*, and the association with extraversion and introversion is a red herring. The transformation of attitude is an integral part of the transformation of personality, and the concept acts as a good bridge between Jung's theories and non-clinical applications.

A second major theme is the relationship between consciousness and the unconscious. **Consciousness** refers to everything that we can see, imagine, think, or feel. We can be conscious of people and objects in the world, or ideas and emotions in ourselves. At the centre of consciousness is the **ego**. This does not have the colloquial meaning of an inflated self-importance. It is a technical term that describes the sense of awareness that we call 'I' or 'me'. When we refer to the ego we are discussing the sense of awareness. The term consciousness refers to everything of which the ego is aware.

Consciousness is only a small part of our personality; it is the tip of the iceberg. The larger part is **the unconscious**. In the film *The Matrix* this is the world of the red pill. It contains everything that is outside our awareness (that is unrelated to the ego). The Jungian concept of the unconscious is different from that used in neuroscience, although there is some overlap. Neuroscience focuses on the biological processes that take place in the brain such as the transmission of information between neurons. The Jungian concept of the unconscious refers to anything that it is outside the reach of the ego.

We can illustrate the relationship between the ego and the unconscious with the analogy of being locked in the room of a house. We can only see the contents of the one room. We can't see anything in the other rooms of the house. In this analogy, the person corresponds to the ego, the room to consciousness, and the rest of the house to the unconscious. Another analogy is that of a sailor in a boat on a murky sea. Everything above the water is visible (conscious). Everything below the water is out of sight (unconscious).

Jung analysed the structure or layers of the unconscious using a number of different models. Most of them are not relevant to this book so we will ignore them. The main model that is relevant is the division between the personal and collective unconscious. The **personal unconscious** contains individual experiences that we have forgotten or repressed. For example, as a very young child, we may have had a frightening experience with a dog that we cannot recall but has instilled in us a fear of dogs. In the boat analogy, the personal unconscious is akin to the flotsam and jetsam that was at one point on the boat but has been deliberately or inadvertently thrown overboard. Some of it may now form a floating mass, just under the surface of the water, and it is interfering with the direction of the boat.

At a deeper level, there is the **collective unconscious**. The term 'collective' refers to anything that we share, that is the same in many people. The collective unconscious refers to ways of thinking or behaving that are instinctive, either within a particular culture or for all humanity. For example, a parent will instinctively protect a child without thinking about it. The term used to describe an instinct is **archetype**. In the boat analogy, the archetypes are akin to the undercurrents that can have a hidden influence on the direction of the boats that are on the surface of the water.

Our whole personality, including consciousness and the unconscious, can be referred to using the terms **psyche** or **self** (see Figure P.1). The term self also has two other meanings (Jung often used the same word to mean several things). It can refer to the centre of the personality, which is in the unconscious. It is akin to the centre of gravity of an iceberg, which is always in the part of the iceberg that is underwater. The self can also be viewed as an archetype. It is the most important archetype of all because it is at the centre of the personality and contains the instinct to develop our unique personality.

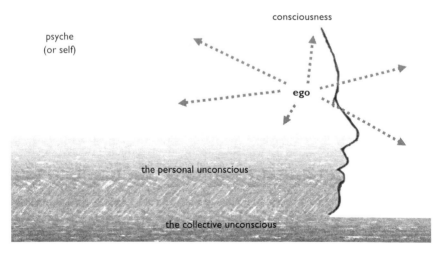

Figure P.1 The psyche or self.

The phrase **ego-self axis** describes the relationship between the ego and the self. That is, it describes the attitude 'I' have towards my whole personality, including the unconscious. The self includes both what I can see above the water and what I cannot see below it. One attitude might be to deny that the unconscious part of the psyche exists. Another attitude might be to recognise that the self is much larger and more powerful than the ego.

The third theme of the present book is a comparison of two theories. **Myers-Briggs typology** is a theory that describes some common preferences we have for thinking or behaving – such as whether we prefer to deal with facts or possibilities. Myers and Briggs developed the *MBTI* instrument to help people discover their preferences. However, in the present book we will be discussing the theory not the instrument. Although the phrase *Myers-Briggs®*, when applied to an instrument, is a trademark that refers to the *MBTI*, in this book we are using the phrase to describe the theory that Myers and Briggs developed:

> Myers-Briggs® is a registered trademark representing the Myers-Briggs Type Indicator® (MBTI®) assessment tool. Where there is no likelihood of confusion, the phrase 'Myers-Briggs' may be used as shorthand for 'Myers and Briggs' when referring to their theory of personality type.
> (Personal correspondence from Consulting Psychologists Press, Inc., Legal Department, 23 March 2018)

The second theory in the comparison is **Jungian individuation**. This is a process of psychological development that Jung describes in *Psychological Types*. It works towards two goals simultaneously – to become a unique individual and to become more whole.

Becoming an **individual** means developing attitudes that are not merely the same as everyone else's but include expressions of our unique potential. In the early part of life, we seek to establish the role that society expects of us, whether by direct demand or by compensating for gaps in social functioning. Our individuality usually remains dormant until later life, when our unique potential can start to emerge.

A **whole** personality means that we are not internally divided between the conscious and the unconscious side. In practice, it is impossible to achieve complete wholeness, because the unconscious is so extensive. However, we can reduce the division and work towards wholeness, which yields benefits for ourselves and society. Wholeness is a synthesis that arises out of the dialectic between one side (thesis) and its opposite (antithesis).

The individuation process of developing individuality and wholeness is often (though not always) a goal of Jungian analysis, which is a form of psychotherapy. Jungian analysis is sometimes called **analytical psychology**, though the term can also refer more generally to Jung's overall system of theories. We will use it in this second, more general sense, as we are concerned with non-clinical applications of individuation. Jung's original vision for his typological theory was that it would promote individuation in the wider population, not just in a clinical setting.

The fourth and final theme is the use of **alchemy** as a psychological metaphor. Alchemy is the ancient art of the transmutation of metals, which originated in the third century and is the forerunner of chemistry. Alchemists conducted experiments to understand the nature of matter, make metals change into (or appear as) other metals, and create the philosopher's stone which could produce gold from a base material.

During the nineteenth century, several writers reinterpreted alchemy as a pseudo-religious or **mystical** practice concerned with the alchemist's own psychological development. Mysticism is a form of religious or spiritual practice which Jung studied when producing his theory. Jung's theory is not itself mystical, nor was he a mystic. He viewed himself as a scientist and he experienced mysticism as part of his research into the workings of the unconscious psyche. He also used alchemy as a psychological metaphor to describe his process of individuation. It is easy to confuse Jung's theory with mysticism – as many do – because his writings often use mystical language to describe psychological processes.

Timelines and references

There are extensive references in this book that are presented in the academic format of in-line brackets – e.g. (Jung 1921, p. 410). Although some readers may have preferred footnotes, which are less intrusive in the text, in-line references can add useful information and save a lot of page turning in the paper edition. Knowing an idea's source can help identify whether it is a quote or paraphrase from Jung, a suggestion by a third party, or my interpretation of the theory. For some readers who work in the Myers-Briggs or Jungian field this may become important. Some of the ideas I present are controversial and challenge long-held beliefs. Therefore, in deciding how to react, those readers may want to see the source of that challenge.

Also, when citing Jung's letters and books, the date can set his comments in context because his theoretical stance changed in various phases of his life. Jung became a psychiatrist in 1900, and in 1906 started collaborating with Sigmund Freud, the pioneer of psychoanalysis. They fell out and terminated their friendship in 1913 after Jung had started developing his own psychoanalytic theory. During the First World War, he worked out many of his ideas in his private notebook, *The Red Book*, which was not published until nearly a century later. Jung published *Psychological Types* in 1921. From roughly 1929 to 1937 there was a gradual shift in his focus from typology to alchemy. In 1944, he suffered a heart attack that led to a greater interest in philosophical questions about the nature of the world and the place of the human psyche within it.

Jung continued to use typology to the end of his life but it was not central to his writing. He died in 1961 when there were a couple of books in progress, which were then published posthumously. One is his alleged autobiography – *Memories, Dreams, Reflections* (Jung 1963) – which was written largely by his personal assistant Aniela Jaffé (Shamdasani 1995). Her leading role in writing the book does not invalidate the information or quotes taken from it. However, we cannot be sure whether Jung had seen the exact wording or whether it is Jaffé's interpretation. Where there are references that contain two or more years, they refer either to the period in which Jung published the material initially as separate papers (e.g. 1930–31) or to the dates when Jung published a paper and later revised it (e.g. 1935/1952). In one case – an important essay 'The Transcendent Function' (Jung 1916/1957) – the two dates refer to when he wrote it and when it was published.

Finally, there are three people who are referenced using the name 'Myers'. Isabel Briggs Myers died in 1980, but some works were published posthumously. Therefore, all dates up to and including 1985 are a reference to her work. A preface to her book was added by her son, Peter Briggs Myers, in 1995. All references to 2009 or later are to publications by me – Steve Myers – no relation to either of the aforementioned.

References

Belbin, M. (1981). *Management Teams: Why They Succeed or Fail.* Oxford: Butterworth-Heinemann, 1993.

Jung, C.G. (1916/1957). 'The transcendent function'. In *CW8.*

Jung, C.G. (1921). *CW6.*

Jung, C.G. (1952). 'Answer to Job'. In *CW11.*

Jung, C.G. (1963). *Memories, Dreams, Reflections.* London: Harper Collins, 1995.

Myers, I.B. (1980). *Gifts Differing.* Palo Alto, CA: Davis Black, 1995.

Myers, S. (2009). 'The cryptomnesic origins of Jung's dream of the multi-storeyed house'. *Journal of Analytical Psychology* 54(4): 513–31.

Shamdasani, S. (1995). 'Memories, dreams, omissions'. *Journal of Archetype and Culture* 50: 115–37.

Thompson, H.L. (1996). *Jung's Function-Attitudes Explained.* Watkinsville, GA: Wormhole Publishing.

Chapter 1

Introduction

In 1921, Carl Gustav Jung wrote a book about one-sidedness. Jung was one of the pioneers of modern psychology and a psychiatrist whose research interests included a wide range of subjects, such as culture, religion, science, literature, education, and human development. One-sidedness is the tendency to favour a certain point of view to the extent of denigrating or failing to understand the opposing point of view. Although this is a simple principle, Jung had seen it have a powerful impact in mental health problems, the breakdown of personal relationships, and international conflicts. This wasn't merely an observation, he had experienced it directly. He saw clinical problems not only in his clients but also in himself, partly as a result of a difficult family upbringing. His working relationship and friendship with Sigmund Freud and other psychoanalysts came to an acrimonious end. And he underwent a prolonged period of self-analysis against the background of living through the First World War in Switzerland, which was surrounded by protagonists on both sides. Through this deep introspection, which came to be known as his 'confrontation with the unconscious' (Ellenberger 1970, p. 670), he saw these various conflicts as symptoms of the same fundamental problem – the one-sidedness of the Western mind. He developed his own version of psychoanalytic theory and laid out its foundations between 1916 and 1921 in a 'book and ... three essays, four works in all, [which] formed the core process ... that distinguishes his system of analytical psychology' (Bair 2003, p. 283).

Jung had high hopes for his book. He wanted the educated layperson to make practical use of his theory in a wide range of applications (Jung 1920, p. xi). The book was relevant to the lay audience because it described a solution to the fundamental problem of one-sidedness in Western culture. And it is still relevant today because the types of problems Jung described continue to occur, although to differing degrees and in different forms. For example, after a decline in casualties due to war in the second half of the twentieth century (Brecke 2017), they started to rise again in the twenty-first century (Allansson *et al.* 2017). The nature of conflict is changing through the increase of terrorism (Global Terrorism Database 2017). There is a resurgence in political conflict, for example in the rise of populist extremist parties in the European Union (Goodwin 2011) or

2 Introduction

in the increasing divide between Republicans and Democrats in the United States (Pew Research 2014a). The political mainstream is shrinking, aided by the echo chambers created in social media (Krasodomski-Jones 2016). This political one-sidedness or polarisation is being exacerbated by our tendency to live and move amongst like-minded people (Bishop and Cushing 2008). There is also increasing hostility by or towards religion (Pew Research 2014b), though the form of this prejudice is also changing. For example, there has been a decrease in violent incidents of anti-Semitism but an increase in verbal and visual forms of it on social media (Porat 2016). There is also a rise in mental health problems. For example, the proportion of people in the UK meeting the criteria for at least one mental health disorder was 15.5 percent in 1993, 17.6 percent in 2007, and 26 percent in 2014 (NHS 2016). There may be some relation between these various trends because mental health problems can arise from violent conflict (Pols and Oak 2007) or prejudice (Loewenthal 2017). The internet and social media may also be playing a role by changing not only how we relate but also the way we think (Balick 2013, p. 158).

Jung did not see his hopes for the book realised, because most readers misunderstood it. His book was about the one-sidedness at the root of the damaging conflict that he saw in himself, his relationships, and wider society. He attributed this one-sidedness to the fundamental nature of consciousness, which is to discriminate between opposites (Jung 1938/1954, p. 96). His book grappled with that problem and described a solution that involved developing out of one-sidedness into a more balanced approach. However, readers tended to view it as describing categories of people or as explaining the common aspects of personality. They missed Jung's analysis of the problem and the solution.

A lost solution

Jung's book has a misleading title – *Psychological Types.* The first English translation, in 1923, made a small step towards correcting the misunderstanding by adding the subtitle of 'the psychology of individuation' (Ress *et al.* 1979, pp. 16, 68). This is only a subtle change, which the more recent English translation does not include, but Jung made clear in later years that the main theme of the book is overcoming one-sidedness:

> In *Psychological Types*, I tried to establish the general lines along which … one-sided developments move … A dominating one-sidedness … leads to disaster.
>
> (Jung 1930, p. 33)

> Our time suffers like none other before it from a deplorably one-sided differentiation about which I have written a thick and – let me tell you in confidence – difficult book, beware!
>
> (Jung 1932, p. 89)

The act of differentiation involves distinguishing between two or more things or groups. It is by differentiating between two things, and then favouring one side, that we become one-sided. Jung's observation was that Western culture tended to differentiate to extreme lengths, creating an acute one-sidedness and division between societies, cultures, and people. It is the process of differentiation that underpins all the political, religious, and personal conflicts discussed above. Jung sometimes referred to this problem (of an overly-differentiated one-sidedness) as the 'problem of opposites' (Jung 1937a, p. 125) or the 'problem of types' (Jung 1921a, p. 8). That phrase, or one very similar, appears in eight of the chapter headings in *Psychological Types*. He discusses his solution to the problem in two of those chapters.

Jung became increasingly aware of the misunderstanding of *Psychological Types* during the 1930s. Readers saw it as describing ways of classifying people, rather than as pointing to forms of one-sidedness that emerge from internal psychological mechanisms. When writing the foreword to the first Swiss edition he said he had aimed his book at a lay audience (Jung 1920, p. xi). In his foreword to the Spanish or Argentine translation – *Tipos psicológicos* – he accused readers of misunderstanding it. He claimed their use of typology to categorise people was 'a childish parlour game [that] serves no other purpose than a totally useless desire to stick on labels' (Jung 1934, pp. xiv–xv). He said he used typology to classify the empirical material rather than to categorise people. He directed readers away from chapter X, which describes the common forms of one-sidedness that readers were interpreting as categories, warning them it is not the main content of the book. He pointed them towards chapters II and V, in which he discusses his solution.

The following year, Jung complained in a letter that the tendency of readers to classify people meant that they missed the book's 'gravamen' (Jung 1935b, p. 186). He acknowledged that he also classified people on occasion, but 'only when I have to explain to certain patients the one-sidedness of their behaviour' (ibid.). Elsewhere, he made an even stronger point that 'if you identify with [a type] you identify with a corpse' (quoted in Shamdasani 2003, p. 87). Jung's criticism of readers was not a superficial objection to putting labels on people. Rather, one of the messages of his book was that identifying with a type could damage the individual. There are some important exceptions, such as development in the early part of life, dealing with situations that do not allow individual freedom, or as a stepping stone for individuation (Jung 1921a, p. 440). However, typology is a collective psychology that in later life can repress individuality – and the development of a unique personality is one of the main goals of his theory.

The popular misunderstandings of Jung's book contributed to a shift in his focus. Although he started looking at alchemy in earnest in the late 1920s, in the early 1930s typology was still a starting point for both his writing and his psychotherapeutic practice (Bair 2003, p. 376). But by 1937, Jung's interests had shifted away from typology and become 'firmly lodged in the realm of

4 Introduction

alchemical writing' (ibid., p. 425). He continued to use typology in all aspects of his work, including material written before his death and published posthumously (e.g. Jung 1964, pp. 45–56), but it became less prominent. The metaphor of alchemy explained his understanding of the problem and his solution in a better way. By the late 1930s, Jung had all but given up on his book being the means by which laypeople could pursue their individuation. He wrote another foreword to *Psychological Types*, saying there was no point in revising or expanding the book 'when not even the elements have been properly understood' (Jung 1937b, p. xii). He had concluded that only professionals could understand *Psychological Types*. He made the same observation in an undated manuscript on the origin of types – that 'lay people could not use [typological theory] correctly' (Shamdasani 2003, p. 87). However, Jung did not give up completely because, after the Second World War, he recommended *Psychological Types* to the United Nations committee who were seeking ways to promote world peace (Jung 1948, p. 613fn).

Myers and Briggs

Although there were many people who read Jung's book, we will focus on the two who have become culturally significant – the mother and daughter Katharine Cook Briggs and Isabel Briggs Myers. During the First World War, Katharine Briggs was prompted to research personalities when she met her future son-in-law, Clarence Myers. Her interest was sustained by a desire to create characters for her fictional writing (Saunders 1991, p. 58). She read *Psychological Types* and, in October 1937, the mother and daughter met Jung when he was on a trip to the United States. After that meeting, he sent them some papers (ibid., p. 59) which include views that are contrary to their version of typological theory. For example, most people do not fall into one or other of the opposite type categories, but into a large middle group (Jung 1923, pp. 515–16). During the Second World War, Isabel Myers wanted to do something for the war effort. She volunteered to use the *Humm-Wadsworth Temperament Scale* to help people find suitable jobs. However, she found the results were not useful. In consultation with her mother, she embarked on the development of the *MBTI* questionnaire using Jung's typological theory as the basis (Saunders 1991, pp. 2–3).

In 1950, Myers sent Jung a copy of the embryonic *MBTI* questionnaire with some explanatory notes and asked to meet him when she was visiting Switzerland. Jung refused, though Myers was not told that. Marie-Jeanne Schmid was his secretary at the time and wrote many replies for him, which he often signed without reading. She wrote a rejection letter in her typically diplomatic style, using health and holidays as an excuse (Myers 2016). A few years later, a psychologist from the University of Houston conducted some lengthy film interviews with Jung. One question asked for Jung's views on the 'misconceptions of [his typological theory] among some writers in America' (Jung 1957, p. 304). Jung replied, 'God preserve me from my friends' (ibid.). He went on to reiterate

Introduction 5

the complaint he made more than 20 years earlier in the Argentinian foreword, that 'the classification of individuals means nothing, nothing at all' (ibid., p. 305).

In 1960, a PhD student (E.A. von Fange) asked him for constructive comments on research that involved the *MBTI* instrument. Jung refused, despite having once regarded typology as 'a critical tool for the research worker' (Jung 1936, p. 555). He said von Fange's research 'certainly does not coincide with the purpose of my book' (Jung 1960, p. 551; see also Myers and McCaulley 1985, p. 308, for a reference to that research). Jung expressed regret that his theory of typology had become a system of classification. He reiterated that readers had misunderstood his book and, as a result, he had become sceptical of typological research.

Myers also recognised there was some divergence of opinion between them. In her later years, she criticised him for overlooking something in his theory along with 'almost all his followers except van der Hoop' (Myers 1980, p. 19). From her viewpoint the differences were relatively minor but Jung regarded them as significant. Today, those who use Myers-Briggs typology believe they present the basic elements of Jung's theory in a more accessible form, albeit with slight modification. As we shall see over the coming pages, from Jung's perspective the popular interpretation of typology misses the most important part of the theory.

The result of this series of events is that the lay audience has lost the opportunity to learn about the typological version of Jung's solution to the problem of one-sidedness. He had wanted many people to read his book, and he believed that half the population could make use of his techniques (Jung 1948, p. 609). However, the version of typology that became popular does not explain the problem nor include any reference to the solution. Jung's later writings describe the problem and its solution using the metaphor of alchemy; but those works are not so well known and they use mystical language that is difficult to understand. At no point does Jung explain the relation of alchemy to the typological version of his theory that he outlined in *Psychological Types*.

What went wrong?

There are several reasons for the divergence of Myers-Briggs typology and Jungian individuation. Much of the responsibility lies at Jung's door. We have already seen that the name of the book is misleading, but there are many other factors. One is Jung's writing style. He admitted that *Psychological Types* is a difficult book and that his writing has 'the result that the layman becomes bewildered and loses his tracks in the maze of parallels' (Jung 1952, p. 10). One reason for this is that he wasn't only trying to explain his theory, but he was also producing a work of literature that was an example and expression of the psychological phenomenon that his theory described. He expected readers to engage with it hermeneutically, interacting with it and interpreting it:

6 Introduction

> Jung has often been criticized for his writing style. At times given to what appears as self-indulgent digressions, many of his essays seem to constitute an excursion around his topic ... In writing, Jung is not just describing the creativity of the psyche, his words also enact and perform it.
>
> (Rowland 2005, p. 2)

This approach can be frustrating for those of us who do not have a literary mind but are looking for a straightforward explanation of his theory. The present book abandons Jung's literary goal and seeks to explore his text purely as an explanation of psychological principles.

A further complication is that many of Jung's later writings use alchemical language, which makes it more challenging to grasp the basics of his psychology. It suggests to readers that his work is mystical rather than psychological, but this was a claim he rejected (Jaffé 1989). He regarded his psychology as scientific, and only included mysticism as one of his subjects of investigation (Jung 1935c, p. 195). Nevertheless, the extensive use of terminology from alchemy makes some of his work difficult to comprehend for all but the most enthusiastic readers who are willing to spend a great deal of time learning the language.

Another problem is that Jung often uses contradictory statements, both in formal writing and in informal discussion, to be witty and make a serious point at the same time. One illustration of this is a discussion with the writer Maud Oakes, who visited Jung to investigate the meaning of a stone mandala in his garden. Jung greeted her by saying 'The stone is nothing ... I did it to amuse myself. It is a holiday thing' (Oakes 1987, p. 15). As she left, Jung said 'I need not have written any books; it is all on the stone' (ibid., p. 16). The stone was both nothing and everything for him. He used paradoxes because his psychology 'arouses everything that is contradictory and unclarified in the human psyche' (Jung 1934, p. xiv). Also, when he reviewed the work of earlier philosophers in *Psychological Types*, he noted that they sometimes expressed truth using contradictions (Jung 1921a, p. 50). He concluded elsewhere that 'a great number of antinomies is required to describe the nature of the psyche satisfactorily' (Jung 1935a, p. 4). But he did acknowledge that contradictions can cause difficulty 'for anyone who thinks there is only one true explanation' (Jung 1921a, p. 493).

Another way in which Jung inadvertently clouds his meaning is by using words in an amorphous and protean manner. In some cases, this is to reflect the nature of a concept, akin to a caterpillar turning into a butterfly. Sometimes he uses the same word to explain very different ideas, to suggest an underlying link. For example, he uses the term myth in at least nine ways (Main forthcoming). Although it is possible to discover the underlying relation between those uses (Myers 2017), Jung does not himself explain it. Also, he avoids closed, rigid definitions where possible, because of the 'experimental, empirical, hypothetical nature of his work' (de Angulo 1952, p. 213). *Psychological Types* was a rare exception because he included a set of definitions in chapter XI, to make clear what he means by the various terms (Jung 1921a, p. 409). Whether he succeeded

Introduction 7

in being clear is a matter of judgment, but we shall look at some of his most significant definitions in the present book.

Another problem with *Psychological Types* is that it does not stand alone; it is not a comprehensive description of his thinking. There are several more essays and lectures that he writes during this time, but they do not form a coherent whole until the late 1950s. For example, he wrote one significant essay in 1916 called 'The Transcendent Function' but for some unknown reason he neglected to publish it until 1957, after someone discovered it amongst other papers.

There are also some translation problems that change his meanings. There is one example that may seem to be splitting hairs but it confused me for many years. In the English version of *Psychological Types*, Jung defines concretism as the antithesis of abstraction (Jung 1921a, p. 420). The meanings of these terms do not matter for the moment. What is significant is that, although they are opposites, elsewhere in the book he suggests that someone can be both concrete and abstract at the same time. This juxtaposition of words might seem to be a deliberate contradiction, but it is not. It is an error in the most recent translation which uses the same English word – concrete – to represent two different German concepts: 'objektiven' (Jung 1921b, p. 390) which means objective; and 'Konkretismus' (Jung 1921b, p. 479) which means concretism. The first translation by H.G. Baynes is correct, because it refers to 'abstract [and] objective sensation' (Jung 1921c, p. 458). The more recent translation by R.F.C Hull refers to 'concrete [and] abstract ... sensations' (Jung 1921a, p. 363). Jung's writing is already hard enough to understand without these extra and unnecessary complications.

Another example of a misleading translation, which has much wider ramifications, is the phrase 'well-differentiated' (Jung 1936, p. 549). We will examine the meaning of the term 'differentiated' later in this book but, for the moment, what matters is the use of the qualifier 'well', which can imply that differentiation is a good thing. However, the adjective translated as 'well' is 'verhältnismäßig' (Jung 1921b, p. 583), which means comparatively or relatively. It is value-neutral and refers only to the proportion or degree. As we shall discover in Chapter 8, differentiation can in some cases be problematic, and more of it can make things worse.

In post-Jungian research, there is an increasing realisation that *Psychological Types* is 'a cryptic work hiding some of Jung's most radical ideas' (Crellin 2014, loc. 189). This hiding of his ideas was not deliberate, for he wanted laypeople to understand and use his theory. Nevertheless, much of his material is difficult to understand. In part, that is because the psychological concepts he describes are inherently complex, contradictory, protean, and amorphous. His style of writing and the translation problems compound the difficulty. Also, Jung wrote *Psychological Types* whilst thinking about the acrimonious breakdown of relationships between himself, Sigmund Freud, and Alfred Adler. As a result, he focuses more on trying to make sense of these events, rather than showing how his theory applies to a lay audience with more general concerns.

8   Introduction

These various problems have contributed to a divergence between his understanding of typology and the popular interpretation of his book. It is therefore unfair for him to blame laypeople for their alleged inability to use typological theory correctly. They have not had the opportunity to use it in the way he intended, because the message has been laid out in a cryptic manner and confounded by a range of other issues.

Aims

More than a century has passed since Jung began to formulate his theory of analytical psychology and distinguish it from Freud's psychoanalysis. During that time, there have been many developments, in both theoretical and empirical research, which have made some aspects of his theory obsolete or inappropriate. His sketch of the psyche was often imprecise or approximate, akin to the rough map of the world drawn by the early cartographers. Also, his ideas reflect the milieu of early twentieth-century Switzerland. For example, he used language that reinforced European stereotypes about gender and other cultures. He also made assumptions about ancient-historical developments, based on the best available evidence at the time, which turned out to be inaccurate. On the other hand, there is recent evidence in quantum physics and brain imaging research that supports some of his most radical ideas, such as the reciprocal influence of psyche and physics, or the influence of the unconscious on conscious decisions. We shall touch on some examples of these post-Jungian developments, though they are not the primary purpose of the present book.

The main aim of the present work is to rediscover the gravamen of *Psychological Types* and make it of practical relevance to contemporary issues of one-sidedness and polarisation. It goes back to *Psychological Types* and extracts the message that Jung complained readers were overlooking. The divergence of theories, between the popular reception of typology and Jung's original intent, is due to a number of factors, not only those discussed above but others such as American psychology being oriented in the early twentieth century towards quantification (Geyer 1995). Katharine Briggs and Isabel Myers were not responsible for the divergence of theories but in the modern era their model has come to represent the popular interpretation. The present book uses *Psychological Types* and some of Jung's other writings to relate the gravamen to Myers-Briggs typology, the alchemy of individuation, and contemporary issues of one-sidedness.

In trying to make the links clear, this book draws comparisons and presents complex theories in a simplified form. For users of the *MBTI* or alternative questionnaires, this approach may appear to set up Myers-Briggs typology and Jungian individuation as a clash of titans and then declare Jung the winner. However, it is not the aim of the present book to reject Myers-Briggs typology but to reframe it, to show that there are further stages of development after type, and to show that the principles of typology can be applied on a much wider basis than is currently the norm. For those working in the field of analytical psychology, the book may seem to oversimplify the process of individuation, imposing unacceptably narrow or specific definitions on Jung's theory, and putting the emphases on some unexpected concepts. Again, the present book does not seek to exclude the nuance and complexities of analytical psychology. However, when seeking to make Jungian concepts available for use by a wide audience, they need to be presented in terms that relate to contemporary culture. There is some evidence that Jung was prepared to tolerate simplifications when they were needed (e.g. Jung 1954, pp. xiii–xiv) and he acknowledged that 'limiting definitions will sooner or later become an unavoidable necessity' (Jung 1936, p. 555). Although the simplifications used in the present book may have gone further than Jung would have liked, they will make *Psychological Types* easier to relate to the practical applications in which he wanted his theory to be used.

Overview

The majority of this book presents a one-sided view of *Psychological Types*, from the perspective of Jung's claim that readers have overlooked its gravamen. It raises questions about the way typology is used in contemporary society. Chapter 2 introduces type as a problem of one-sidedness, using the character of Capulet from *Romeo and Juliet*. It shows how a one-sided attitude can lead to intrapersonal, interpersonal, and inter-societal conflict, and how it can limit or distort a person's judgment. It examines three types of attitude – societal, common psychological, and individual. It contrasts how Jung and Myers viewed typology by looking at their different uses of the same metaphor – an army commander. These analogies show that Myers was interested in describing a personality. Although she also includes some development, she was guided by the past and the present, by how we express our inborn or developed nature in the here and now. Jung was interested in the transformation of a personality, by developing something radically different from what was there before. Although he took account of the past and present, he looked forward to what we could become in the future, to the realisation of our hidden uniqueness and potential.

Chapter 3 provides an overview of Jung's solution. It introduces the central concept in his solution, 'the transcendent function'. This term does not imply anything mysterious; it simply suggests the development of a psychological function that goes beyond the limits of the previous function. This chapter introduces the transcendent function and other aspects of Jung's solution with the example of the Northern Ireland Peace Process. It considers the opinions of some of the prominent politicians who were involved. Although some suggest that talking to terrorists was key to achieving peace, David Trimble lays the emphasis on the Irish Republican Army (IRA)'s realisation that they could not win. We will examine these perspectives in the light of Jung's solution to the problem of opposites, which involves giving equal respect and parity of power to the two sides. This chapter also uses Northern Ireland as an example to provide an

10 Introduction

overview of eight principles that describe how Jung's solution is relevant to overcoming one-sidedness. The following eight chapters will examine these principles in more detail.

Chapter 4 compares the attitudes of Robert Mugabe and Nelson Mandela when they became presidents of Zimbabwe and South Africa, respectively. The former was one-sided, and he brutally repressed opposition. The latter unknowingly developed Jung's solution – the transcendent function – at an early stage of life. He also gave it a prominent role in South African society by giving the two sides parity, by holding the opposites in tension. That is, the two sides disliked each other and wanted to separate, but Mandela brought them together and held them together. Holding the tension between opposites, or between people with opposite attitudes, is like holding two magnets together with the same poles facing each other. Each of the magnets is trying to push itself away from the other and a lot of strength and control is needed to keep them together and aligned. Chapter 5 examines how the solution described in *Psychological Types* can resolve many forms of conflict. To do so, it looks at Jung's analysis of Carl Spitteler's *Prometheus and Epimetheus*, an epic poem that Jung uses to illustrate his solution to the problem of opposites. Chapter 6 shows how Jung's theory applies differently to the individual, relationships, groups, and society.

The next five chapters explore other aspects of Jung's typological theory and relate them to his later writings on alchemy. Chapter 7 introduces the links between typology and alchemy, using the image of the caduceus. This is the staff of Hermes, the messenger of the gods, which is entwined by two snakes with wings at the top. It is used in the alchemical metaphor to represent the communication between consciousness and the unconscious. Before looking at alchemy in more detail, we will examine some criticism of Jung's approach from contemporary researchers. Chapter 8 summarises the alchemical process of individuation as consisting of two movements – *separatio* and *coniunctio* – which are alchemical terms for separating and joining. We will use the metaphor of a jigsaw puzzle to show how these movements correspond to two forms of 'differentiation'. Chapter 9 relates the alchemical principle of the axiom of Maria to the solution that Jung outlines in *Psychological Types*. An axiom is a statement that is accepted as a basic truth, and Maria was one of the earliest alchemists. The axiom of Maria was viewed as a basic truth throughout the history of alchemy and Jung used it to summarise his alchemical metaphor of psychological development. Chapter 10 returns to a key theme, the transformation of attitude. It shows how Jung's model of development leads to greater flexibility of perspective, which enables us to make better judgments. Chapter 11 looks at some of the theories discussed in Jung's other works, and how they relate to the problem and solution outlined in *Psychological Types*.

Chapter 12 concludes the book by examining some of the implications of the divergence of Myers-Briggs typology and Jungian individuation for the communities who use those ideas. It also provides a summary of the key issues facing individuals. There are two substantial appendices. Appendix A provides a summary of Spitteler's epic poem *Prometheus and Epimetheus* (Spitteler 1881). Jung uses Spitteler's poem to explain his solution to the problem of opposites. It forms the basis of the largest chapter in *Psychological Types*, and is one of two chapters that Jung suggests contain the gravamen of the book (Jung 1934, p. xv). Appendix B provides a summary of *Psychological Types* that shows how each section relates to the theme of one-sidedness and the reconciliation of opposites.

In summary, the essential argument of the present book is as follows. Jung's book on typology describes a problem, of individual and social one-sidedness, and a method for resolving that problem. Myers-Briggs typology is the contemporary manifestation of an interpretation that runs counter to Jung's goals. It redefines the problem and thereby removes the need for Jung's solution. Myers-Briggs typology and Jungian individuation are therefore two overlapping but separate theories that address different problems. From the perspective of users of Myers-Briggs theory, Jungian individuation has largely receded into the background. The challenge that faces us is how to bring it back into the foreground, for the benefit of individuals and society as a whole.

References

Allansson, M., Melander, E., Themnér, L. (2017). 'Organized violence, 1989–2016'. *Journal of Peace Research* 54(12): 574–87.

Bair, D. (2003). *Jung: A Biography*. New York: Back Bay Books.

Balick, A. (2013). *The Psychodynamics of Social Networking: Connected-up Instantaneous Culture and the Self*. London: Karnac Books.

Bishop, B., Cushing, R.G. (2008). *The Big Sort: Why the Clustering of Like-Minded America Is Tearing Us Apart*. New York: Houghton Mifflin.

Brecke, P. (2017). 'Conflict catalog: Violent conflicts 1400 A.D. to the present in different regions of the world'. Centre for Global Economic History, Utrecht University. Online at: www.cgeh.nl/data#conflict, accessed 14-Oct-17.

Crellin, C. (2014). *Jung's Theory of Personality: A Modern Reappraisal (Research in Analytical Psychology and Jungian Studies)*. Hove: Routledge, Kindle Edition.

de Angulo, X. (1952). 'Comments on a doctoral thesis'. In *C.G. Jung Speaking*. Princeton, NJ: Bollingen Paperbacks, 1977.

Ellenberger, H.F. (1970). *The Discovery of the Unconscious: The History and Evolution of Dynamic Psychiatry*. New York: Basic Books.

Geyer, P. (1995). *Quantifying Jung: The Origin and Development of the Myers-Briggs Type Indicator*, MA Thesis. University of Melbourne, VIC: Department of History and Philosophy of Science.

Global Terrorism Database (2017). 'Full global terrorism database dataset'. National Consortium for the Study of Terrorism and Responses to Terrorism, University of Maryland. Online at: www.start.umd.edu/gtd/contact/, accessed 14-Oct-17.

Goodwin, M. (2011). *Right Response: Understanding and Countering Populist Extremism in Europe*. London: Chatham House.

Jaffé, A. (1989). *Was C.G. Jung a Mystic and Other Essays*. Einsiedeln: Daimon.

Jung, C.G. (1920). 'Foreword to the first Swiss edition'. In *CW6*.

Jung, C.G. (1921a). *CW6*.

12 Introduction

Jung, C.G. (1921b). *Psychologische Typen*. Ostfildern: Patmos, 1995.

Jung, C.G. (1921c). *Psychological Types, or The Psychology of Individuation*, trans. H.G. Baynes. London: Routledge & Kegan Paul, 1923.

Jung, C.G. (1923). 'Psychological types'. In *CW6*.

Jung, C.G. (1930). 'Some aspects of modern psychotherapy'. In *CW16*.

Jung, C.G. (1932). 'Letter to M. Vetter, 12 March 1932'. In *Letters 1*.

Jung, C.G. (1934). 'Foreword to the Argentine edition'. In *CW6*.

Jung, C.G. (1935a). 'Principles of practical psychotherapy'. In *CW16*.

Jung, C.G. (1935b). 'Letter to G.A. Farner, 18 February 1935'. In *Letters 1*.

Jung, C.G. (1935c). 'Letter to Pastor Ernst Jahn, 7 September 1935'. In *Letters 1*.

Jung, C.G. (1936). 'Psychological typology'. In *CW6*.

Jung, C.G. (1937a). 'Psychological factors affecting human behaviour'. In *CW8*.

Jung, C.G. (1937b). 'Foreword to the seventh Swiss edition'. In *CW6*.

Jung, C.G. (1938/1954). 'Psychological aspects of the mother archetype'. In *CW9i*.

Jung, C.G. (1948). 'Techniques of attitude change conducive to world peace'. In *CW18*.

Jung, C.G. (1952). 'Foreword'. In F. Fordham (1953). *An Introduction to Jung's Psychology*. London: Penguin.

Jung, C.G. (1954). 'Foreword'. In E. Neumann (1954). *The Origins and History of Consciousness*. Princeton, NJ: Bollingen Paperbacks, 1970.

Jung, C.G. (1957). 'The Houston films'. In *C.G. Jung Speaking*. Princeton, NJ: Bollingen Paperbacks, 1977.

Jung, C.G. (1960). 'Letter to E.A. von Fange, 8 April 1960'. In *Letters 2*.

Jung, C.G. (1964). *Man and His Symbols*. London: Picador, 1978.

Krasodomski-Jones, A. (2016). 'Talking to ourselves? Political debate online and the echo chamber effect'. DEMOS (research charity). Online at: www.demos.co.uk/wp-content/uploads/2017/02/Echo-Chambers-final-version.pdf, accessed 14-Oct-17.

Loewenthal, K.M. (2017). 'Anti-Semitism and its mental health effects'. Royal College of Psychiatrists. Online at: www.rcpsych.ac.uk/pdf/kateloewenthallantisemitismandits mentalhealtheffects.pdf, accessed 14-Oct-17.

Main, R. (forthcoming). 'C.G. Jung's uses of myth'. In *Explanation and Interpretation: Theorizing about Religion and Myth: Contributions in Honor of Robert A. Segal*, edited by Nickolas Roubekas and Thomas Ryba. Leiden: Brill.

Myers, I.B. (1980). *Gifts Differing*. Palo Alto, CA: Davis Black, 1995.

Myers, I.B., McCaulley, M. (1985). *Manual: A Guide to the Development and Use of the Myers-Briggs Type Indicator*. Palo Alto, CA: Consulting Psychologists Press.

Myers, S. (2016). 'The five functions of psychological type'. *Journal of Analytical Psychology* 61(2): 183–202.

Myers, S. (2017). *Mythology for Christians: An Investigation and Empirical Test of C.G. Jung's Proposal that Protestant Theologians and Adherents Should Think of God as a Mythologem*. Colchester: University of Essex Research Repository. Online at: http://repository.essex.ac.uk/20065/1/mythology%20for%20christians%20-%20author%20 final.pdf, accessed 13-Mar-18.

NHS (2016). *Key Facts and Trends in Mental Health*. London: National Health Service Confederation. Online at: www.nhsconfed.org/~/media/Confederation/Files/Public ations/Documents/MHN%20key%20facts%20and%20trends%20factsheet_Fs1356_3_ WEB.pdf, accessed 14-Oct-17.

Oakes, M. (1987). *The Stone Speaks: The Memoir of a Personal Transformation*. Wilmette, IL: Chiron Publications.

Pew Research (2014a). '7 things to know about polarization in America'. Pew Research Center. Online at: www.pewresearch.org/fact-tank/2014/06/12/7-things-to-know-about-polarization-in-america/, accessed 16-Mar-17.

Pew Research (2014b). 'Religious hostilities reach six-year high'. Pew Research Center. Online at: www.pewforum.org/2014/01/14/religious-hostilities-reach-six-year-high/, accessed 16-Oct-17.

Pols, H., Oak, S. (2007). 'War and military mental health: The US psychiatric response in the 20th century'. *American Journal of Public Health* 97(12): 2132–42. Online at: www.ncbi.nlm.nih.gov/pmc/articles/PMC2089086/, accessed 14-Oct-17.

Porat, D. (ed.) (2016). *Antisemitism Worldwide 2016*. Tel Aviv: Kantor Center. Online at: http://humanities1.tau.ac.il/roth/images/general-analysis_2016.pdf, accessed 14-Oct-17.

Ress, L. *et al.* (compilers) (1979). *General Bibliography of C.G. Jung's Writings*. Princeton, NJ: Princeton University Press.

Rowland, S. (2005). *Jung as a Writer*. Hove: Routledge.

Saunders, F.W. (1991). *Katharine and Isabel*. Palo Alto, CA: Consulting Psychologists Press.

Shamdasani, S. (2003). *Jung and the Making of Modern Psychology: The Dream of a Science*. Cambridge: Cambridge University Press.

Spitteler, C. (1881). *Prometheus and Epimetheus*, trans. James F. Muirhead. London: Jarrolds Publishers.

Chapter 2

The type problem

William Shakespeare's *Romeo and Juliet* is a tragedy, though it does have a hint of hope and transformation in its ending. It opens with a conflict between two respectable families which affects many other people in Verona. The prince has to rebuke the heads of the families – Capulet and Montague – for repeatedly fighting and having 'disturb'd the quiet of our streets' (Shakespeare 1982, *Romeo and Juliet*, I.i.96). Capulet, caring for his daughter Juliet's future, arranges a respectable marriage to Paris, a member of the royal household. However, Juliet falls in love with Romeo, who is a member of the opposing family, the Montagues. The conflict between the families thereby becomes a dilemma for Juliet. The story ends in tragedy, with the deaths of Romeo and Juliet, which resolves the conflict between the families and restores peace to Verona. The Chorus explains the plot in his opening summary:

> Two households, both alike in dignity,
> In fair Verona, where we lay our scene,
> From ancient grudge break to new mutiny,
> Where civil blood makes civil hands unclean.
> From forth the fatal loins of these two foes
> A pair of star-cross'd lovers take their life;
> Whose misadventur'd piteous overthrows
> Do with their death bury their parents' strife.
>   (Shakespeare 1982, *Romeo and*
>   *Juliet*, I.i.1–8)

In the four centuries since Shakespeare wrote his plays, many things have changed. For example, modern technology enables us to interact with people on the other side of the planet, and it gives us the ability to destroy all life on earth within minutes. However, our psychology is largely the same, and Shakespeare's ability to capture our emotions has not diminished. We love, we hate, we struggle with relationships, and we struggle with ourselves. And it sometimes takes a tragedy to make us face up to the problems that we are otherwise unable to acknowledge. *Romeo and Juliet* is a compelling and moving story because it reflects significant and enduring truths about ourselves and the societies in which we live. Capulet points to an aspect of our contemporary Western psychology.

Capulet's 'attitude'

Shakespeare gives the opening words to the Chorus, someone who is independent of the two families. The Chorus is not independent of the play, for he has a certain perspective and role. He engages the audience by setting the scene and, later, by giving them a link to the second act. But the Chorus is independent of the families, which enables him to describe their feud in a balanced way. He sees the Capulets and the Montagues as alike in dignity.

In theory, Shakespeare could have given the opening words to Capulet. He is the head of a prominent household in Veronese society, a central figure in the story, and the person who takes the first step of reconciliation at the end of the play. If Capulet had spoken at the start, he would have presented a one-sided view. He has strong values that he uses to judge what is right and wrong which means he can only see the dignity of his household and the evil of the other. The Montagues do not live up to his values and they pose a threat to the security of his family. He sees himself as the hero – someone who is good and defeats evil – and he sees Montague as the villain. Capulet excludes from his perspective both Montague's positive attributes and his own negative ones. He sees things in a very one-sided way.

There are also two sides to Capulet's character, which are related to his one-sided perspective. One is a noble, prosperous, and respected man. He does what is best for his daughter, according to the culture of the time, by organising her marriage to a worthy husband. He also ensures that his family adheres to the standards of behaviour expected of prominent citizens of Verona. For example, when he holds a feast in his house later in the play, Capulet admonishes Tybalt, a member of his own family, for wanting to attack Romeo, a member of the Montague family. When Tybalt rejects the admonishment, Capulet makes Tybalt withdraw from the party.

The other side of Capulet's character is an unconscious aggression; he cannot see it in himself. It is autonomous, having a life of its own, and sometimes takes over his conscious attitude. This emotional hijacking makes him think or behave in a way that is contrary to his preferences. For example, early in the play, servants from the Capulet household provoke a fight with servants of the Montagues. Benvolio, who is a Montague, enters and tries to calm things down. Tybalt then comes onto the scene, attacks Benvolio, and draws him into the fight. Various members of the two households join in, and it escalates into a fray. Hearing the noise, Capulet enters the scene and calls for his sword. His wife wittingly points out that he is too old to use a sword and asks why he wants it. Capulet, seeing that Montague is about to enter, justifies himself by falsely accusing Montague of drawing his sword first:

16 The type problem

> *Cap.* What noise is this? – Give me my long sword, ho!
> *La Cap.* A crutch, a crutch! – Why call you for a sword?
> *Cap.* My sword, I say! – Old Montague is come,
> And flourishes his blade in spite of me.
> *Enter* Montague *and* Lady Montague
>   (Shakespeare 1982, *Romeo and Juliet*, I.i.80–83)

The scene illustrates four essential things about Capulet's attitude. The first is that Capulet reacts automatically. When he hears the noise, there is no need for him to get involved. He could try to calm the situation down, as Benvolio had done. He could call on members of his household to withdraw, just as he does with Tybalt at the feast. But none of this occurs to Capulet. His automatic reaction is to call for his sword and enter the fray, which escalates the conflict. He is ready to react in a certain way; he is up for a fight. Capulet's automatic reaction, his readiness to fight, inflicts damage to his reputation and makes his family more unpopular with the other citizens who want a peaceful Verona.

Secondly, Capulet has limited judgment. He misjudges the situation because he cannot see his own aggression, he projects it into Montague (see Figure 2.1). The process of psychological projection involves one person denying a characteristic in themselves but seeing it in another person instead. In this case, Capulet's projection means that he fails to see his own aggression but sees Montague's aggression and exaggerates it. This is demonstrated by his reaction when his wife challenges him. Capulet justifies calling for his sword by claiming that Montague is approaching and brandishing his sword. But Capulet calls for his sword first, in response to the noise and fray, and before Montague enters. Although Montague also reacts in an aggressive way, Capulet sees only Montague's aggression and wrongly blames Montague for starting the fight.

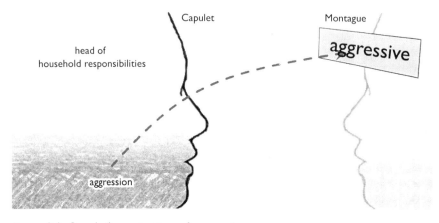

Figure 2.1 Capulet's projection of aggression.

The type problem 17

Thirdly, Capulet's attitude is extreme. The fact that there is a fight at all – and problems later in the story – is due to the strength with which Capulet adheres to his values. He takes his responsibilities very seriously, including finding his daughter a good husband and protecting his family. He does what Verona society expects the head of the household to do. The problems in the play lie not in the social attitudes themselves, but in Capulet going too far with them. He defends his household so vehemently that he becomes aggressive, and it leads to others becoming aggressive as well. He is so determined to find Juliet a good husband that he rides roughshod over her feelings.

Finally, there is a fundamental split within Capulet's psyche. His conscious attitude is to be a responsible citizen and a good head of the household. He upholds the values of Verona society, he looks after his family, and he fulfils his responsibilities. His unconscious attitude is to create unnecessary conflict and stir up aggression. This split between the conscious and unconscious side leads to an inner conflict, which he cannot see in himself. He is also unable to recognise the connection between the conflict in himself and the conflict in the world around him. The battle between Capulet and Montague, and between their households, is due in part to the split within Capulet between the two sides of his character.

Capulet's one-sidedness means that he is unable to see how his behaviour is undermining those things that he holds dear. It affects his reputation, his relationship with Montague, and the conflict between the two sets of servants. It also damages Juliet and is a factor in her death when she cannot get her father to recognise her feelings. Capulet creates for himself a reassuringly safe world-view. He wants certainty, and he avoids ambiguity, contradiction, and paradox. He achieves it by ignoring or repressing those things that are not compatible with his viewpoint. He will not face up to the split in himself, so he unwittingly transfers the conflict into Juliet. She falls in love with Romeo and discovers that he is a member of the opposing family, which creates turmoil between her love for Romeo and her family's hatred of the Montagues:

> My only love sprung from my only hate!
> Too early seen unknown, and known too late!
> Prodigious birth of love it is to me,
> That I must love a loathed enemy.
> > (Shakespeare 1982, *Romeo and Juliet*,
> > I.v.138–41)

Capulet's one-sidedness is not solely a bad thing; it is also responsible for his family having a position of respect in Verona society. 'The capacity for … one-sidedness is the secret of success – of a sort, for which reason our civilization assiduously strives to foster it' (Jung 1917/1926/1943, p. 72). In contemporary life, one-sidedness leads to outstanding achievements in the fields of science, economics, politics, religion, and many more. It is a natural result of the way the conscious mind works, the essence of which is to distinguish between opposites

18   The type problem

(Jung 1921, p. 112). To develop consciousness, we need to become one-sided, even though it causes problems. This means that 'one-sidedness is an unavoidable and necessary characteristic ... It is an advantage and a drawback at the same time' (Jung 1916/1957, p. 71). To overcome the problems, we then need to develop further, so that we can see both sides and use them in a more balanced way. In the long term, the major problems do not arise from one-sidedness per se but from it becoming excessive or involuntary.

> A *conscious* capacity for one-sidedness is a sign of the highest culture, but *involuntary* one-sidedness, i.e. the inability to be anything but one-sided, is a sign of barbarism.
>
> (Jung 1921, p. 207, original italics)

One-sided attitudes

When Jung started to investigate the breakdown of relations between himself, Freud, and Adler, he initially found an explanation in the philosophy of William James. The latter's two psychological types – tough-minded and tender-minded – coincided with the different theoretical views expressed by Freud and Adler. In his first paper on the problem, now appendix 1 of *Psychological Types*, Jung adapted James' ideas and coined the expressions extraversion and introversion (Jung 1913, p. 500). Freud is extraverted, so his theory is extraverted. Adler is introverted, so his theory is introverted. Their theories are one-sided because their personalities are one-sided (Jung 1921, p. 62). Their one-sidedness creates conflict in their relationship and between the two groups of psychoanalysts who base their work on either Freud or Adler. We can see a similar pattern in *Romeo and Juliet.* The one-sidedness of both Capulet and Montague distorts their view of themselves and each other, which leads to conflict in their relationship, and in the relationship between the two families. There is a close link between the one-sidedness of leaders and the one-sidedness of groups.

Having recognised the problems caused by one-sidedness in himself and others, Jung wrote *Psychological Types* to describe how to overcome it. As part of his critique of Western culture, he described the typical forms of one-sidedness that lie at the root of personal and societal conflict. The central theme, or gravamen, of *Psychological Types* is his theory of how that conflict can be resolved, though it takes a bit of investigation to uncover. Jung weaves it into the book alongside extensive historical analysis of the development of ideas by earlier philosophers and psychologists. Jung illustrates it using texts with which few modern readers will be familiar. And, although Jung dedicates an entire chapter to definitions, he sometimes obscures his meaning through the extensive use of cross references. We have to follow a chain of references to understand one of the central concepts in the book, a psychological type. He begins the definition of a type, which is a page long, by describing the common or general understanding of the term, and he then explains how he uses the word in the book:

The type problem 19

In the narrower sense used in this particular work, a type is a characteristic specimen of a general *attitude* (q.v.).

(Jung 1921, p. 482, original italics)

The psychological types are therefore forms of attitude which, if we follow the cross reference, has a much longer definition. It extends for more than three pages and begins with a brief history of the term. Jung then describes how it leads to one-sidedness:

For us, attitude is a readiness of the psyche to act or react in a certain way ... A selection or judgment takes place which excludes anything irrelevant ... The selection is implicit in the attitude and takes place automatically ... This automatic phenomenon is an essential cause of the one-sidedness of conscious *orientation* (q.v.).

(Jung 1921, pp. 414–15, original italics)

Attitudes automatically select some things and exclude others, thereby causing one-sidedness. Jung gives the example of oppression, in which 'an oppressed person has a conscious attitude that always anticipates oppression' (Jung 1921, p. 416). He is not suggesting that the person imagines their oppression. Rather, through being habitually oppressed, the person develops an attitude that starts to expect it. There are more examples of attitude in the cross reference to the definition of *orientation*, which is the 'general principle governing an *attitude* (q.v.). Every attitude is oriented by a certain viewpoint' (Jung 1921, p. 456, original italics). Jung gives the examples of a power attitude, a thinking or logical attitude, and a sensation or facts-oriented attitude.

Two of these examples relate to a basic concept in Myers-Briggs typology. Jung's use of the word 'thinking' in this context does not have the usual generic connotation – of something happening in the mind – but it has a very specific meaning; it refers to a particular typological function. In Jung's theory, a function is a psychological activity that is the same in a variety of conditions or circumstances (Jung 1921, p. 436). There are four basic typological functions that, in any and all circumstances, produce the same attitude – sensation produces an attitude that notices facts, intuition notices possibilities, thinking notices logical connections, and feeling notices values. In his definition of orientation, referred to above, Jung mentions the psychological functions of thinking and sensation as producing a logical and facts-oriented attitude, respectively. However, two more examples in the discussion are unrelated to typological functions – oppression and power. That is, a typological function is a form of attitude but there are many others.

In his definition of attitude, Jung describes three types – social, typological, and individual. In later works, he writes much more about archetypes, which are unconscious and instinctive ways of behaving that can be viewed as unconscious attitudes. These have the same basic nature as typology; they are part of our

20 The type problem

phylogenetic inheritance. The difference is that typology is primarily concerned with consciousness and archetypes with the unconscious. I am therefore going to rename the middle category as 'common psychological attitudes', to include both typology and archetypes.

Social attitudes

'Social attitudes [are] those on which a collective idea has set its stamp' (Jung 1921, p. 417). Much of Jung's definition of social attitude is in evidence in Capulet. For example, he has a readiness to find Juliet a good husband – an attitude that is part of the culture of the time. The governing principle is that the head of the household plays a leading role in making important decisions that affect the members of that household. Capulet's view of his responsibilities dominates many of his actions throughout the play.

Jung suggests that one way to identify social attitudes in contemporary life is to look at words ending in 'ism'. He gives the examples of 'materialism, atheism, communism, socialism, liberalism, intellectualism, [and] existentialism' (Jung 1936/1954, p. 62). However, he also suggests many other examples that don't rhyme with 'ism' (Jung 1935a, p. 6). Isms are usually one-sided because they promote one principle and neglect the opposite.

The primary way in which we meet social demands is through an ad hoc, adopted attitude – termed the persona. This attitude is a mask that we put on to mediate between ourselves and the expectations or needs of society. It is a 'segment of the collective psyche' (Jung 1928, p. 156) which means that it includes attitudes that many people share or that serve a collective purpose. People often have two personae, using one at work and another at home, but neither represents the true individuality. The use of social attitudes can potentially repress and damage the development of the individual (Jung 1934/1950, p. 349).

Common psychology

The attitudes that Jung describes in *Psychological Types* are common elements of human psychology; they are innate, part of our phylogenetic inheritance. Just as most of us are born with two arms and two legs, so too there are four psychological functions that are present in all of us. We may have specific talents that make us more suited to use some attitudes more than others. In addition, there are two orientations – extraversion and introversion – that can be combined with each of the four functions.

In the context of typology, extraversion and introversion describe ways of dealing with the outer world of people and things – whether we invest interest in it or withdraw interest from it. Put simply, extraversion takes action in the world, introversion thinks about it. In *Psychological Types*, Jung argued that Freud and Adler had developed these attitudes in a one-sided way. However, in ordinary life, they 'should contribute equally' (Jung 1923, p. 518). Jung borrowed an analogy from Goethe to compare the harmonious cooperation of extraversion and introversion with the movements of the beating heart. Like the diastolic and systolic flows that alternate, a 'rhythmical alternation of both ... would perhaps correspond to the normal course of life' (Jung 1921, p. 5).

The four psychological functions create attitudes that focus on certain types of information and ignore others. Although they can undergo some degree of change, these functions are more or less the same in individuals who are at the same stage of development. Sensation, intuition, thinking, and feeling each focus on facts, possibilities, logic, and values. We can illustrate the differences between these functions by looking at the type of art they produce (see Figure 2.2).

Sensation pays attention to what is known – facts, reality, or actuality – which are perceptions that come from conscious sources. If artists make primary use of sensation when creating a painting, they will portray a tangible reality – such as the objects, people, ambience, or aesthetic qualities in a landscape.

Intuition focuses its attention on the unknown – possibilities, implications, or potential – which are perceptions that come from unconscious sources. Paintings based on this attitude will have more of a dream-like appearance, where the meaning or content of the image is far from clear. As we look at the picture, we animate it from within our imagination.

Thinking is oriented towards a logical structure – the objective connections between ideas and objects. This type of art would have a systematic arrangement, for example suggesting to the viewer how the parts of the image connect with each other, or with people, things, and ideas that are outside the painting.

Feeling is oriented towards the inherent value or importance of something – which might take the form of personal liking or disliking, or moral evaluation. This type of art might focus on images that are personally meaningful, such as friends or family, or depict acts of compassion or relationship.

Jung paired the functions together as opposites – sensation vs intuition, and thinking vs feeling – because there is a see-saw, dynamic relationship between them. Using one of them in the conscious attitude tends to repress the other, so it becomes an unconscious attitude. If we use sensation to focus on facts, then it tends to inhibit our awareness of possibilities, and vice versa. If we use thinking to focus on the objective connections between things, then we tend to repress

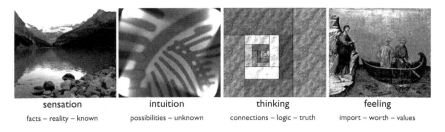

Figure 2.2 Four types of art.

22 The type problem

feeling and be unaware of their inherent worth, and vice versa. These four functions are present in all of us, and we can use all of them to differing degrees. Typology is concerned with the cases when the conscious use of functions becomes habitual and one-sided:

> When a function habitually predominates, a typical attitude is produced. According to the nature of the differentiated function, there will be ... a typical thinking, feeling, sensation, [or] intuitive attitude.
>
> (Jung 1921, p. 417)

> When any of these attitudes is *habitual* ... I speak of a psychological type.
>
> (Jung 1921, p. 482, original italics)

> Each of these types represents a different kind of one-sidedness.
>
> (Jung 1923, p. 519)

These four functions combine with extraversion and introversion to create eight function-attitudes, such as introverted thinking or extraverted intuition. They are each a different form of one-sidedness, a different kind of Capulet. And, as with Capulet, each type has two sides to the personality – consciousness tends to have good qualities, and the unconscious tends to be more problematic. In chapter X of *Psychological Types*, Jung describes the conscious and unconscious characteristics of each of the one-sided types of personality.

A typological function arises from within us, from our phylogenetic inheritance, but it is also a social function because we use it to fulfil a social role. Typological functions are therefore associated with the persona (Jung 1916, p. 297). They are developed from the interaction of inner dispositions and environmental conditions. They are a compromise between who we are and what society expects us to be. They lie in the 'ectopsychic sphere' (Jung 1935b, p. 44) which is the part of the psyche that we use to adapt ourselves to the outer world.

There is another form of common psychology – archetypes. They are deep, instinctive patterns within the collective unconscious part of the psyche. They can appear at the surface in the form of behaviours or thoughts that are associated with common images or characters – such as a father, mother, or hero. When an unconscious archetype is activated, we instinctively react in a fatherly, motherly, or heroic way. For example, Capulet's unconscious, archetypal instinct as a father was to protect and defend his daughter.

As with the typological functions, these unconscious, archetypal attitudes can serve both the individual and society. For example, instinctively knowing how to father a child is vital to both. The relationship between Capulet and Juliet was influenced and reinforced by both social expectations and archetypal instincts. When Capulet expressed both attitudes in a one-sided way, there was no room to take account of Juliet's feelings or wishes. He could not see the importance of accommodating the views that his wife and Juliet expressed.

Archetypes can therefore be beneficial or damaging. For example, the instinct of the hero archetype might prompt us to take quick action and save someone in danger. But if our heroic behaviour becomes habitual or one-sided, we might use it when it is not suitable. We might start interfering in other people's trivial affairs, trying to give help when it is not wanted. Or we might project the hero and its opposite into other people – seeing one person as heroic and another as a villain – and thereby exaggerating the differences between them.

The projection of archetypes into other people can sometimes change their actual behaviour. If we see people as heroes and villains they might start acting like heroes and villains, through the psychological process of 'projective identification'. That is, they start to conform to the expectations of the projections. We can see this projective identification in many political movements, when supporters project heroic qualities into their leader. The heads of populist parties, for example, might come to believe they are the saviours of the people against the political elite, who in turn are portrayed as corrupt – irrespective of whether there is any actual corruption. The hero archetype is especially relevant to the problems of one-sidedness and polarisation, as we shall see in Chapter 11.

Individual

The third kind of attitude is a uniquely 'individual phenomenon' (Jung 1921, p. 417), which refers to a standpoint that is different from that taken by other people. It can make use of societal beliefs and common psychological functions, even though the personal attitude is unique. What is different is how we organise those shared beliefs and the place they have within our overall worldview (Jung 1921, p. 448).

We can illustrate the relationship between individual and collective attitudes with the analogy of a unique image printed from a computer. Although it is unique, it can incorporate material drawn from other sources. For example, the cover to the present book is different from others, but it includes words such as 'Jungian' that are widely used elsewhere. Also, the spiral around the black hole has been printed using the same four colours that all other printers use – cyan, magenta, yellow, and black. What is different about the picture is the way the colours are blended to form new ones (e.g. shades of red, yellow, green, and blue) and create a unique image. Similarly, every individual attitude is different but can draw on many social and common psychological attitudes. What is unique is the way we blend and arrange those attitudes to form our own, individual viewpoint. Just as a one-sided picture uses only one or two colours to produce a more monochrome image, a one-sided personality type tends to use some functions more than others, leading to a monochrome view of the world.

24 The type problem

Myers-Briggs typology vs Jungian individuation

One of the main differences between Isabel Briggs Myers and Carl Gustav Jung is how they view the problem of a one-sided attitude. Myers sees the type problem primarily as the need for 'balance between judgment and perception, and between extraversion and introversion' (Myers 1980, p. 17). Jung sees it as a much broader problem, as the balance between many different pairs of opposites, and primarily as a split between consciousness and the unconscious. Because of their different views of the problem, they come to different views of the solution. Myers solves her version of the problem through the cooperation of two functions. One deals with extraversion, the other with introversion. One deals with perception, the other with judgment. For Jung, even if we use two or three functions we are still one-sided and have not yet begun the process of individuation (Fordham 1953, pp. 45–46). The use of three functions is akin to printing a computer image using, say, only yellow, cyan, and black.

Myers based her view on a small section at the end of chapter X of *Psychological Types* (Myers 1980, p. 18). After Jung describes the eight types of one-sided attitude, he suggests that such pure forms do not arise in actual life. People tend to make some use of a second attitude in a supporting role. There are sixteen combinations that tend to occur in practice. Jung starts to list them but he does not finish the list. Myers viewed this section as suggesting that the 16 combinations are no longer one-sided, but well-balanced. Jung saw these 16 types as frequently occurring types that were less extreme but still one-sided. Despite the presence of an auxiliary attitude, there is still a split between consciousness and the unconscious within the individual. This split lies at the heart of his critique of Western culture.

Although Myers acknowledged the presence of the unconscious (ibid., p. 84), she viewed the problem as a need for balance in consciousness, which the second, auxiliary function provides. As a result, we can regard being a type as a virtue, and we can stay one type throughout our personal development. For Jung, being a type is a problem, because it helps sustain the split between consciousness and the unconscious. We can see how the two models of development differ by examining how Myers and Jung made different use of the same analogy.

An army commander

Isabel Briggs Myers uses the analogy of an army general working from a command tent to illustrate how to balance extraversion and introversion. In Myers-Briggs typology, the four basic functions are arranged in a hierarchy according to their influence on consciousness, as determined by their personality type. The function with the most influence is called the dominant, and the second most important is the auxiliary. It is these two functions that, through their cooperation, provide the balance within consciousness. (The third function in the hierarchy is the tertiary, and the least important or fourth function is referred to as the inferior.)

The type problem   25

To illustrate how balance is achieved, Myers equates the general with the dominant function and his aide with the auxiliary. If the general is extraverted, he goes outside the tent, and his introverted aide tends to stay in the tent. If the general is introverted, he remains inside the tent and sends his extraverted aide outside the tent (Myers 1980, p. 13). We achieve a balance between introversion and extraversion through the cooperation of the dominant and auxiliary, because each works primarily in the opposite world to the other.

Jung uses a similar military analogy, but his view of the problem of balance is much wider, and he presents a different solution. He does not describe this analogy in *Psychological Types* but in an essay produced a few years later called 'Analytical Psychology and *Weltanschauung*' (Jung 1928/1931). A *Weltanschauung* is a worldview or philosophy of life – an overarching attitude that shapes, structures, and guides an individual's consciousness. The individual has many other attitudes it can call upon, but the *Weltanschauung* is the most important attitude and it is ever present – 'the conscious attitude is always in the nature of a *Weltanschauung*' (Jung 1923, p. 523). To illustrate how this overall worldview relates to other attitudes, Jung equates the ego with an army commander:

> *Weltanschauung* embraces all sorts of attitudes to the world ... Attitude is ... oriented towards a goal or directed by some kind of ruling principle. If we compare ... attitude to military dispositions then attention, for example, would be represented by ... standing to arms ... As soon as the strength and position of the enemy are known, the disposition changes: the army begins to move in the direction of a given objective. In precisely the same way the psychic attitude changes ... The army stands under a simple and unified command ... The ego is the army commander.
>
> (Jung 1928/1931, pp. 358–60)

The ego, as army commander, has an overall worldview, a tentative and ever-developing 'picture of the world and of oneself, to know what the world is and who I am' (Jung 1928/1931, p. 362). This *Weltanschauung* embraces a wide range of conscious attitudes, including typological functions, social attitudes, and individual attitudes. But a *Weltanschauung* is itself also an attitude. It can be philosophical, aesthetic, religious, idealistic, realistic, or of any other nature. This overall worldview is akin to military strategy, and the various attitudes it calls upon are akin to military tactics. Each attitude, whether strategy or tactics, is characterised by a dominant principle or idea.

Figure 2.3 shows the relation between various attitudes and the ego. The *Weltanschauung* or overall worldview is the most important, but other attitudes are available for use whenever needed. We could regard the *Weltanschauung* as the dominant attitude, and all others as subordinate. This relationship is evident in the behaviour of Capulet and Benvolio in the fight scene of *Romeo and Juliet.* Capulet had a very limited worldview which was dominated

26 The type problem

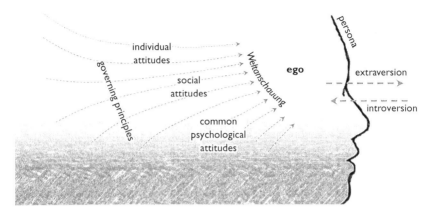

Figure 2.3 Weltanschauung draws on a range of attitudes.

by the governing principle that he had to protect his family from existential threats. When he saw the fray developing in the street between members of his household and the Montagues, the only attitude he could call upon was to fight. Although in other situations he had other attitudes at his disposal – such as making decisions about his daughter's future – in the street scenario there was only one option that was relevant and available to him, so he called for his sword. Benvolio, however, had a broader worldview and saw that there were various ways to deal with conflict. In this situation, he was able to call on two attitudes. He used the first attitude when he entered the scene and could see the fight developing; he tried to calm things down. He used the second attitude when the first one did not work and Tybalt attacked him; Benvolio then started to fight, to defend himself. In this context, Benvolio's worldview was much broader than Capulet's, and he had a wider range of attitudes on which he could draw.

There are some similarities between Jung's and Myers' versions of the military analogy. For both, the ego is the army commander, guided by a dominant attitude, with a degree of flexibility to deal with various aspects of everyday life. Where they differ is that, for Myers, the dominant attitude is one of the basic typological functions and it stays that way throughout all psychological development:

> Full development of type involves getting to be expertly skilled with the dominant process, which actually bosses the other three processes and sets the major goals in life. Type development also depends on skilled use of the auxiliary process, which is vital for balance … Finally, full type development requires learning to use the two less-favored and less-developed processes appropriately. The less-developed processes are always a problem.
>
> (Myers 1980, pp. 193–94)

The type problem   27

In Jung's military analogy, the ego is the commander of an army that, through development, becomes much more flexible. The goal of the Jungian model is akin to changing one's character from being Capulet-like to being Benvolio-like; we develop a broader range of attitudes on which we can call. Significantly, in the Myers-Briggs metaphor the army led by the ego commander is fighting primarily on one front, there is a single battle. It is concerned with consciousness and the outer world – either directing energy into it (extraversion) or withdrawing energy from it (introversion). In the Jungian metaphor there are two fronts. The ego fights not only with consciousness and the outer world but also with the unconscious and the inner world of the person's instinctual nature. This is – to use the word in a more general sense – an even more introverted activity because it looks at adapting to the world of impulses, dreams, spirituality, individual potential, and the whole personality that includes the unconscious. The ego stands between these two worlds as if they were two different opposing forces attacking the one army. Myers-Briggs typology focuses on the western front. Jungian individuation focuses on both the western and the eastern fronts.

Another difference between Myers and Jung is that the former associates the ego primarily with a basic psychological function, but the latter associates the ego with a *Weltanschauung*. In Jungian individuation, the typological functions stay at the disposal of the ego, but they do not dominate it. The development of an increasingly wide range of attitudes can happen naturally, because 'every increase in experience and knowledge is a step in the development of a *Weltanschauung*' (Jung 1928/1931, p. 361). However, there is one attitude that is particularly important – the attitude towards the unconscious:

> If ... I had to name the most essential thing that analytical psychology can add to our *Weltanschauung*, I should say it is the recognition that there exist certain unconscious contents ... with which the conscious mind must come to terms, whether it will or no.
>
> (Jung 1928/1931, p. 370, original italics)

The importance of typology to Jung is that it describes some frequently occurring conscious attitudes on which the ego can call. Also, the dominant and inferior functions are two significant poles between which development takes place. The individual becomes unique *between* the opposites in a dialectical exchange which also promotes wholeness. The individual does not become unique by developing one of the opposites, which promotes one-sidedness. Jung illustrated this principle with the analogy of the blacksmith forging a unique sculpture:

> It is the old game of hammer and anvil: between them the patient iron is forged into an indestructible whole, an 'individual'. This, roughly, is what I mean by the individuation process.
>
> (Jung 1939, p. 288)

The type problem

If an attitude becomes excessively or involuntarily one-sided, it causes problems because it 'limits a person's judgment' (Jung 1963, p. 233). The attitude filters out important aspects of reality before they reach conscious awareness. Such a distortion of our view of the world affects ourselves and our relationships, and it has made its mark 'in the history of human thought' (Jung 1936, p. 553). Such 'one-sidedness ... is a mark of barbarism' (Jung 1929, p. 9) even when it occurs in fields that we regard as amongst the greatest advances of humanity. It does not matter if the attitude is intellectual, philosophical, scientific, psychological, or otherwise. There is nothing wrong with an attitude per se because we need to filter out information – there is just too much for us to deal with at any one time. The problem of one-sidedness occurs when an attitude is overdeveloped or over-valued to the extent that we forget the opposite, or ignore it, or consider it to have no worth:

> The tendency to separate opposites as much as possible ... is absolutely necessary for clarity of consciousness ... But when the separation is carried so far that the complementary opposite is lost sight of, and ... the evil of the good ... is no longer seen, the result is one-sidedness.
>
> (Jung 1955–56, p. 333)

The phrase *evil of the good* suggests that even the noblest of actions can have an evil flipside if it is one-sided. The good side of Capulet is that he has a strong social conscience. He is protecting his family. He is carrying out the father's duty of arranging a good marriage. But this good also has an inadvertent evil side, which is not a separate part of his character but a direct consequence of his goodness. He is unable to recognise how his determination to arrange a good marriage is riding roughshod over Juliet's feelings. He cannot see how protecting his family is putting them in greater danger because it is creating conflict with the Montagues. He cannot see how his devotion to Juliet's future life is creating the turmoil within her that contributes to her death. He cannot see any of this because he thinks he is rational, reasonable, unprejudiced, and many-sided – which is how one-sidedness sees itself (Jung 1916/1957, p. 70).

We all think that we make balanced judgments. The type problem suggests that we are all one-sided in some way but are unable to see it. Capulet saw Montague as the evil enemy, whom he needed to defeat, but the conflict was primarily due to the split between the conscious and unconscious part of Capulet's own psyche. The essence of the type problem is coming to terms with the location of evil. We start out by thinking it is in other people or cultures. To individuate, we have to recognise this location as being due to projection and see the evil as actually being within ourselves. Many writers recognise that making this step of awareness is a difficult challenge, for example:

The type problem   29

If only it were all so simple! If only there were evil people somewhere insidiously committing evil deeds, and it were necessary only to separate them from the rest of us and destroy them. But the line dividing good and evil cuts through the heart of every human being. And who is willing to destroy a piece of his own heart?

(Solzhenitsyn 1973, p. 168)

This principle applies not only to interpersonal relations but also to conflicts that occur between opposing theories, politics, philosophies, religions, etc. We see one side as evil – or immoral, or incompetent, or out of touch, etc. – and the other as noble. Such a tendentious perspective is rarely based on the facts, although we can usually find facts to justify our view. It is based on the principle of one-sidedness. Therefore, we can reconcile political and other forms of conflict only by focusing on the underlying psychology:

As a rule, the partisans of either side attack each other purely externally, always seeking out the chinks in their opponent's armour. Squabbles of this kind are usually fruitless. It would be of considerably greater value if the dispute were transferred to the psychological realm, from which it arose in the first place.

(Jung 1921, p. 488)

Jung saw this squabbling between the psychoanalysts who followed Freud and Adler. The problem originated in the one-sidedness of the two leaders, in their typology. *Psychological Types* is not concerned with the classification of people; it is concerned with how to solve the 'problem of opposites' (Jung 1935c, p. 186). Becoming a type is both an advantage and a drawback. It achieves a degree of personal development but it also creates new problems and is not the final stage of development.

One of the criticisms of Myers-Briggs typology is that it lacks a means of 'changing how we see the world' (Bennet 2010, p. 32). Yet this change of attitude is the gravamen of *Psychological Types*. In Jung's original vision, typology is the scaffolding of individual identity. It is not the individual building itself but it is a necessary step in the construction process. Another analogy is that type is a stepping stone, a 'necessary transitional stage on the way' (Jung 1921, p. 440). However, just as one needs to step onto a stone to make progress, so too we then need to step off it to make further progress. There is great value in the stepping stone of Myers-Briggs typology, but if we linger there too long the danger is that it becomes an obstacle to individuation.

References

Bennet, A. (2010). *The Shadows of Type: Psychological Type Through Seven Levels of Development.* Morrisville, NC: Lulu Enterprises.

30 The type problem

Fordham, F. (1953). *An Introduction to Jung's Psychology: An Exposition for the General Reader of the Theories and Technique of the Foremost Living Medical Psychologist.* London: Penguin Books.

Jung, C.G. (1913). 'A contribution to psychological types'. In *CW6.*

Jung, C.G. (1916). 'The structure of the unconscious'. In *CW7.*

Jung, C.G. (1916/1957). 'The transcendent function'. In *CW8.*

Jung, C.G. (1917/1926/1943). 'On the psychology of the unconscious'. In *CW7.*

Jung, C.G. (1921). *CW6.*

Jung, C.G. (1923). 'Psychological types'. In *CW6.*

Jung, C.G. (1928). 'The relations between the ego and the unconscious'. In *CW7.*

Jung, C.G. (1928/1931). 'Analytical psychology and *Weltanschauung*'. In *CW8.*

Jung, C.G. (1929). 'Commentary on the secret of the golden flower'. In *CW13.*

Jung, C.G. (1934/1950). 'A study in the process of individuation'. In *CW9i.*

Jung, C.G. (1935a). 'Principles of practical psychotherapy'. In *CW16.*

Jung, C.G. (1935b). 'The Tavistock lectures'. In *CW18.*

Jung, C.G. (1935c). 'Letter to G.A. Farner, 18 February 1935'. In *Letters 1.*

Jung, C.G. (1936). 'Psychological typology'. In *CW6.*

Jung, C.G. (1936/1954). 'Concerning the archetypes and the anima concept'. In *CW9i.*

Jung, C.G. (1939). 'Conscious, unconscious, and individuation'. In *CW9i.*

Jung, C.G. (1955–56). *CW14.*

Jung, C.G. (1963). *Memories, Dreams, Reflections.* London: Harper Collins, 1995.

Myers, I.B. (1980). *Gifts Differing.* Palo Alto, CA: Davis Black, 1995.

Shakespeare, W. (1982). *Romeo and Juliet. The Illustrated Stratford Shakespeare.* London: Chancellor Press, 701–28.

Solzhenitsyn, A. (1973). *The Gulag Archipelago, 1918–56, Volume 1: An Experiment in Literary Investigation.* New York: Harper Perennial Modern Classics, 2007.

Chapter 3

The solution

Psychological Types is a difficult book to read. Its purpose is to explain the problem of opposites and the solution. However, Jung structures the book as a literature review. The first nine chapters (330 pages) review the writings of prior philosophers, psychologists, and poets. Jung discusses the gravamen of the book – the problem of opposites and the solution – in chapters II and V, which examine works by Schiller and Spitteler. The last two chapters (150 pages) are pseudo-appendices, listing the most common forms of one-sidedness and giving a set of definitions. Jung explains the reason for this strange structure in the foreword to the first Swiss edition.

> [I wanted] to show how the ideas … can be linked up … with an existing body of knowledge … [This puts them in a] context which will enable the educated layman to derive some profit from them.
>
> (Jung 1920, p. xi)

In my view, Jung's structure has the opposite effect to his intent. Rather than making his solution accessible to the layperson, he makes it incomprehensible and easy to miss. At the centre of Jung's theory is the transcendent function, which is omitted from Myers-Briggs typology. We will take a detailed look in Chapter 4 at what this function is. Throughout the rest of this book we will examine how it develops. For the moment, we will get an overview by using a contemporary political example – the Northern Ireland peace process. Although Jung was not alive when the Troubles started, his analysis shows why this peace process has had more success than, say, the Israeli–Palestinian conflict. It is also an exemplar of the role the transcendent function plays in overcoming otherwise intractable problems.

Northern Ireland

There is a close relationship between politics and religion in the island of Ireland. The complex roots of the conflict go back centuries, to the Norman invasion of Ireland in the twelfth century. The conflation of the political and religious

32   The solution

divides began in the sixteenth and seventeenth centuries, after the Reformation, Henry VIII's break from the papacy, and the mass colonisation known as the Ulster Plantation. There was a series of uprisings which the English contained until the nineteenth century. Resentment then grew during the potato famine, in which one million people died, another two million emigrated, and the total population eventually fell by more than 50 percent. At the time of writing – 2018 – the number of people living on the island still has not recovered to its pre-famine level.

The conflict between the Irish and British reached a climax in the twentieth century. During the Irish War of Independence, shortly after the First World War, the UK partitioned Ireland and agreed that the southern partition could become independent. Northern Ireland remained a part of the UK, though it gained a devolved parliament. The Irish constitution later laid territorial claim to Northern Ireland and enshrined the primacy of the Catholic Church's teaching over Protestant beliefs. A court case made the practical implications of this political and religious alignment very public in 1950. A Dublin judge ordered that a Protestant father should lose custody of his children and return them to their Catholic mother (Moloney 2008, p. 23). The Catholics living in Northern Ireland also felt oppressed. In 1968, the police used excessive and inflammatory violence against a peaceful civil rights march, which was protesting the institutional prejudice towards Catholics. Although there was a long history that led up to this incident, it became the spark for the latest period of violence, the Troubles (McKittrick and McVea 2012, pp. 46ff.). This conflict between religious and political attitudes captures many of the facets of one-sidedness covered in Chapter 2. The Protestant community is primarily unionist, wanting to keep Northern Ireland as a part of the UK. The Catholic side is mostly nationalist, wanting a united Ireland. Many people have shared these collective attitudes. One prominent example is Ian Paisley.

Ian Paisley

Paisley was born in 1926, into a fundamentalist Baptist family. At the age of 16, with the help of his father, he enrolled at the Barry School of Evangelism. He was ordained as a Presbyterian minister and quickly became involved in politics. He joined the National Union of Protestants, whose aim was to oppose the increasing influence of Roman Catholicism in the Anglican Church (Moloney 2008, pp. 19–20).

Paisley was a man who had strong beliefs and values, which would eventually lead to him setting up both a new church (Free Presbyterian) and a new political party (Democratic Unionists). In many ways he was a modern-day Capulet, standing up for the values he believed in and opposing the many Montagues who threatened those values. Like Capulet, Paisley did not recognise his part in worsening the conflict and how his rhetoric stirred up aggression and violence (ibid., p. 85). In 1997, during negotiations for the Good Friday

The solution   33

Agreement, Paisley adhered so firmly to non-violent values that he refused to negotiate with the IRA. His stance was still the same in 2006:

> No unionist who is a unionist will go into partnership with IRA-Sinn Fein. They are not fit to be in partnership with decent people. They are not fit to be in the government of Northern Ireland. And it will be over our dead bodies that they will ever get there.
>
> (Paisley 2006)

However, soon after in May 2007, there was an event that signalled a remarkable transformation. In the gallery of Stormont (the parliamentary building in Northern Ireland) was an array of politicians who usually took centre stage, rather than acting as observers. They included the British Prime Minister, Tony Blair, and the Irish Taoiseach, Bertie Ahern. Just a few feet away, there were key figures from the Irish Republican Army, including the Quartermaster General, the military commander in Belfast, the head of intelligence, and the man who persuaded Colonel Gaddafi to arm the IRA (Powell 2009, loc. 122ff.). The members of the gallery looked down on two men who had been bitter enemies for nearly four decades. One was Ian Paisley; the other was Martin McGuinness, a former IRA member and one of the leading members of Sinn Fein along with Gerry Adams. They swore oaths of allegiance to share power with each other in running Northern Ireland. This alone was 'nothing short of sensational' (McKittrick and McVea 2012, p. 38) but, shortly after, a photographer caught Paisley and McGuinness on camera together in raucous laughter. Various news organisations transmitted the image around the world (Bowcott 2007) and it sent shock waves through Paisley's unionist supporters. Within a few weeks of taking the oath of allegiance, Paisley and McGuinness acquired the nickname 'The Chuckle Brothers' (BBC 2007). They developed a good working relationship and an enduring friendship. The image of the two men smiling and laughing together became a symbol that cemented a remarkable transformation in Northern Ireland's politics.

Analysis

Those with intimate knowledge of the peace process offer various reasons for its success. Jonathan Powell, the Downing Street Chief of Staff during Tony Blair's premiership, suggests the key was 'refusing to accept "no" for an answer ... by never letting the talking stop' (Powell 2009, loc. 174). David Trimble offers a subtly different but significant view. He was the leader of the Ulster Unionist Party during the negotiations leading up to the Good Friday Agreement, joint winner of the Nobel Peace Prize in 1998, and Northern Ireland's First Minister until the suspension of the devolved parliament in 2002.

Trimble criticises the arguments that attribute the progress in Northern Ireland to persistent talks. Although he recognises the importance of dialogue, he sees

34   The solution

the context in which the dialogue takes place as being more important. He compares the failure of the ceasefires in the 1970s with the progress made in the 1990s. In the earlier years, the IRA were allowed to enter talks too easily; they could continue with violence. In the latter years, the British laid down stricter criteria for the IRA to be involved in official negotiations; their violence would need to end. The crucial factor that forced the IRA to alter their approach was 'a growing sense among senior republicans that the organisation's "armed struggle" had reached a point of deadlock' (Trimble 2008, p. 16).

Trimble's analysis adds a new dimension to the oft-used mantra of engaging in dialogue to achieve peace. Talking alone cannot bring peace, nor can it transform a divided society. As Powell points out, there have been many conflicts where talking has not led to a lasting resolution, such as the Middle East 1993 Oslo accord, 2002 Tamil Tigers ceasefire, and the 2006 ceasefire of the Basque separatist group ETA. These agreements 'gradually unravelled, returning the dispute to violence' (Powell 2009, loc. 167). The civil war in Syria is another example. At the time of writing, the United Nations have discussed the problem for more than six years, but there is still no end in sight. What was different in Northern Ireland was the recognition by both sides that neither could win. Peter Hain was the Secretary of State for Northern Ireland for two years leading up to and including the reinstatement of power-sharing in 2007. He recognised that engaging in dialogue carries with it 'the danger of encouraging an armed group in the belief that its campaign is working' (Hain 2007).

A psychological perspective

Although Jung wrote a great deal about political conflict, his interest lay in the psychology that underpins it, rather than the political issues per se. He saw psychological explanations as better than political ones (Jung 1936, p. 564). For example, he dismissed many of the political and economic analyses of the Second World War – in one of his humorous exaggerations – as being 'about as useful as explaining the Hiroshima explosion as the chance hit of a large meteorite' (Jung 1947/1954, p. 218). The roots of the war were primarily psychological; they lay in the split between the ego and the unconscious in many individuals, aggregated to the level of society, and represented in political leaders. People wanted a one-sided truth, and their degree of one-sidedness gave their collective, unconscious projections a fanatical quality (ibid., p. 219).

In the next few pages, we will examine eight principles that show how Jung's psychological solution is relevant to the peace process in Northern Ireland. Then, in the following eight chapters, we will look at them in more detail, and apply them to examples in the fields of politics, the arts, personal development, and others. These principles are derived from a variety of Jung's writings, not just *Psychological Types*. Although he clarified and developed his ideas between 1921, when he wrote the book, and 1961, when he died, he did not revise *Psychological Types* apart from some minor corrections. We therefore need to take account of his other work to get a clearer picture of his typological theory of individuation and how it relates to the metaphor of alchemy that he used in later years.

Principle one: The transcendent function

The solution to the psychic split between the ego and the unconscious is the transcendent function. As with many other words, the term 'transcendent' has a variety of meanings, some of which conjure up the image of a mysterious, spiritual, or metaphysical experience. However, in respect of the transcendent function in *Psychological Types*, this was not what Jung meant. 'There is nothing mysterious or metaphysical about the term' (Jung 1916/1957, p. 69). The verb 'to transcend' simply means to go beyond the limits of something. In the context of typology, it means to go beyond the limits of the current conscious and unconscious attitudes. The transcendent function helps change those attitudes to be broader, more whole, more flexible, and more integrated. In the case of Ian Paisley, for example, his initial attitude was that the IRA and Sinn Fein were evil and should never be allowed in power. He 'transcended' that attitude when he took the view that he could collaborate with Martin McGuinness when governing Northern Ireland.

The transcendent function acts as a form of peace and reconciliation process between consciousness and the unconscious. However, it is difficult to describe, for several reasons. One is that it does more than merely bridge the divide. It is a 'function which [not only] mediates opposites [but also] facilitates a transition from one psychological attitude ... to another' (Samuels *et al.* 1986, p. 150). That is, the transcendent function is a form of psychological development that reconciles the opposites by ushering in a new attitude that embraces and 'transcends' both sides. Another difficulty, when describing the transcendent function, is that it evolves. It takes different forms throughout the process and eventually becomes the new attitude itself. It is the means of bringing the solution about and it is the solution itself. It is an ongoing process that continually reinvents itself, emerging and re-emerging as the conflict becomes progressively less one-sided and less polarised.

The Northern Ireland peace process is an example of a transcendent function. It evolved through many forms, such as the formal attempts at power-sharing in the 1970s, the 1985 Anglo-Irish agreement, the 1993 Downing Street Declaration, the 1998 Good Friday Agreement, and the restoration of power-sharing in 2007. There were also informal aspects of the process, such as the 'web of talks over the years, most of which were held in strict secrecy' (McKittrick and McVea 2012, p. 215).

As an ongoing process, the transcendent function often produces a gradual rather than immediate change in attitude. For example, at the start of the peace process, the IRA hated the British and viewed terrorism as a legitimate means of achieving a united Ireland. It was only after a quarter of a century of the peace process that they abandoned terrorism, sought to achieve their goals through purely political means, and respected the rights of the majority of Northern

36 The solution

Ireland who wished to stay in the UK. Similarly, unionist politicians such as Ian Paisley started out with a hatred of Sinn Fein and the IRA. It took four decades for his attitude to change sufficiently to enter power-sharing with Sinn Fein.

From the perspective of Jung's typology, two psychological factors helped to produce these new attitudes. Trimble's analysis points to one of them, which was the realisation by both sides that they could not win. The IRA had to change their approach because their armed struggle had reached the point of deadlock. There was also recognition on the unionist side that they could not win, they could not achieve stability merely by asserting the supremacy of UK law and demanding compliance from the Irish nationalists. For Paisley, this moment of acceptance arrived publicly two years before the final power-sharing agreement. He acknowledged in a radio interview that 'I'll have to face up to the fact that I've got to do business with them' (Paisley 2005).

The acceptance on both sides that neither can win is a crucial factor in Jung's theory. For the transcendent function to realise its full psychological potential, there must be a 'balance of power' (Jung 1928a, p. 229). Each side must reach the point where they cannot – or will not – inflict defeat on the other side; they must treat the other with equal seriousness and respect:

> When there is full parity of the opposites [it] leads to ... a standstill, a damming up of vital energy results, and ... the tension of opposites produce[s] a new, uniting function that transcends them ... It thus forms the middle ground on which the opposites can be united.
>
> (Jung 1921, p. 479)

The second psychological factor was the role played by symbols, which have the power to change deeply embedded attitudes. Whilst the transcendent function is a mechanism to unite the opposites, it does not always give people the motivation to do so. Something needs to force them to abandon the one-sided attitude and adopt the new, mediatory attitude. In Northern Ireland, the old one-sided attitudes were very persistent. Before 2007, all attempts at power-sharing had collapsed because many in the two communities deeply distrusted those on the other side. One of the major challenges to this distrust was the image of Paisley and McGuinness laughing together and seeming to enjoy each other's company. The photograph acted as a symbol that helped change the attitudes of those who still opposed the power-sharing arrangement:

> His warm relations with McGuinness certainly surprised observers ... who imagined that civil servants would have to mediate between the IRA man and the unionist who had repeatedly called for such people to be executed. The photographs of Paisley and McGuinness grinning in each other's company shocked many on both sides. The 'Chuckle Brothers', as they were dubbed, seriously challenged the entrenched divisions.
>
> (Bruce 2009, p. 271)

A symbol can change entrenched attitudes because it can 'canalise libido' (Jung 1928b, p. 47). It deflects the focus of interest (or psychic energy) in a different direction. It is like a beaver that fells trees and uses them to dam up a river. The dam diverts the water in a new direction, down a new canal (ibid., p. 42).

Principle two: Various forms of opposite

This process of resolution is relevant to any intractable conflict that has a psychological component. The opposition can be political, religious, economic, or of any other form that depends on human behaviour, relationships, or identities. It is not relevant to mathematical or physical opposites, such as Newton's third law of motion (every action has an equal and opposite reaction), even though there are some analogies between them. Nor is Jung's solution necessary when there is a rational compromise available (Jung 1921, p. 105).

In the case of Northern Ireland, there are two sets of attitudes that overlap and establish different identities. The first is religious, which pits the Catholic and Protestant communities in opposition to each other. The second is territorial, in which nationalists seek a return to a united Ireland, and unionists wish to stay part of the UK. There is a significant overlap between these two groups of people: Catholics tend to be nationalists, and Protestants tend to be unionists. Many other forms of opposite also play a role, such as the different views about civil rights for minorities such as the LGBT (lesbian, gay, bisexual, and transgender) community. But the central conflict arises through the religious and territorial differences that have their roots in earlier centuries.

Psychological Types examines a wide range of opposites – religious, political, psychological, and others. One of the key pairs of opposites is the conflict between good and evil. We usually associate good (or some other form of superiority, such as truth, integrity, or loyalty) with our viewpoint, with our close family and friends, or with the groups and isms with which we identify. We project evil (or some other form of inferiority, such as delusion, dishonesty, or selfishness) into the opposite viewpoint – into other people, groups, or nations – and we make them scapegoats. When these projections aggregate unconsciously across large numbers of people, they accumulate into cultural and international conflict:

> These projections ... are dangerously illusory. War psychology has made this abundantly clear: everything my country does is good, everything the others do is bad. The centre of all iniquity is invariably found to lie a few miles behind the enemy lines ... The normal person ... acts out [his own internal schism] socially and politically, in the form of ... wars.
>
> (Jung 1916/1948, pp. 271–72)

38   The solution

Principle three: Various levels of development

Jung's process of transformation can also be relevant to differing levels of psychology. It can address problems within and between individuals, in groups, and in culture. In the case of Northern Ireland, there was a remarkable change within Ian Paisley, in his relationship with McGuinness, and in various other relations between Catholics and Protestants, nationalists and unionists, and the governments of Ireland and the UK. These transformations had to overcome centuries of troubled history and the legacy of violent conflict from the 1920s that 'left a deep and bitter imprint on many in both communities' (McKittrick and McVea 2012, p. 4).

There are often two main political parties in Western countries, which attack each other and portray each other in highly negative terms. What keeps them apart is not politics, for in many cases their policies are similar. Rather, the source of the schism lies in the underlying identity of the individuals who make up the two collective groups. Each needs a heroic cause with which to identify and a villainous political enemy to carry the projections of their unconscious attitudes:

> It is in the nature of political bodies always to see the evil in the opposite group, just as the individual has an ineradicable tendency to get rid of everything he does not know and does not want to know about himself by foisting it off on somebody else.
>
> (Jung 1957, p. 299)

The solution to political conflict is not to overcome or defeat the enemy. This only changes the ruling power. It leaves the psychological problems intact, which can therefore reappear at some point in the future in a different form. Any political or societal change depends on a psychological change within each individual. The solution lies firstly in looking at our own inner split, between our ego and the unconscious, and then seeking their reconciliation and transformation. Jung recognised that this argument is difficult to accept:

> It is impossible to convince anybody that the conflict is in the psyche of every individual, since he is now quite sure where his enemy is. Then, the conflict which remains an intrapsychic phenomenon in the mind of the discerning person, takes place on the plane of projection in the form of political tension.
>
> (Jung 1955–56, p. 363)

Another important but complex aspect of political transformation is leadership. Leaders are at the same time individuals, representatives of a group, and expressions of a collective unconscious phenomenon. Paisley was not the cause of the conflict, but he was symbolic of it and he expressed the views of one side:

The solution   39

It remains a moot point whether [the leaders'] message is their own ... or whether they merely function as a megaphone for collective opinion ... Responsibility is ... shuffled off by the individual and delegated to a corporate body. In this way the individual becomes more and more a function of society, which in its turn usurps the function of the real life carrier.

(Jung 1957, p. 254)

There was a symbiosis between Paisley, as a megaphone leader, and the organisations that both supported him and opposed him. 'No one was better able to articulate all [the] threats to Protestantism than Ian Paisley' (Moloney 2008, p. 148). He dealt with the negative aspects of this one-sidedness by setting up two corporate bodies in Northern Ireland to which he could delegate responsibility. The Free Presbyterian Church of Ulster and the Democratic Unionist Party took responsibility for religious and political attitudes, respectively. Psychologically, this enabled Paisley to 'disclaim responsibility for sectarian violence caused by his anti-Catholic tirades' (Moloney 2008, p. 85; see also p. 132 for evidence of a link). Paisley was also of value to the IRA, though inadvertently so. He provided them with someone who could carry their projections:

The IRA and Paisley were politically dependent upon each other ... they fed off each other's success ... The relationship was one reason why the IRA never contemplated assassinating Paisley when the Troubles did break out. As the outward symbol ... of what Nationalists had to endure in Northern Ireland, he was much more useful alive. Equally, IRA violence and the threat it represented to Unionists' political security provided the nourishment that sustained Paisley's political and religious outlook and recruited his supporters in their droves. That symbiotic relationship between Paisley and the Provisionals was to flower in the years of the peace process and would, arguably, even enable its final resolution.

(Moloney 2008, p. 351)

The IRA served Paisley, and Paisley served the IRA, by each conforming to the other's expectations of evil. This enabled them both to 'point a finger at the shadow [which] is clearly on the other side of the political frontier' (Jung 1957, p. 289). The term 'shadow' refers to a particular area of the unconscious that is projected into other people and is directly opposite to the current conscious attitude. For example, if I have a one-sided conscious attitude that believes in peace rather than violence, then I see myself as peaceful, but my shadow contains violence. I then project this violence into other people which enables me to point at them and declare 'I am peaceful but you are violent'. This naturally leads to political conflict, and the solution begins not with political policies but with the recognition of our own shadow:

A political situation is the manifestation of a parallel psychological problem in millions of individuals. This problem is largely *unconscious* ... It consists of a conflict between a conscious ... standpoint and an unconscious one ... You find this conflict in nearly every citizen of any Western nation. But one is mostly unconscious of it ... [To overcome it] the unconscious must be slowly integrated without violence and with due respect for our ethical values ... The discovery of the unconscious means an enormous spiritual task, which must be accomplished if we wish to preserve our civilization.

(Jung 1949, pp. 535–37, original italics)

Jung provides further criticism of political debate by suggesting that, when it does take account of psychology, it focuses on the wrong level. It takes place exclusively at the level of collective psychology, treating everyone as if they are the same. The policymakers 'forget the existence of the individual psyche altogether' (Jung 1933/1934, p. 136). A political conflict can occur between different countries, or opposing groups in the same country, or even in relationships between individuals. But its resolution begins with the recognition that the conflict reflects an unconscious aspect of ourselves (Jung 1957, p. 297). That is, to a greater or lesser extent, our views of the political parties and leaders reflect our own one-sidedness. Once we have recognised the split in our own psyche, and the nature of our projections, we are then able to make better contributions to the public political debate.

Principle four: The caduceus

The metaphor of alchemy expresses the process of transformation more clearly than the cryptic writings within *Psychological Types*. The caduceus is an alchemical image (see Figure 3.1) that illustrates how consciousness can advance (become more individual and more whole). It also provides a link between typology and alchemy. In Greek mythology, the caduceus is a staff entwined by two snakes with wings at the top that belongs to Hermes the messenger of the gods. Movement up the caduceus represents progress in reconciling the opposites:

Figure 3.1 The caduceus.

> It is a *longissima via*, not straight but snakelike, a path that unites the opposites in the manner of the guiding caduceus, a path whose labyrinthine twists and turns are not lacking in terrors.
>
> (Jung 1944, p. 6, original italics)

The moving apart of the snakes and their coming together higher up represents a combination of circular and forward progress, which we can see in Northern

Ireland. The Troubles began in 1968, after the violent response to the civil rights protests. The government laid the seeds of the peace process straight away, with immediate reforms and a commission to investigate the causes of the disturbances (McKittrick and McVea 2012, p. 310). In the next four decades, there were periods in which the two sides came close together, for example in attempts at power-sharing or in agreeing how to deal with IRA prisoners. There were also times when they were far apart, during periods of violence, a refusal to engage in talks, or the banning of Sinn Fein voices from media broadcasts.

Principle five: Two movements

One aspect of making progress up the caduceus is that there are two types of movement. There are times when the opposites separate and other times when they come together. Sometimes we make progress and at other times we seem to regress. Progression involves developing a new attitude and then using that attitude to deal with the current situation. An example of progression is Paisley's acceptance that he would have to share power with Sinn Fein. On the IRA side, they were willing to achieve goals using purely political means, calling a ceasefire and engaging in dialogue. Examples of regression are the collapse of IRA ceasefires, or Paisley returning to his rhetoric of never doing business with Sinn Fein/IRA.

Whenever we make progress, it 'is not something that is achieved once and for all' (Jung 1928b, p. 32). We can easily lose the ground we have gained if the attempts to deal with the situation are frustrated. If this happens, the opposites split again, they create 'tension [that] leads to conflict' (ibid., p. 33), and there is a regression to earlier, more primitive, and more unconscious attitudes and behaviours. In other words, if the peace talks break down then both sides regress to their prior states of using violence, refusing to talk, repressing the opposite in themselves, and condemning the opponent as evil.

However, these periods of regression can be very productive and are a vital part of the overall process. Although they seem to be a step backwards, they also contain 'valuable seeds' (ibid., p. 35) for development. For example, in a regressive state we might behave childishly or take things less seriously. Whilst this might be inappropriate in the circumstances, it can also bring to our attention a new aspect of the split in our psyche. It can reveal something new that will help in further progression. For example, Paisley had for many years refused to shake hands with the Irish Taoiseach, Bertie Ahern. In 1999, he explained: 'I will not shake hands with a prime minister of a country which still has a claim over my country' (Moloney 2008, p. 406). When RTÉ radio interviewed him, a few years later, 'Paisley laughed and joked [and] said he would shake hands with Bertie Ahern if they had something to shake on' (Paisley 2005). Paisley's playfulness brought out a subtle but significant shift in his attitude towards Ahern, and they did, in fact, shake hands in 2007, shortly before the restoration of power-sharing.

42   The solution

Psychotherapists sometimes take advantage of this principle by encouraging adults to play with sand or toys and talk about their experience. The therapist encourages a degree of regression – to childhood creativity – that can sometimes bring up new and valuable attitudes that the individual has not yet acknowledged. The value of such play is that it not only encourages the creative imagination, but it also treats the opposites with equal seriousness. In an irreconcilable conflict, 'the opposition between the two functions, or function groups, is so great [that] a third factor is needed, which at least can equal the other two' (Jung 1921, p. 107). If we treat both sides of the self with the same, low level of seriousness, then we can more easily see any third thing that emerges as being superior. By engaging in the two movements – progression and regression – we bring new, hitherto-unconscious material into consciousness and develop new attitudes that overcome the conflict.

Principle six: The axiom of Maria

The two movements take the conscious attitude through four main states or stages, illustrated by a verbal alchemical metaphor. Maria was one of the pioneers of alchemy who lived around the third century AD. She developed a cryptic axiom that was used throughout the history of alchemy and which Jung adopted to represent the process by which a person's attitude is transformed. The wording of the axiom is 'one becomes two, two becomes three, and out of the third comes the one as the fourth' (Jung 1951, p. 153).

In summary, we start out in stage one by viewing everything as the same. In stage two, we separate the opposites and give priority to one over the other, making the former conscious and repressing the opposite into the unconscious. In stage three, we treat both equally, giving them parity of respect and seriousness, and tolerating the conflict or paradox that their opposition creates. Finally, in stage four, we reconcile the two sides with a solution that emerges from the unconscious.

The first stage involves there being little or no discrimination between the opposites. In the Northern Ireland example, this refers to the political and religious condition of Ireland before the twelfth century. The second stage consists of the separation of opposites, a political differentiation that began when the Normans invaded Ireland in the twelfth century. The period of English or British rule lasted until 1921 when the southern part of Ireland gained its independence. There were no distinctions between Protestants and Catholics until the sixteenth century, which is when Protestantism emerged as a separate religious movement.

In this second stage, each side has a tendentious and one-sided perspective. We can easily find facts to sustain the superiority of our viewpoint, through cognitive biases and logical fallacies. That is, unconsciously we find supporting evidence or arguments that seem correct but may have a subtle flaw or ignore something important. For example, confirmation bias notices evidence that supports our view and shows the harm or deficiencies in the opposite. It does not see the balancing evidence, which shows the damage that results from our approach and the good that flows from the opposite. Another example is the association fallacy, which rejects a point of view because it shares a characteristic with something that is known to be wrong. There are many such forms of biases and fallacies.

It was a cognitive bias that underpinned Paisley's view of Sinn Fein/IRA as 'fiendish Republican scum' (Moloney 2008, p. 328) and as the source of violence. It is true that they were violent, but Paisley's rhetoric in crowds could itself become 'violent and even menacing' (ibid., p. 284). He could not see any connection between his actions and those of the loyalist paramilitaries. He denied the evil in himself, and in the collective attitude that he represented, and projected it into the IRA. He was able to do this because the IRA were indeed committing atrocities. The IRA's violence helped the loyalists avoid coming to terms with the violence on their own side:

> The real existence of an enemy upon whom one can foist off everything evil is an enormous relief to one's conscience. You can then at least say, without hesitation, who the devil is; you are quite certain that the cause of your misfortune is outside, and not in your own attitude.
>
> (Jung 1916/1948, p. 272)

The third stage in the axiom of Maria involves the withdrawal of projections and giving both opposites parity of respect and seriousness. We recognise that the harm or evil we see in the other is based partly on projection, and that some of it lies in our own individual or collective attitude. An example of this in the peace process is the setting up of the inquiry into the events of Bloody Sunday, a civil rights march in 1972. British armed forces opened fire and killed 13 people who were posing no threat. By setting up the inquiry, which took more than a decade to complete, the British withdrew the collective projection of evil into the IRA. They stepped back from the view that the state always acted honourably and only the nationalists engaged in unjustified violence. They began to recognise the good and evil on both sides. Prime Minister David Cameron formally acknowledged this in 2010, when he issued an apology on behalf of the British Government (BBC 2010).

Although this third stage involves treating both sides with equal respect and seriousness, it does not imply moral equivalence. There may, indeed, be more good or evil on one side rather than the other. But that judgment is not the primary concern. What matters is treating them with parity, giving both sides equal power in the dialogue:

> One is forever trying violently to suppress the other in order to bring about a so-called harmonious solution of the conflict. Unfortunately, too many people still believe in this procedure, which is all-powered in politics; there are only a few here and there who condemn it as barbaric

44 The solution

and would like to set up in its place a just compromise whereby each side ... is given a hearing.

(Jung 1933, p. 809)

Reaching the fourth stage of the axiom of Maria depends on holding the tension of opposites in stage three, to give fantasy the time and opportunity to do its work. The only prospect of finding a resolution to a psychological paradox – or a no-win, no-win scenario – is to give free rein to the creative imagination. Even the smallest of obstacles or distractions will inhibit the creativity of the unconscious because it is fragile and easily destroyed. If we can quieten the conscious mind so that creative ideas can foment and emerge into conscious awareness, then fantasy will at some point come up with a way of reconciling the opposites. We can sometimes find this time and space through meditation, or creative techniques such as art or play, or a solution might appear in a dream because the conscious mind is at its least active during sleep. In a group, we can encourage the creative imagination using techniques such as brainstorming or group dreaming (the sharing of dreams in a workshop environment).

Unstructured time can also play a significant role in developing a new attitude. We cannot rush the process of imagination or fantasy, or make it stick to a schedule. Even a small amount of structure or guidance from the conscious mind can inhibit unconscious creativity. In the negotiations for the Good Friday Agreement, there were often meetings at Hillsborough Castle that were loosely structured, or not structured at all. The lack of an agenda allowed participants to interact informally. At one point, the negotiations moved to Weston Park, to encourage a shift in mindset. It worked, as the Sinn Fein leader 'Gerry Adams revealed a new side of himself ... by wandering around the park hugging the stately trees' (Powell 2009, loc. 3445). Gerry Adams started tree hugging as a joke, but he found it was a calming influence (BBC 2001). Such meetings hold the opposites in tension in a loose way. They enable solutions to emerge that can transcend otherwise insurmountable differences.

The axiom of Maria describes reaching this final stage by saying 'out of the third comes the one as the fourth' (Jung 1951, p. 153). That is, by holding the opposites in tension (stage three), something forms in the unconscious (the one) that emerges into consciousness to reconcile and unite the opposites (the fourth). In the case of the Northern Ireland peace process, the environment enabled the conflicting parties to come together on equal terms (out of the third). It encouraged a more creative approach (comes the one), as shown by the tree hugging. It eventually led to a new attitude that transcended the two sides, i.e. the Good Friday Agreement (as the fourth).

Principle seven: Flexibility of perspective

When psychological or cultural development follows the path outlined by the axiom of Maria, it leads to a more flexible perspective. Those who have reached

The solution   45

the fourth stage for any particular pair of opposites can see the viewpoint of all the prior stages. Jung implies this in his *Weltanschauung* essay, and in his view that a conscious capacity for one-sidedness is a sign of culture. Marie-Louise von Franz says it more overtly when describing the development of the typological functions. A new attitude emerges that can use none or all of the functions at the same time (von Franz 1971/1986, pp. 27–28).

One-sidedness sees things from its own perspective. It cannot see – or rejects or disparages – other viewpoints that do not fit with its own. At the end of the process of transformation, the individual can call on any of the attitudes associated with the four stages of the axiom of Maria. Such flexibility does not necessarily mean always taking a middle view, nor agreeing with one side or the other. Nor does it involve developing all the knowledge or skills of both sides. It means being able to see and respect what each of the perspectives can see, thereby enabling us to make a much more informed judgment. We recognise how things are the same or share something that is common (stage one), how each side sees itself as better than the other (two), how their values or beliefs conflict (three), and how we can move towards reconciling the two sides (four).

Principle eight: One-sidedness and analytical psychology

One final but important question concerns the relationship between typology and other parts of analytical psychology. Many people view them as separate theories. For example, the psychoanalyst Anthony Storr argued that 'the quaternity of the four functions has been discarded by all except the most dedicated Jungians' (Storr 1973, p. 73). Although there have been challenges to that view (e.g. Samuels 1985, p. 84), it reflects a widely held assumption that typology is primarily concerned with the organisation of consciousness. In contrast, analytical psychology is concerned (so this argument goes) with the integration of consciousness and the unconscious. However, this portrayal of typology as different from the rest of analytical psychology was part of Jung's frustration with its popular interpretation. For him, typology was not a separate theory; it was an integral part of the foundation of analytical psychology. Its primary purpose was not to classify individuals, nor even to classify the contents of consciousness. Its value was in identifying the problem of one-sidedness, of conflict between the conscious and unconscious psyche, and in furnishing a solution based on the symbol and the transcendent function. For example, in the Northern Ireland peace process the typological preferences of the main actors involved had little bearing on the resolution. What mattered was bringing the political and religious opposites together and holding that tension in an environment where neither could win. Typology is an example of that principle, but it is not the principle itself, nor is it separate. It is part of the same overall theory that has the ultimate goal of restoring balance and wholeness.

There are many ways to overcome the split between consciousness and the unconscious in analytical psychology, including dreams, myths, religion,

46   The solution

philosophy, and others. These theories are part of the same overall framework that has the transcendent function as its central theme (Miller 2004). They all address the same topic of how to reconcile consciousness and the unconscious, and transform the personality. The bulk of the present book examines how to do this using the theory Jung outlines in *Psychological Types*. In Chapter 11, we will examine how that typological goal is achieved using other aspects of analytical psychology.

References

BBC (2001). 'Gerry Adams admits to tree hugging'. British Broadcasting Corporation. Online at: http://news.bbc.co.uk/1/hi/uk/northern_ireland/1424096.stm, accessed 5-Feb-18.

BBC (2007). '"Chuckle brothers" enjoy 100 days'. British Broadcasting Corporation. Online at: http://news.bbc.co.uk/1/hi/northern_ireland/6948406.stm, accessed 1-Apr-17.

BBC (2010). 'Bloody Sunday: PM David Cameron's full statement'. British Broadcasting Corporation. Online at: www.bbc.co.uk/news/10322295, accessed 5-Feb-18.

Bowcott, O. (2007). 'Paisley and McGuinness mark new era'. *The Guardian*. Online at: www.theguardian.com/uk/2007/may/08/northernireland.northernireland, accessed 1-Apr-17.

Bruce, S. (2009). *Paisley: Religion and Politics in Northern Ireland*. Oxford: Oxford University Press.

Hain, P. (2007). 'Peacemaking in Northern Ireland: A model for conflict resolution? Speech at Chatham House, 12 June 2007'. Ulster University's CAIN Web Service (Conflict and Politics in Northern Ireland). Online at: http://cain.ulst.ac.uk/issues/politics/docs/nio/ph120607.pdf, accessed 5-Feb-18.

Jung, C.G. (1916/1948). 'General aspects of dream psychology'. In *CW8*.

Jung, C.G. (1916/1957). 'The transcendent function'. In *CW8*.

Jung, C.G. (1920). 'Foreword to the first Swiss edition'. In *CW6*.

Jung, C.G. (1921). *CW6*.

Jung, C.G. (1928a). 'The relations between the ego and the unconscious'. In *CW7*.

Jung, C.G. (1928b). 'On psychic energy'. In *CW8*.

Jung, C.G. (1933). 'Foreword to Harding: "The Way of All Women"'. In *CW18*.

Jung, C.G. (1933/1934). 'The meaning of psychology for modern man'. In *CW10*.

Jung, C.G. (1936). 'Press communique on visiting the United States'. In *CW18*.

Jung, C.G. (1944). 'Introduction to the religious and psychological problems of alchemy'. In *CW12*.

Jung, C.G. (1947/1954). 'On the nature of the psyche'. In *CW8*.

Jung, C.G. (1949). 'Letter to Dorothy Thompson, 23 September 1949'. In *Letters 1*.

Jung, C.G. (1951). *CW9ii*.

Jung, C.G. (1955–56). *CW14*.

Jung, C.G. (1957). 'The undiscovered self (present and future)'. In *CW10*.

McKittrick, D., McVea, D. (2012). *Making Sense of the Troubles: A History of the Northern Ireland Conflict*. London: Penguin Books.

Miller, J.C. (2004). *The Transcendent Function*. Albany, NY: State University of New York Press.

Moloney, E. (2008). *Paisley: From Demagogue to Democrat?* Dublin: Poolbeg Press.

Paisley, I. (2005). 'RTÉ radio interview, 28 February 2005'. *The Irish Times*. Online at: www.irishtimes.com/news/paisley-says-he-will-share-power-on-democratic-principles-only-1.418812, accessed 5-Feb-18.

Paisley, I. (2006). 'Making history or history made? Speech to the Independent Orange Demonstration, 12 July 2006'. Ulster University's CAIN Web Service (Conflict and Politics in Northern Ireland). Online at: http://cain.ulst.ac.uk/issues/politics/docs/dup/ip120706.htm, accessed 5-Feb-18.

Powell, J. (2009). *Great Hatred, Little Room: Making Peace in Northern Ireland*. London: Vintage Digital, Kindle Edition.

Samuels, A. (1985). *Jung and the Post-Jungians*. London: Routledge, 1986.

Samuels, A., Shorter, B., Plaut, F. (1986). *A Critical Dictionary of Jungian Analysis*. Hove: Routledge.

Storr, A. (1973). *Jung*. New York: Routledge, 1991.

Trimble, D. (2008). 'Misunderstanding Ulster'. The website of David Trimble. Online at: www.davidtrimble.org/publications_misunderstanding.pdf, accessed 1-Apr-17.

von Franz, M.L. (1971/1986). 'The inferior function'. In *Lectures on Jung's Typology*. Putnam, CT: Spring Publications, 2013.

Chapter 4

The transcendent function

The transcendent function is one of Jung's most protean and amorphous concepts. There is nothing mysterious or metaphysical about it. It is a psychological function, like the typological functions of sensation, intuition, thinking, and feeling. But there are also significant differences. We can describe typological functions because they generate attitudes that focus on facts, possibilities, logic, and values. Although they undergo some limited changes depending on development, their features are similar in people who are at the same stage. Hence, typological functions are a collective psychology, because they are the same in many people. They are basic functions that we acquire as part of our phylogenetic inheritance and they serve a collective or social purpose – either to meet direct demands or to compensate for what the family or society is missing. Importantly, because the development of a typological function involves repressing the opposite, it also has the effect of creating a division between the ego and the unconscious.

We cannot describe the transcendent function formally or precisely because it can have a wide range of characteristics in different individuals. However, we can recognise it by more general criteria, such as the effect it has on the opposites, the conditions under which it emerges, or relating it to some clear examples. Another difficulty in describing the transcendent function is that it has a life cycle and takes many different forms.

In a similar manner to the life cycle of a business project, the transcendent function starts off on a small scale, expands its role, brings about significant changes, and then becomes a permanent feature of the way things are done. It may be followed by another 'project' that has a different focus. Just as business projects are often driven by the need to solve problems, the ongoing development of transcendent functions can be driven by intra-psychic difficulties or the problems we encounter in daily life.

The life cycle of the transcendent function begins when we hold the opposites in tension. It forms in the unconscious, then takes on the role of holding the tension itself. It helps to produce appropriate symbols and finally emerges as a new conscious attitude. The life cycle then begins again, either to facilitate an even closer relation between those opposites or to reconcile a different pair of

The transcendent function   49

opposites. It also leads to a better relationship between the ego and the unconscious part of the psyche.

Therefore, just as a ladybird goes from egg to larva, pupa, and insect, so too the transcendent function goes through various stages of psychological metamorphosis. We saw this in the Northern Ireland peace process, which emerged from the conflict in the late 1960s but eventually became a process that held the two parties together. In its final form, it became a new attitude of power-sharing that dominated the political life of Northern Ireland. But the process of change was not complete, and further processes are needed to ensure that opposing views in Northern Ireland continue to be acknowledged and reconciled.

South Africa and Zimbabwe

There are two more examples of a peace process that we will look at in this chapter, one that was very successful, the other highly problematic. These outcomes were due, in no small degree, to the personal qualities of the leaders involved – Nelson Mandela and Robert Mugabe. Their lives have been chronicled by the biographer of African leaders, Martin Meredith, who provides an independent comparison of Mandela's and Mugabe's development and impact.

There were many similarities between the two men. They were both born in the early twentieth century. They lived in similar, neighbouring countries – South Africa and Rhodesia, later called Zimbabwe. They were both victims of colonialism, in which white settlers took land from the indigenous peoples and violently repressed them. Mandela and Mugabe became leaders in the resistance to white dominance. Both decided to go to armed struggle after the failure of dialogue with the whites. They were sent to prison for their violent opposition and released as part of peace negotiations. They went on to become presidents of their respective countries and inherited deeply divided societies. Blacks (and other ethnicities) had been disenfranchised for decades and whites feared the consequences of blacks getting political power. During peace negotiations, both men said they wanted to overcome the differences and promote reconciliation. However, from that point on, their stories diverge significantly. Mandela had learned to hold the tension of opposites in his private life and brought that approach into the political life of South Africa. As a result, most people viewed Mandela as one of the world's greatest leaders of state. In contrast, Mugabe took a one-sided approach, seeking to acquire power and defeat his opponents. As a result, he polarised views and exacerbated the divisions within Zimbabwe. Some saw him as a hero and others as a brutal dictator.

Robert Mugabe

When Mugabe left prison, there were due to be all-party discussions about Zimbabwe's future. Mugabe was 'hostile to any idea of negotiations [because] imprisonment had only hardened his resolve to pursue revolution' (Meredith

50   The transcendent function

2007, p. 2). This demonstrates the most extreme form of political one-sidedness – to violently overthrow the existing order and replace it with a completely new one. But Mugabe's attitude led to Zambia and Mozambique threatening to withdraw their support from him. He therefore agreed to attend a conference to negotiate a transition from British-ruled Rhodesia to independent Zimbabwe. But this was only a tactic to get to the stage of independence where he could do what he wanted. After that, he had no intention of adhering to a negotiated solution. He planned to put the white exploiters on trial, shoot them, and take their land from them. He wanted 'the ultimate joy of having militarily overthrown the regime' (ibid., p. 7). Immediately after the conference, Mugabe was unexpectedly conciliatory. He initially called for moderation and unity, but this was only a part of his strategy to increase his power. Over the next few years, he neglected the needs of those who did not support him, and he blamed the whites:

> Year after year, Mugabe sustained his rule through violence and repression – crushing political opponents, violating the courts, trampling on property rights, suppressing the independent press, and rigging elections. [He threatened] to act like a 'black Hitler' against the opposition ... [Meanwhile,] Zimbabwe's people ... faced mass unemployment, soaring inflation, hunger, and destitution ... Far from addressing their grievances, Mugabe's regime responded with ever harsher oppression through arrests, detentions, banning orders, beatings, and torture.
>
> (Meredith 2007, p. 18)

Mugabe persecuted whites and was undisturbed by them being tortured (ibid., pp. 53–54). His attitude inevitably led to an exodus, with the white population dropping by 50 percent within three years of Zimbabwe's independence (ibid., p. 55). Whites were not his only victims. Anyone who was other, whose identity was different from Mugabe's, received similar treatment, including blacks who had a different ethnicity (ibid., p. 57) and homosexuals (ibid., p. 129). His aim was the acquisition of power from political opponents and his citizens (ibid., p. 85). Even though there was a semblance of democracy, his tactics in keeping power were brazen. They included a television advert that said, 'Don't commit suicide, vote Zanu-PF and live' (ibid., p. 91). Mugabe's story was one of 'growing megalomania' (ibid., p. 148), even to the point of passing legislation 'making it a criminal offence to criticise the president' (ibid., p. 226). Mugabe looked for absolute, unopposed dominance. 'Power for Mugabe was not a means to an end, but the end itself' (ibid., p. 241). Any form of negotiated settlement was unacceptable to him:

> Whereas Nelson Mandela used his prison years to open a dialogue with South Africa's white rulers, Mugabe emerged from prison adamantly opposed to any idea of negotiation ... His aim by then was to overthrow white society by force and to replace it with a one-party Marxist regime ...

The transcendent function 51

[Even] when a negotiated settlement was within reach ... Mugabe still hankered for military victory, 'the ultimate joy'.

(Meredith 2007, pp. 242–43)

Mugabe dealt with the legacy of the past by replacing the one-sided white domination of the blacks with the one-sided black domination of the whites. His attitude later became a one-sidedness that favoured his own people and organisation at the expense of everyone else.

Nelson Mandela

Nelson Mandela was also prepared to use violence, though for him the aim was reconciliation rather than domination. There is a widespread misapprehension that Mandela, like Gandhi, was part of a 'tradition of nonviolent resistance to colonial power' (e.g. CNN 2013). Such a view is a misunderstanding of his legacy. We can see how Mandela used violence, to overcome one-sidedness and hold the opposites in tension, by tracing his attitude towards it throughout his career.

Mandela became committed to the use of violence in the early 1950s. At that time, most of the other members of the African National Congress (ANC) leadership advocated non-violence, having been inspired by Gandhi's success in India. Mandela dissented, arguing that Gandhi's non-violent approach worked because he 'had been dealing with a foreign power that ultimately was more realistic and far-sighted' (Mandela 1994, p. 182). In 1953, Mandela explained his support of violence to a crowd at an ANC meeting:

I said, violence was the only weapon that would destroy apartheid and we must be prepared, in the near future, to use that weapon ... Non-violent passive resistance is effective as long as your opposition adheres to the same rules as you do. But if peaceful protest is met with violence, its efficacy is at an end. For me, non-violence was not a moral principle but a strategy; there is no moral goodness in using an ineffective weapon.

(Mandela 1994, pp. 182–83)

Mandela argued that Gandhi's non-violent resistance led to change in India because of British values. They were embarrassed and ashamed when Gandhi exposed their use of violence to suppress non-violent protest. In South Africa, the government would not feel the same shame, so non-violence would not have the same effect. However, Mandela put his argument too strongly at the ANC meeting, and the crowd became overly excited and agitated. The ANC leadership rebuked him. He accepted it but 'in my heart, I knew that non-violence was not the answer' (ibid., p. 183). Ten years later, the ANC leadership changed their mind and agreed that he could set up an armed branch – the MK (*uMkhonto we Sizwe*, which translates as the spear of the nation). Even whilst setting up the

52 The transcendent function

MK, which would become branded as a terrorist organisation, his long-term vision was one of reconciliation:

> In planning the direction and form that MK would take, we considered four types of violent activities ... It made sense to start with the form of violence that inflicted the least harm against individuals: sabotage. Because it did not involve the loss of life, it offered the best hope for reconciliation among the races afterwards.
>
> (Mandela 1994, p. 336)

A couple of years later, in 1963, Mandela was arrested and put on trial. He again made clear his commitment to violence. He explained that his aim was not to win a battle over the ruling whites but to end oppression and build better relations between the two communities. At the trial, he said:

> I planned [violence] as a result of calm and sober assessment of the political situation that had arisen after many years of tyranny, exploitation, and oppression of my people by whites ... I have fought against white domination, and I have fought against black domination. I have cherished the ideal of a democratic and free society in which all persons live together in harmony and with equal opportunities.
>
> (Mandela 1994, pp. 433, 438)

He still held this view 20 years later. In 1985, the president of South Africa (P.W. Botha) offered Mandela his freedom 'on condition that [he] gives a full commitment [to not] committing acts of violence for the furtherance of political objectives' (Meredith 2010, p. 351). Mandela rejected that offer:

> I am not a violent man [but dialogue] was ignored [and] in vain. It was only then, when all other forms of resistance were no longer open to us, that we turned to armed struggle. Let Botha ... renounce violence. Let him say that he will dismantle apartheid ... Let him guarantee free political activity so that people may decide who will govern them ... I cannot and will not give any undertaking at a time when I and you, the people, are not free.
>
> (Mandela 1985)

The white rulers were not prepared to discuss political equality. They still wanted to subjugate the blacks and other ethnicities. In those circumstances, Mandela saw no alternative other than to retain the policy of violence (Dash 1985). It was an essential part of his goal of achieving parity in negotiations, of holding the tension of opposites between the oppressor and the oppressed. Mandela continued to retain the right to use violence, even after his release from prison in 1990. Whilst the rest of the world was euphoric about his release,

Mandela kept the all-important focus on having the right conditions for reconciliation – parity between the opposites.

Mandela was far from perfect. For example, there were many criticisms of his autocratic leadership style and lack of organisation within the ANC, which Mandela accepted (Meredith 2010, pp. 439–40). However, the one principle on which he was consistent over many decades was the need to reconcile whites and non-whites in South Africa. Mandela viewed violence as means of achieving a balance of power between black and white. He created a 'no-win, no-win' situation that forced both sides to make a negotiated solution their number one priority.

Different paths

Mugabe and Mandela pursued very different routes to power. Both men were strongly associated with one side of the conflict but Mugabe despised the opposing side. He took the psychologically easier route by seeking to eliminate all opposition and remove any challenges to his authority. He paid lip service to reconciliation – to achieve power – and used violence to impose one-sidedness and maintain his personal dominance.

Nelson Mandela took a route that was psychologically harder. He was one of the oppressed and imprisoned but he respected the other. He sought to engage with his opponents as equals and give them parity. This was riskier because he did not have full control of the outcomes; he relied on the two sides coming together as collaborators, and he risked being criticised or rejected by one or other side. His use of power – whether through violence or the spoken word – was part of his long-term ambition to build harmonious relations between black and white. The sole purpose of the armed struggle was to make the government negotiate and bring them to the table on equal terms.

The difficulty of Mandela's task in reconciling the two sides was immense. There was not just one conflict but many. There were disputes between the different ethnicities, often involving violence and criminality, whom he had to bring to the negotiating table and keep there. His party, and even his wife, often engaged in crime to further their aims and agendas. Mandela also had to deal with the unrealistic expectations laid upon him by different people. Some saw him as a hero of almost messianic proportions who was going to solve all South Africa's problems. Others saw him as a terrorist whom they could never trust.

But the task was not Mandela's alone. For the South African peace process to succeed, many others had to play their part in bringing the opponents together. South Africa's prime ministers – first P.W. Botha and then F.W. de Klerk – had to engage constructively in discussions with people they regarded as terrorists. Botha made his offer to release Mandela in the context of increasing pressure not only from black violence but also from many white South Africans, other governments, international sports bodies, economic sanctions, cultural events, etc. They had also seen how badly things turned out in Zimbabwe, partly because

54 The transcendent function

the white rulers had been too intransigent in the lead up to independence. Their attitude had resulted in a lengthy black guerrilla war which contributed to the eventual ascendancy of a Marxist government led by Mugabe. It was a lesson from which the white South Africans could learn (Meredith 2010, p. 392). There were many factors in forcing the white rulers to negotiate.

An evolving peace process

Once the peace process had started, it went through various forms. It began out of the public eye with secret talks between Botha's government and the ANC. After Mandela's release, negotiations led to an interim constitution. In 1994 there were elections for a transitional government of national unity, which guaranteed the white minority a degree of representation and influence in the South African parliament. A few years later, South Africa had a more conventional form of government, based directly on democratic representation.

In the late 1990s, the peace process took the form of the Truth and Reconciliation Commission (TRC). They revisited South Africa's violent past – 'a journey that Mandela insisted should be undertaken' (Meredith 2010, p. 551). There was much debate about its purpose. Some in the ANC argued for Nuremberg-style trials, which would have reopened and worsened the historical divisions. Many in the white community were fearful of what it would achieve and opposed the idea. In the end, Archbishop Desmond Tutu chaired the commission, with the aim of investigating only the extreme violations of human rights, on all sides. Its role at the end of apartheid was 'to enable South Africans to come to terms with their past on a morally accepted basis and to advance the cause of reconciliation' (Omar 1995). It was a forum for perpetrators to confess to their crimes, receive a pardon, and for the two sides to reconcile themselves with each other.

The final report of the commission generated a hostile reaction on both sides, and there have been critics of the TRC who suggest that it did not achieve anything. For example, it allegedly failed in one of its main aims, 'to give back to the victims their dignity or compensate them' (Borowski 2014). Also, the TRC fudged some issues, such as Winnie Mandela's responsibility for the murder and violence carried out by the Mandela United Football Club (Meredith 2010, pp. 555–60).

If we focus on the practical shortcomings of the TRC, such as the lack of financial compensation or its failure to name those responsible for some atrocities, then we focus on only one aspect. As we saw in the case of Capulet, the conflict between people is closely related to the conflict between consciousness and the unconscious within the individual. To hold the tension in relationships, individuals need to hold the tension within themselves. Even if the TRC had produced no tangible outcome – no report, no decisions, no restoration, or no compensation – it still played a vital role in South Africa's transformation. It facilitated political forgiveness and repaired some of the brokenness between the

The transcendent function   55

two communities by dealing with some of the unconscious conflicts within and between the two sides (Gobodo-Madikizela 2008). The transformation in individuals and relationships helped to cement the transformation in society.

The role of symbols

Throughout the campaign against apartheid, various social symbols emerged to help change or galvanise attitudes. In the 1980s, Mandela's imprisonment became the symbolic focus of many international campaigns. He took on an importance that transcended his significance as an ANC leader. There was worldwide television coverage for events such as the Nelson Mandela concert at Wembley in 1988 and his short walk through the prison gates in 1990. His release from prison gave hope to both sides, that blacks would get equal democratic rights and that whites need not fear the type of retribution that had taken place in Zimbabwe. His release changed the nature of his symbolism. 'In an instant he switched from being a symbol of the oppressed to the global symbol of courage and freedom that he remains today' (Smith 2010). Mandela's influence was not due to his personal negotiating skill, although that played an important role. It was primarily because he became a widely shared symbol that 'touches a corresponding chord in every psyche ... [to] embrace what is common to a large group ... Herein lies the potency of the living, social symbol' (Jung 1921, p. 477).

A person, image, principle, or event can become viewed as symbolic in one of two ways. It can happen spontaneously or we can develop an attitude that looks at the image as symbolic (Jung 1921, pp. 475–76). Both these factors were at play in South Africa. For many, Mandela's significance was a spontaneous reaction. He took on numinous qualities in the sense defined by Rudolf Otto, as a *mysterium tremendum et fascinans*, a fearful and fascinating mystery (Otto 1923). Mandela was a mystery because the public had not seen or heard him since the early 1960s. He was a fearful character for some because he was a terrorist whose release from prison might unleash further campaigns of violence. Such fears were not without foundation, for some parts of the ANC were 'running amok [having] been taken over by gangsters, warlords, and renegade ... guerrillas' (Meredith 2010, p. 465). For others, Mandela was a fascinating character, someone who represented hope for the future, even though no one knew how he could bring that better future about or what it might involve. Some people chose to take a symbolic attitude, putting Mandela's release at the centre of an international campaign. They recognised that he represented something far more than just an individual who sought freedom from prison. He was symbolic of the end of apartheid and a potential new beginning for South Africa.

Mandela not only became a symbol, but he also used symbols when holding the tension of opposites. After his election as president, he made blacks and whites work together in his administration on an equal footing. He preserved

56 The transcendent function

symbols of identity on both sides and made them shared symbols of South Africa. One striking example was his treatment of the 'Springboks' (the South African rugby team) when the country hosted the World Cup in 1995.

The blacks hated the term 'Springboks' because they associated it with white nationalism. Following Mandela's election, there was 'strong pressure within the ANC to give a new name to the national team' (Meredith 2010, p. 525). Mandela opposed the change, partly because of his determination to prevent black domination that oppressed whites. He persuaded blacks to rally behind the rugby team, and he wore publicly a Springbok cap. He also persuaded the white rugby players to sing the black anthem *Nkosi Sikelel' iAfrica*. What happened next was something of a miracle – the rugby team realised Nelson Mandela's highest hopes. South Africa went on to reach the final, and they won it with a drop goal in extra time:

> The whole of South Africa erupted in celebration, blacks as joyful as whites. Johannesburg became a giant street party. In the northern suburbs, domestic workers rushed out on the streets shouting: 'We've done it! We've done it.' Never before had blacks had cause to show such pride in the efforts of their white countrymen. It was a moment of national fusion that Mandela had done much to inspire.
>
> (Meredith 2010, p. 527)

These symbols changed the deeply entrenched attitudes in South Africa. They canalised the collective libido (the focus of interest) away from the opposition between the two communities into a single, unified channel. Furthermore, they transformed the energy of both sides, from violently opposing the other to being more constructive, to building a new, united South Africa. It is akin to the transformation of energy in a water power station, which takes the flow of water and converts it into electricity (Jung 1928, p. 42). It channels the energy in a new direction, where it can be more useful and productive.

Symbols are not always beneficial, and they do not always produce a positive outcome. It depends on the attitude we take towards them. If we ignore symbols, it can sometimes lead to disaster, as we shall see in Chapter 5. A symbolic attitude significantly increases the chance that the symbol will have a reconciling impact. It sees beyond the literal truth or falsity of something to recognise that it represents some unconscious contents. A conscious attitude cannot create a symbol, but it can pay attention to the meaning of symbols that are emerging from the unconscious and value them. Nelson Mandela took such an attitude to the various symbols in South Africa. He recognised the potential for one-sided symbols to create division and strife. He also realised that combining the white name of the rugby team and the black national anthem had the potential to unite the country. He not only held the tension of opposites and valued the symbols himself, but he encouraged those symbols to take centre stage in the South African peace process.

The transcendent function in typology

Within the individual, the transcendent function is a form of peace process between consciousness and the unconscious. Like the peace processes in Northern Ireland and South Africa, it can go through various stages. Initially, the conflict seems to be entirely in the outer world; it is between our attitude and the hostile attitudes of other people. We act like Capulets; we see the problems of the world as being caused by the Montagues. As we withdraw projections, it becomes clear that there is also a conflict between the conscious and unconscious in ourselves. There may still be a conflict in the outer world, but we can deal with it more effectively because there is less complication due to our unconscious projections. If Capulet had developed greater self-knowledge, he would have come to terms with his own inner conflicts, reconciling his care for Juliet's future with his disregard for her feelings. He may still have had disagreements with the Montagues, or with other members of his own family, but he would have developed a new attitude and been able to deal with them more constructively.

The new attitude emerges from between conflicting principles when we give them equal value or respect. If we hold that inner tension – which may be reflected in holding external tensions as well – then the transcendent function starts to form in the unconscious. This is a natural process in which the unconscious seeks to resolve the contradiction through creative imagination or fantasy. As ideas on how to reconcile the opposites start to take shape, they begin to emerge into consciousness in the form of a uniting symbol. For many people in South Africa, Nelson Mandela was a social symbol who pointed towards the potential resolution between the races. This work needed to be undertaken by many people, because the reconciliation of the divisions in South African society depended on the reconciliation of divisions within each of its citizens.

It can take some time for the meaning of a reconciling symbol to unfold. In the initial stages of South Africa's transformation, it was not apparent how Mandela would bring the two sides together. Some people wanted Mandela to replace white domination with black domination, but he opposed this. His approach became clear as time went on, for example when he refused to replace white symbols with black ones and insisted that blacks and whites work collaboratively as equals and with mutual forgiveness. Mandela not only focused attention on symbols of reconciliation, but he acted as a symbol himself. These various social symbols began to reconcile the racial divisions in the individual psyches of many South African citizens.

The symbol and the transcendent function can themselves start to hold the opposites in tension. That is, when the possibility of a solution becomes realistic enough, it motivates those involved to continue with the process of reconciliation. The peace process in South Africa gained enough momentum that people on both sides of the divide became increasingly committed to it. The process made people reconsider their attitude towards those they had previously considered as being enemies, oppressors, or terrorists.

58 The transcendent function

In the final stage of the process, the transcendent function becomes a new attitude; it 'reveals itself as a mode of apprehension, [which is a combination of] intellectual understanding [and] understanding through experience' (Jung 1917/1926/1943, p. 109). In South Africa, the peace process became the new attitude. As the possibility of sharing power became a reality, there was an increasing desire to be reconciled, and they eventually shared power.

For those familiar with Myers-Briggs typology, this raises a practical but tricky question. How can a new attitude reconcile the attitudes of the typological functions when they are contrary to each other? For example, the dynamics of type suggest that if we pay attention to facts, then we ignore intuitive possibilities, and vice versa. The most we can achieve (so this argument goes) is that we manage the polarities. That is, we alternate between facts and possibilities, but at any one instant we must give priority to one or the other.

We can indeed reconcile typological opposites, in things that are both fact and possibility at the same time. For example, in a talent management system, sensation (oriented towards facts) might focus on current performance levels. Intuition (oriented towards possibilities) might see the individual's long-term potential. A good talent management system provides us with a measure of potential, which is both a fact and a possibility. This new attitude is a third thing between sensation and intuition that reconciles the two. We can still take account of measures of current performance and the intuition of potential, but now we have a third perspective, which combines the other two and tends to take precedence over them.

However, the reconciliation of facts and possibilities is not the most crucial aspect of the transcendent function. What matters is the reconciliation of consciousness with the unconscious, especially when there are one-sided attitudes involved. The intra-psychic divide has a significant impact on the individual and society, and it damages relationships by distorting our view of other people. For example, if a one-sided sensation attitude represses intuition, then possibilities take on a primitive character. We mix them up (or concrete them together) with all sorts of emotions, instincts, childish fears, and exaggerations. We then project them into someone else. Therefore, when other people suggest new or untested possibilities, these people become the carriers of our projections. We might dismiss them and their ideas as irresponsible, unrealistic, immature, or not worthy of consideration.

Although such projections can lead to interpersonal conflict, due to the misperceptions they create of the other person, they can also act as a mirror to help us see the neglected or repressed side of our personality. If we can recognise and withdraw those projections, to integrate the unconscious into our *Weltanschauung*, that greater self-knowledge can improve the nature of any real conflict with other people, making it more constructive and productive. The transcendent function does not destroy differences; it establishes a better relationship between them and produces a new attitude that goes beyond the limits of each of the opposites.

The transcendent function   59

Jung draws the idea of the transcendent function from one of his philosophical predecessors. Friedrich Schiller proposed a mediating function to reconcile opposing psychological functions. However, Jung needed to modify Schiller's concept because it raised a 'very complex problem' (Jung 1921, p. 115fn), which we will consider in Chapter 9. Jung explains his modified solution in chapter V of *Psychological Types*, in which he analyses Carl Spitteler's epic poem *Prometheus and Epimetheus*. It is to Spitteler's work that we shall now turn.

References

Borowski, M. (2014). 'Truth and reconciliation's checkered legacy'. Deutsche Welle. Online at: www.dw.com/en/truth-and-reconciliations-checkered-legacy/a-17589671, accessed 5-Feb-18.

CNN (2013). 'Nelson Mandela dead at 95; people who knew Mandela speak about him'. Cable and News Network. Online at: http://transcripts.cnn.com/TRANSCRIPTS/1312/05/sitroom.01.html, accessed 5-Feb-18.

Dash, S. (1985). 'A rare talk with Nelson Mandela'. *The New York Times*. Online at: www.nytimes.com/1985/07/07/magazine/a-rare-talk-with-nelson-mandela.html, accessed 5-Feb-18.

Gobodo-Madikizela, P. (2008). 'Trauma, forgiveness and the witnessing dance: Making public spaces intimate'. *Journal of Analytical Psychology* 53(2): 169–88.

Jung, C.G. (1917/1926/1943). 'On the psychology of the unconscious'. In *CW7*.

Jung, C.G. (1921). *CW6*.

Jung, C.G. (1928). 'On psychic energy'. In *CW8*.

Mandela, N. (1985). 'Statement read out by Zindzi Mandela at a mass rally in Soweto, 10 February 1985'. Quoted in Meredith 2010, pp. 351–52.

Mandela, N. (1994). *Long Walk to Freedom*. London: Abacus, 1995.

Meredith, M. (2007). *Mugabe: Power, Plunder, and the Struggle for Zimbabwe*. New York: PublicAffairs.

Meredith, M. (2010). *Mandela: A Biography*. London: Simon & Schuster.

Omar, D. (1995). 'Introduction by the Minister of Justice'. Truth and Reconciliation Commission. Online at: www.justice.gov.za/trc/legal/justice.htm, accessed 5-Feb-18.

Otto, R. (1923). *The Idea of the Holy: An Inquiry into the Non-Rational Factor in the Idea of the Divine and its Relation to the Rational*. Oxford: Oxford University Press, 1958.

Smith, A.D. (2010). 'Why FW de Klerk let Nelson Mandela out of prison'. *The Guardian*. Online at: www.theguardian.com/world/2010/jan/31/nelson-mandela-de-klerk-apartheid, accessed 5-Feb-18.

Chapter 5

Many forms of opposite

The typological functions are frequently occurring psychological opposites, but there are many others – 'the phenomenon of life consists of a great many pairs of opposites' (Jung 1938, p. 247). The index to Jung's Collected Works has 120 or so entries under the category of pairs of opposites, but it is an abridged list. It does not include the basic typological functions, nor other opposites that he discusses elsewhere, such as truth vs falsehood. Examples in the index include real/ imaginary, doubt/credulity, being/not-being, heaven/hell, love/hate, moral/ immoral, classic/romantic, idealism/materialism, male/female, and life/death. Within *Psychological Types*, he points to many other opposites, such as desire and anger, hunger and thirst, care and folly, honour and disgrace, and various forms of fluctuating emotions (Jung 1921, pp. 195–97). He also discusses how to reconcile opposites in his final work *Mysterium Coniunctionis*. The concluding chapter is concerned with philosophy, particularly epistemology, and the relation between the opposites of matter and spirit, which are principles that underpin science and religion. It is the culmination of his research into alchemy and his collaboration with the physicist Wolfgang Pauli into the relation of psyche and matter. The reconciliation of matter and spirit involves recognising the nature of the universe as not just matter, nor even matter and spirit. It is one world, an *unus mundus*, and matter, spirit, and psyche are related aspects of, or different perspectives on, that one world. The distinctions between them are useful but there may also be a fundamental level of reality in which they are the same or connected.

The diversity of opposites, to which Jung's theories apply, began to appear during the research that led to the publication of *Psychological Types*. In Jung's early research, he thought of the problem as being theoretical difference – between Freud's and Adler's theories – which also related to their interpersonal conflict. In Jung's first paper on types, he said he was looking to construct a theoretical solution that would be equally fair to both views (Jung 1913a, p. 509). That paper also suggests, even at this early stage of his thinking, that Jung was not only looking at interpersonal conflict, but was also considering what intrapersonal impact typology has. He was seeking 'to maintain the balance between the two psychological opposites of extraversion and introversion' (ibid.,

p. 505). He highlighted the work of Schiller, whose analysis took an important turn from considering types of people to considering the 'psychological mechanisms which might be present in the same individual' (ibid., p. 506).

In 1914, Jung gave a lecture that suggests he was also considering the developmental aspect of the problem of opposites. He compared Freud's reductive or causal standpoint, which offers explanations, with his own constructive method, which is concerned with 'the process of becoming' (Jung 1914, p. 183). Although Jung's comparison might be 'less than fair to the reductive standpoint' (Samuels 1985, p. 135), it provides a clue as to why Jung was unhappy with the popular interpretation of typology. He saw readers using his theory in, what he considered to be, a Freudian reductive way rather than using it for the constructive purpose he had in mind. The Freudian approach of explanation dominates the contemporary view of typology. For example, Isabel Briggs Myers stressed that 'to be useful, a personality theory must portray and explain people as they are' (Myers 1980, p. 18). Jung's theory is more concerned with becoming and realising potential:

> For, in the last resort, we are conditioned not only by the past, but by the future, which is sketched out in us long beforehand and gradually evolves out of us.
>
> (Jung 1926/1946, p. 110)

When Jung started to delineate his approach from Freud's, he acknowledged that the constructive method is reductive to some extent. That is, it still breaks things down into types. But this is not merely to explain; it is 'to widen the basis on which the construction is to rest' (Jung 1914, p. 187). During the next few years, in his confrontation with the unconscious, he described other aspects of the problem in his personal working notes, *The Red Book* (Jung 2009). For example, he noted there are philosophical opposites, concerned with the nature of existence, that are related to typological opposites: 'What a thinker does not think he believes does not exist, and what one who feels does not feel he believes does not exist' (Jung 2009, p. 248).

By the time Jung wrote *Psychological Types*, the most significant opposites were consciousness and the unconscious. A small degree of one-sidedness is not usually of concern because the unconscious can 'act compensatorily to the conscious contents of the moment' (Jung 1915, p. 15). For example, if people find their work to be mundane, the unconscious mind may compensate (restore balance) through imaginative daydreaming, or by stimulating discussions with colleagues, or by having other interests that are more challenging. This process of compensation is akin to the keel of a sailing boat. Above the water, the wind may push the boat sideways. Below the water, the keel stops the boat from overturning. Problems tend to arise only with greater degrees of one-sidedness. This is akin to the wind becoming much stronger so the keel breaks or the boat capsizes. We can see what this means in practice in the example of Capulet. He was a civilised man, taking very seriously his responsibilities as the head of the household and as a leading citizen in Verona. But he took things too far, focusing so much on social expectations that he overlooked the personal feelings of his daughter. He became too 'civilised', and being overly civilised is one way that the keel of the boat can break:

> [The] purpose [of the unconscious] is to compensate or correct, in a meaningful manner, the inevitable one-sidednesses ... of the conscious mind ... The differentiated consciousness of civilized man [runs] all the more danger ... of his getting lost in one-sidedness ... The more differentiated consciousness becomes, the greater the danger.
>
> (Jung 1940, pp. 162–63)

One-sidedness can take many forms – psychological, political, religious, social, philosophical, etc. Jung discusses some of these opposites in his analysis of Spitteler's epic poem *Prometheus and Epimetheus* (1881). This poem is of significance because Jung regards it as visionary, as reflecting something of profound significance in the cultural or phylogenetic layers of the unconscious psyche.

A visionary poem

In analytical psychology, there are two forms of artistic work – psychological and visionary (see Figure 5.1). Psychological art draws its content from conscious sources, for example by collating or adapting text or images that appear in other artistic creations. Visionary art is inspired; it comes from the fantasy or imaginative activity of the collective unconscious (Jung 1930/1950, pp. 105–6). It goes deeper than the personal unconscious, which holds material that has been

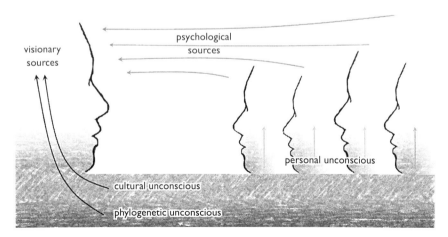

Figure 5.1 Psychological vs visionary sources.

forgotten or repressed due to individual life experiences. It goes to the collective layers that contain material that is repressed by culture or is part of our phylogenetic inheritance. Spitteler's poem is a visionary myth; it is a product of fantasy that points to the state of the collective unconscious. We can use it to understand some of the most profound aspects of not only our individual psyches but also our contemporary culture and civilisation.

We can illustrate the role of visionary myth using the analogy of sailors who want to understand the currents of the sea. Sailors cannot see the depths directly, but they can infer some of the undercurrents from the surface. They can see various features that give clues to the depth and direction of the currents, such as the waves, colours, debris floating on the surface, and rocky features. Similarly, just as the surface of the water is the intermediate stage between the air and the depths of the water, so too myth is the intermediate stage between consciousness and the depths of the unconscious (Jung 1963, p. 343). We cannot see what is happening in the unconscious psyche but we can infer it, using our observations of visionary myths and interpreting them symbolically. That is, we do not consider the story to be literal truth, or merely entertainment, or even a cryptic message. Instead, we view it as a dim echo of those parts of the psyche that we cannot access directly.

Spitteler's work is of value to Jung, and to the problem of conflict within and between individuals and societies, because he is in that class of poets, artists, and thinkers whose work is visionary. Jung regards visionary work as more significant because it comes from such a deep source; it has a more fundamental impact on the individual and society. Spitteler points to a solution for the problem of opposites that is relevant to Western culture (Jung 1921, p. 190).

Spitteler's poem deals directly with a few opposites, including the conflict between consciousness and the unconscious, extraversion and introversion, social conscience and individual soul, and opposing psychological functions. In chapter V of *Psychological Types*, Jung analyses the poem and then goes on to consider related opposites in Brahmanism, Chinese philosophy, the writings of Meister Eckhart, and others. The overall theme of Jung's analysis is that the West has been developing in an increasingly one-sided way, and Spitteler's story offers a solution. This solution may not be apparent from *Psychological Types* because Jung does not tell Spitteler's story, perhaps because he might have assumed that most readers would already be familiar with it. Spitteler wrote the poem in German in 1881 and Jung wrote *Psychological Types* in German in 1921. However, although Jung's book was translated into English within a couple of years, Spitteler's was not translated until 1931. Even then, it did not become a popular work because the style of the poem did not appeal to an English-speaking audience. Therefore, very few English readers are familiar with it. For that reason, we will examine Spitteler's story now, to help make sense of the analysis of it in *Psychological Types*.

Spitteler based his poem on two brothers from classical Greek mythology, Prometheus and Epimetheus, but he changes the nature of the brothers and their

64　Many forms of opposite

story significantly. He also introduces many other characters, including animals, objects, and anthropomorphisms. They all stand for aspects of the personality of one person. Some representations are explicit, such as characters called Soul and Conscience. God and the Angel of the Lord represent divinity, and a Lambkin represents a Christian attitude. Dogs and lions represent animal instincts.

These characters give the story an intrapersonal meaning. The conflict between Prometheus and Epimetheus is 'a struggle between the introverted and extraverted lines of development in one and the same individual' (Jung 1921, p. 166). The story is concerned only with people who are one-sided, and not the 'normal, middle-of-the-road man' (ibid., p. 170). For this last group of individuals, the relationship between intrapersonal and interpersonal conflict is not particularly relevant, because 'his neighbour [does not] appear to him in the least problematical' (ibid.). The story itself does not deal directly with societal conflicts, though Jung expands its application to these areas in his analysis. In the English translation, it runs to over 300 pages. We will briefly review the synopsis here. There is a more detailed summary in Appendix A.

Prometheus and Epimetheus

At the start of the poem, the two brothers Prometheus and Epimetheus live together. The Angel of the Lord needs to appoint a new king over the people of Earth. He wants to offer the position to Prometheus but cannot do so because Prometheus is too closely allied to Soul. So, he appoints Epimetheus, who declares his allegiance to Conscience. After his appointment, Conscience guides Epimetheus as to what is right and wrong in each situation. Epimetheus cares for his people and has a happy life, but Prometheus suffers by having to do menial chores and being isolated. He becomes ill, and his eyesight starts to fail. One evening, he happens to meet Epimetheus, who points out to Prometheus all his mistakes.

There is a 'Pandora interlude', in which God is sick (which mirrors Prometheus' suffering). God's daughter Pandora makes a jewel that will relieve the suffering of people. God blesses the treasure, and Pandora leaves it in the land of the people of Earth. Some peasants find the jewel and take it to the king, thinking they will get a reward. However, Conscience finds it alarming, so Epimetheus rejects it. The peasants take the treasure to various other people – priests, teachers, goldsmiths, and market sellers – but they all think it is worthless. Eventually, the peasants lose the treasure. Then, the Angel of the Lord visits Epimetheus, expecting the people of Earth to be celebrating the arrival of the jewel. As life is carrying on as normal, he calls them to account for not recognising the treasure and asks for its return, but they can't find it.

One of Epimetheus' responsibilities is to protect Mythos, Hiero, and Messias, the three sons of the Angel of the Lord. The Angel falls sick and, expecting to die, tries to hide his illness from his enemy Behemoth, until the Angel can crown his son Mythos as his successor. However, Behemoth realises the Angel is sick

Many forms of opposite   65

because he sees a vulture hovering, so he hatches a plan with Leviathan to capture the sons of God. They pretend to be friends with the people of Earth, build relationships with them, and remove the borders between their two lands. Epimetheus is deceived by the plan and Behemoth captures the three sons. Then, Behemoth and Leviathan kill Mythos. The people of Earth embark on a rescue mission for the other two sons. But Leviathan dissuades them from attacking Behemoth's land through a clever response. Behemoth then kills Hiero and the same thing happens – the people of Earth start to attack but are turned back.

There is then a fortunate twist in the story, because Behemoth and Leviathan do not get the opportunity to kill the third son of God (Messias). Behemoth's princes revolt (for other reasons) and return him to the people of Earth to make Behemoth and Leviathan fall out. Behemoth assembles an army to surround the people of Earth and force them to hand Messias back. The people, being afraid, want to hand him over, but Conscience will not let Epimetheus agree. To get out of the situation, Epimetheus agrees a deceitful plan with Leviathan. He arranges for Messias to be handed back with apparent guarantees of safety but knowing privately that he will be killed. Finding himself in an untenable position, Epimetheus sees no alternative but to resign as king.

The wife of the Angel of the Lord goes to find Prometheus, to see if he can do anything to save Messias. She meets Soul, who agrees to help by asking Prometheus to intervene. As the people of Earth lead the last Child of God to be handed over to Leviathan, Prometheus tricks them and rescues Messias. Although the Angel of the Lord is unhappy with the actions of the people of Earth, he commits his remaining son to their protection again, with a warning that their fate is inextricably bound to his. He offers the position of king to Prometheus, but he does not want it and goes searching for Epimetheus to reconcile their relationship. In the final scene, Prometheus meets the Angel of the Lord's wife and a caterpillar appears between them and runs off.

Jung's analysis

There are many parallels between Spitteler's poem and Jung's psychological solution to the conflict of opposites. He makes some of the connections at the start of chapter V of *Psychological Types*. Prometheus and Epimetheus represent various conflicts within an individual, between introvert and extravert attitudes, between individual conscience and soul, between two psychological functions, etc. They start the story living together in harmony, which represents an undifferentiated attitude (we will examine what this means in more detail in Chapter 8). They separate, and Epimetheus becomes king, which stands for an extraverted function becoming a dominant, one-sided attitude. Pandora's jewel appears, which stands for a psychological symbol from the unconscious that can potentially reconcile the intra-psychic split. The treasure is a divine wonder-child (Jung 1921, p. 259) so Pandora's jewel has the same symbolic meaning as Messias. The priests, teachers, etc. reject the treasure, which represents a failure

66   Many forms of opposite

by the conscious religious and educated attitudes to see its value. Instead, they strike a deal with Behemoth and Leviathan, which represents being so one-sided that they experience an enantiodromia (turning into the opposite). That is, their society (representing the conscious attitude) goes from being stable and driven by social conscience to making a pact with evil and facing a disaster. Prometheus saves the situation at the bidding of Soul, which stands for a compensatory attitude from the unconscious forcing itself on consciousness. Epimetheus resigns as king, and Prometheus refuses to become king. This stands for there being no dominant function, and the holding of the opposites in tension.

A different ending

At the end of the story, Jung's interpretation takes a slightly different turn from the story itself. Spitteler finishes the poem with the image of a caterpillar, an empty throne, and Messias in the care of the people of Earth. However, Jung adds an implied epilogue that Spitteler does not include in his text; he suggests that Messias takes the place of Epimetheus as king. Messias is a symbol that represents a function and an attitude:

> In their stead a new function appears, symbolized by the divine child Messias ... Messias is the mediator, the symbol of a new attitude in which the opposites are united.
>
> (Jung 1921, p. 271)

Spitteler leaves the question of kingship open. By the end of the story, Messias has become the divine heir, because he is the only surviving son of the Angel of the Lord. But the Angel of the Lord has not appointed Messias king; he has told the people of Earth to 'guard him and watch over him' (Spitteler 1881, p. 299). The Angel says he does not know who to appoint as king: 'Perhaps, another day may bring us a solution of this problem' (ibid.).

Jung implies that Messias goes from being cared for by the people to becoming sovereign over them. He represents the third thing, the symbol or function that transforms the personality and creates a new attitude. If this happens, Messias would be no ordinary king but a divine child king who rules in both heaven and earth. Therefore, he unites not only extraversion and introversion but also consciousness and the unconscious. He stands for not only a new psychological function and attitude but also a greater degree of wholeness and the emerging potential of the individual. At the start of the story, the individual was divided. Now, there is a new, unified attitude represented by Messias.

A surprising aspect of Jung's analysis is that he does not mention the caterpillar, which appears on Spitteler's final page. The caterpillar is a significant symbol that can represent a forthcoming transformation. Given that Spitteler finishes his story with this image, which is relevant to his solution, Jung's failure to mention it is striking. It is possible that this omission may have been due to an

Many forms of opposite 67

assumption that readers are familiar with the story. There was no need for Jung to explain that the caterpillar points to a forthcoming transformation because this symbolism is so obvious. Alternatively, it may have been because, in earlier years, he had associated the image of a caterpillar with Freud's psychoanalytic theory that was based on sexual development (e.g. Jung 1913b, p. 105). His break-up with Freud was bitter, and there is evidence of that bitterness in many of Jung's writings and actions up until Freud's death in 1939. When he wrote *Psychological Types* in 1921, he may have been inclined to avoid expressing an essential part of his theory using imagery that he saw as being associated with Freud.

Pandora's solution

In the second section of chapter V, Jung compares *Prometheus and Epimetheus* with two of Goethe's works which use the same characters – *Prometheus* and *Pandora*. Whilst there are some similarities, Jung finds Goethe's solution to the conflict between the brothers to be unsatisfactory. Goethe concludes with each character developing a better understanding of the other, of their underlying motivations, through the marriage of their offspring. This approach – of developing mutual understanding – is often used in conflict resolution, including approaches that are based on Myers-Briggs typology. Whilst there is nothing wrong with learning about other people's psychology, Jung is looking for a deeper solution that resolves the problem of one-sidedness. In that context, Goethe's solution is 'not sufficient as an explanation' (Jung 1921, p. 186). Goethe chooses his symbols consciously, rather than allowing them to come up from the unconscious. Jung lays the blame for this on the influence of classical Greek mythology. Goethe's symbols may have been suitable for ancient Greece, but there have been many intervening centuries of Christianity (ibid., p. 187). The value of allowing symbols to appear from the unconscious is that they produce solutions that are relevant to contemporary attitudes.

This analysis suggests there are two types of solution that may not work. The first is the attempt to understand the conscious motivations or psychology of the other. This lacks the power to change attitudes when there is entrenched one-sidedness or polarisation. The value of the symbol is that it canalises libido; it emerges from the creative power of the unconscious, and it forces people to take a different attitude merely by its presence. The second type of solution that may not work, in extreme cases of one-sidedness, is a formula that has succeeded in another time or another place. Although we need to retain links with our cultural history, every situation is different. Therefore, we need to develop a unique and contemporary solution whenever there is a new conflict. If the solution comes from the unconscious, it will naturally have links to both the present and the past.

In Spitteler's Pandora interlude, the unconscious produced a relevant symbol – the jewel – that had the potential to reconcile and heal the division in the

68   Many forms of opposite

psyche. If the people of Earth had recognised its value, and treated the symbol with respect, they could have avoided the disaster that later occurred. That would have meant acknowledging Pandora's jewel as a valuable symbol, and giving time and space for its meaning and message to unfold. That is, taking a symbolic attitude could have resolved the split within the psyche without having to experience an enantiodromia.

A symbolic attitude would have looked at the jewel and said: 'I don't like this, it's horrible. My abhorrence of it must mean something. What does it mean?'. However, all the elements of the conscious world, including the representatives of social conscience, academic learning, established religion, etc., rejected it. They saw the jewel as something repugnant, and they did not even recognise there was a division that needed to be overcome. They represented one-sided attitudes that were unable or unwilling to understand anything that did not fit into their viewpoints. This conscious one-sidedness was the cause of the suffering and illness that afflicted Prometheus and God.

From a Jungian perspective, there is a tendency in contemporary Western culture for scientific and religious attitudes to reject numinous symbols (Hall and Young-Eisendrath 1991, p. 33). In many of Jung's writings, he acknowledges that the development of science has ushered in a more advanced form of thought, and that it shares some of his goals such as wholeness (Jung 1952, p. 451). But he also criticises it for being one-sided – or, rather, he criticises Western culture for its 'one-sidedness [in the] overvaluation of scientifically attested views' (Jung 1947/1954, p. 220). Scientific knowledge has an important role in human understanding, but Western culture privileges rational, conscious thought whilst rejecting symbolic modes of thinking that engage with the irrational unconscious. Goethe fell into this trap by imposing a conscious, rational meaning on the symbols in his story, thereby destroying their emergent, unconscious significance. Whereas Goethe's solution was too superficial, Spitteler allowed the solution to emerge from the unconscious; he allowed the significance and meaning of the symbol to unfold. This was a deeper and more powerful solution.

Disaster as the ultimate solution

The psyche is a self-correcting system. Therefore, if the ego will not take a symbolic attitude and pay attention to symbols, then the unconscious might try to force the ego to pay attention, sometimes through a life-changing event or disaster. Disasters can occur for many reasons that are unrelated to our attitude. Some are the result of nature or due to actions by other people over whom we have no influence. Spitteler's story shows, however, that some disasters can inadvertently be of our own making; they occur when the psyche tries to heal itself and repair the split caused by one-sidedness. If we ignore the symbols that can reconcile, they may reappear later in a more powerful and potentially damaging form. What Jung particularly liked about Spitteler was that he explored the consequences of the first symbol being rejected. The unconscious tried even

Many forms of opposite 69

harder to compensate until it escalated out of control. There was an enantiodro-mia. Epimetheus, whose life had been dominated by social conscience, found himself making a pact with evil.

This theme – that certain types of disaster can result from our own attitudes – occurs in both Spitteler's poem and Shakespeare's *Romeo and Juliet*. Capulet had a strong social conscience but he did not take a symbolic attitude, nor pay attention to the evidence of his unconscious attitude. It led to a disaster in which his life was turned upside down and he got the very thing he was trying to avoid. He wanted the best for his daughter but, by ignoring the signs of Juliet's stress, it resulted in the worst, her death. In Spitteler's story, Epimetheus wanted the best for the people of Earth, and to adhere to his social conscience. But he ignored the signs of the psychic split – the uniting symbol that was Pandora's jewel – and it nearly led to the people of Earth falling under the complete control of Behemoth and Leviathan. It was only due to a combination of luck and Prometheus' intervention that the second symbol (Messias) was saved.

This argument is not exalting the Promethean attitude over the Epimethean one. It is highlighting the consequences of one-sidedness. Earlier in Jung's ana-lysis, he shows how Prometheus is as one-sided as Epimetheus, but in a different direction. The point is not to value one opposite over the other, but to treat them with equal respect and seriousness. If we do not, the unconscious will try to compensate, and it may take the extreme form of broken relationships, loss of reputation, financial loss, economic downturn, international conflict, etc. Spitteler's story highlights the danger of one-sidedness and of ignoring or reject-ing symbols that have the potential to reconcile.

The religious alternative

There are various lessons from Jung's analysis that still have contemporary relevance. Established religions come out poorly from Spitteler's story and from Jung's analysis 'because [they are] lacking insight' (Jung 1921, p. 194). They often merely assert a dogma or pursue a rigid form of social conscience. This perpetuates a split between the ego and the unconscious, and neglects the indi-viduality or spirituality that is represented by Soul. Religion can be of great psychological value if it takes a symbolic attitude. This is not a question of whether one believes in the existence of God or gods. The relation between God and the unconscious is a separate and complicated question (White 1952). Reli-gion can play a constructive role in reconciling opposites when it takes the form of a spiritual quest for discovering those aspects of ourselves and the world that are unknown.

Jung viewed the words *religio* or *religare* as having originally meant to con-sider or reconnect with the numinous (Jung 1950, p. 596 and fn). Symbols often have a numinous quality and, when religion pays attention to them, they can provide a powerful way to bridge conscious and unconscious attitudes. This involves 'allowing the symbol plenty of room to unfold' (Jung 1921, p. 193) and

70   Many forms of opposite

coming to terms with our inner instincts. A religious attitude pays attention to the unknown, to the irrational contents that appear from the unconscious, and it allows time for the meaning of the symbol to become clear. This type of religious attitude is aware of the inner division and the need to bridge it.

There is a danger in being 'civilised' if as a result we pay attention to only one side of our personality. We avoid internal contradictions or absolve ourselves from blame by adhering to a social conscience and projecting the other side of our psyche into other people. For this reason, those who are neurotic – and realise it – can be more 'individuated' than those who seem to be civilised:

> The man with a neurosis who knows that he is neurotic is more individuated than the man without this consciousness. The man who is a damned nuisance to his surroundings and knows it is more individuated than the man who is blissfully unconscious of his nature ... If a man is contradicted by himself and does not know it, he is an illusionist, but if he knows that he contradicts himself, he is individuated.

(Jung 1956, p. 324)

When we acknowledge and reconcile the opposites in ourselves, it does not lead to their disappearance or to the destruction of the differences. It leads to a new attitude that is based on a psychological function that transcends them (goes beyond their limits). Prometheus and Epimetheus are still there at the end of the story, but they have much less influence on the people of Earth; the conflict between the opposites no longer dominates the personality. We can see a practical example of this in South Africa. Before the 1990s, the system of apartheid dominated many aspects of society, leading to restrictions on various political, financial, cultural, and sporting activities. In the twenty-first century, there are still differences in ethnic background and subculture, but they no longer dominate South African politics and there are no longer any restrictions on the country's participation in international affairs. This is a new form of civilisation, one that enables the opposing sides to interact with a much greater parity of respect.

References

Hall, J.A., Young-Eisendrath, P. (1991). *Jung's Self Psychology: A Constructivist Perspective.* New York: The Guildford Press.
Jung, C.G. (1913a). 'A contribution to psychological types'. In *CW6*.
Jung, C.G. (1913b). 'The theory of psychoanalysis'. In *CW4*.
Jung, C.G. (1914). 'On psychological understanding'. In *CW3*.
Jung, C.G. (1915). 'The role of the unconscious'. In *CW10*.
Jung, C.G. (1921). *CW6*.
Jung, C.G. (1926/1946). 'Analytical psychology and education: three lectures'. In *CW17*.
Jung, C.G. (1930/1950). 'Psychology and literature'. In *CW15*.
Jung, C.G. (1938). 'Letter to V. Subrahamanya Iyer, 29 August 1938'. In *Letters 1*.
Jung, C.G. (1940). 'The psychology of the child archetype'. In *CW9i*.

Jung, C.G. (1947/1954). 'On the nature of the psyche'. In *CW8*.

Jung, C.G. (1950). 'Foreword to the "I Ching"'. In *CW11*.

Jung, C.G. (1952). 'Synchronicity: an acausal connecting principle'. In *CW8*.

Jung, C.G. (1956). 'Letter to Henry A. Murray, August 1956'. In *Letters 2*.

Jung, C.G. (1963). *Memories, Dreams, Reflections*. London: Harper Collins, 1995.

Jung, C.G. (2009). *The Red Book: Liber Novus*, edited by Sonu Shamdasani, trans. M. Kyburz, J. Peck, and S. Shamdasani. New York: W.W. Norton.

Myers, I.B. (1980). *Gifts Differing*. Palo Alto, CA: Davis Black, 1995.

Samuels, A. (1985). *Jung and the Post-Jungians*. London: Routledge, 1986.

Spitteler, C. (1881). *Prometheus and Epimetheus*, trans. James F. Muirhead. London: Jarrolds Publishers.

White, V. (1952). *God and the Unconscious*. Dallas, TX: Spring Publications, 1982.

Chapter 6

Individuals, relationships, groups, society

The solution to the conflict of opposites is relevant to any level of psychological functioning, from the individual to international relations, but in different ways. Jungian analysts and academics have applied the concepts of analytical psychology to individuals, relationships, groups (e.g. Stein and Hollwitz 1992), society (e.g. Mattoon 1993), and culture (e.g. Singer and Kimbles 2004). Some academics have raised objections to some of these developments (e.g. Lu 2013; Samuels 2010). They argue, for example, that it is too simplistic to transfer individual concepts to large groups, or that writings based on Jungian theory often fail to take sufficient account of other psychological and sociological research.

Jung's primary focus was on the psyche of the individual, which he saw as having a different nature from collective functioning. In later years he turned his attention to bigger questions about the nature of human existence, including the collective processes that drive society, but he did not simply transfer individual concepts to the shared domain. In this chapter, we will examine how Jung applied his theory to four distinct levels – individuals, relationships, groups, and society – whilst being mindful of some of the concerns raised about their application. Once we have examined all four categories, we will then consider the different ways in which Jung's transcendent function is relevant to the individual and to the collective.

Collectivity is the result of the aggregation or sharing of attitudes in a multitude of people. The term 'collective consciousness' has two aspects. It refers firstly to the same attitudes that occur within all those individuals who are members of a group. For example, if the television news shows a major international disaster and the group of viewers react with horror, then that reaction is a collective attitude because the viewers share it. The second aspect is, to use the terminology of systems theory, an emergent property of the group. Culture is an example of an emergent property because it is more than the aggregation of individual attitudes. It includes processes, laws, infrastructure, etc., that arise from the shared attitudes.

An analogy that illustrates these two aspects of the term 'collective' is listening to a barbershop quartet that sings a harmonious chord. The chord itself is an emergent property; one person cannot sing a chord on their own. The feeling of

Individuals, relationships, groups, society   73

harmony is a shared, collective feeling; it is a subjective reaction that occurs in parallel within the people listening. Comparably, Jung's term 'collective' describes both the emergent properties of a group of people (the chord) and the parallel attitudes of individuals (the feeling of harmony).

Individual

The four categories of this chapter's title are not Jung's distinctions but they are a useful framework to examine his various writings on collective functioning. The difference between them is the number of conscious egos involved. At the individual level, there is a single ego – the sense of awareness that constitutes 'me' or 'I'. Everything that is within consciousness is related to the ego. For example, if I can smell a rose, then the ego is conscious of that smell. If I have an idea, or can see an implicit connection, then the ego is conscious of that idea or relation. When I cannot perceive something then it is outside my awareness; it is unconscious, which means it has no relation to the ego.

The ego makes the individual inherently different from the other levels, which involve interactions between egos. Just as the behaviour of a single bird is different from that of a flock of birds, so too the action of a person is not the same as that of a group or society. Some theorists believe that when more than one person is involved there is a new entity to which we need to pay attention, i.e. 'a group ego and a group self' (Stein and Hollwitz 1992, p. 191). Although Jung does refer to 'group-consciousness' (Jung 1933/1934, p. 136) or collective consciousness, he does not treat it as a distinct ego. Collective consciousness can describe an attitude that is shared by or emergent from the members of the group, but it is not a distinct sense of awareness.

Layers of the unconscious

The most important problem of opposites within the individual is the schism between consciousness and the unconscious. The unconscious is a 'psychological borderline concept' (Jung 1921, p. 483) which means we cannot see what it is; we can only see the border that appears in conscious awareness. We can illustrate a borderline concept by thinking of our ego as a person locked inside a room in a house. We are unable to move out of the room. We are prisoners in our consciousness. Although there may be lots of other rooms or cellars in the house, we cannot see them. All we can see are the walls and the doors of our room. These walls are the borderline between what we can see and what we cannot. We can only surmise what lies beyond those walls by the clues we get – such as the sound of activity through the walls, or light seeping under the door. Most of Jung's theories are concerned, in one way or another, with raising awareness of the unconscious, of what lies beyond conscious awareness. Although we are prisoners in the room of consciousness, the walls are movable. We can push them back, expand the room, excavate the cellars, and rearrange

74 Individuals, relationships, groups, society

the layout. By integrating contents from the unconscious, the area that we see becomes more extensive and more open plan. In the West, we do not tend to do this, we do not pay attention to the unconscious (Jung 1928b, p. 198); as a result, we have become increasingly one-sided. Many contemporary psychologists might challenge that assertion, pointing to modern tools and models that are used to raise awareness of unconscious contents. However, many of these are related to the personal unconscious, which may actually be exacerbating the problem rather than solving it.

In *Two Essays* (*CW7*), Jung makes an assertion that has significant implications for typology but might seem very perplexing. He suggests that raising awareness of the personal unconscious makes us more collective whilst raising awareness of the collective unconscious makes us more individual and unique. For example, he writes that 'raising the personal unconscious to consciousness ... [makes one] less individually unique, and more collective' (Jung 1928b, p. 148). The Jungian analyst Jolande Jacobi makes a similar point when she describes the analysis of the personal unconscious as an adjustment to external reality (Jacobi 1958). Through raising awareness of the personal unconscious, we think and act more like everyone else in the culture. By raising awareness of the collective unconscious, we begin to develop an attitude that is more unique. Although this may seem counter-intuitive, we can illustrate it by comparing what happens in a performance appraisal at work with the process of raising awareness that takes place in Jungian analysis.

A performance appraisal often includes 360-degree feedback, which involves colleagues at all levels – bosses, peers, subordinates – giving the person feedback on their behaviour. The common themes from this feedback will include the collective cultural values of the organisation and how well the individual fits with those values. For example, a restaurant manager might tell a waiter 'to be more professional, don't smile at the customers so much'. This type of feedback is a form of socialisation; it encourages the person to change to be more in line with the working culture. There might be a conscious element (such as the waiter realising his need to be more professional) and an unconscious one (he might not have been aware of the degree to which he smiles). The manager pointed it out to him because it does not fit with the restaurant culture. When the waiter recognises this and changes his behaviour, he is becoming more collective.

In Jungian analysis, the therapist often helps the client to go deeper than the personal unconscious, into the collective unconscious, which includes cultural and phylogenetic layers. If we become aware of the cultural layer, it raises our awareness of contents of which other people in the culture are unconscious. It gives us an insight into various problems and issues in society that other people do not recognise. By withdrawing collective cultural projections, we develop an individual perspective that may be contrary to the prevailing, cultural view.

In the restaurant example, the cultural layer of the unconscious includes things that are relevant to everyone working in that environment, but is unknown to them. By raising awareness of this layer, it gives the person a new insight that

Individuals, relationships, groups, society 75

is different from everyone else's. For example, the waiter might have a dream in which a customer places an order for two meals. Through the Jungian analysis, the waiter might conclude that the dream is suggesting the restaurant does not serve enough food for most customers' tastes. The waiter then develops a new attitude – a wish to serve larger portions – that is different from the current collective attitude in the restaurant. The waiter becomes more individual and unique; but it also creates a conflict between the prevailing cultural view and the waiter's view. If both sides engage in a constructive dialogue based on their different perspectives, it can potentially lead to the restaurant changing their approach in a way that improves its service to customers.

Figure 6.1 illustrates – in a highly simplified form – how raising awareness of the personal and collective layers of the unconscious affects the collectivity or individuality of the person. It calculates an illustrative 'collectivity score' that shows how similar the person's attitude and behaviour is to the psychology of the collective group or culture. Higher scores are more collective. There are three factors – the conscious attitude, the personal unconscious, and the collective unconscious.

In the first column, at the start, the person has already differentiated a conscious attitude that is collective (for example, becoming a good waiter, or becoming a type). As this attitude is similar to other people's, it has a score of plus one. The personal unconscious is unique to the individual, being the result of their own life experiences, so this has a score of minus one. The cultural and phylogenetic layers of the collective unconscious are similar, so they have a score of plus one. When we add the scores in the first column, we get a total collectivity score of one. That is, before raising awareness of the unconscious, the person is somewhat collective.

The second column shows what happens after raising awareness of the personal unconscious, as shown by the example of the waiter's 360-degree

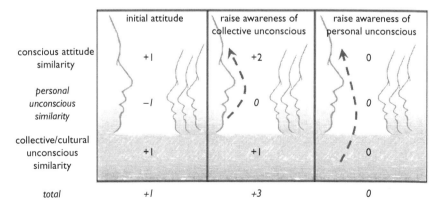

Figure 6.1 Raising awareness of personal vs collective unconscious.

76 Individuals, relationships, groups, society

feedback. Such knowledge makes the person develop a more collective attitude and act more collectively, so the top number goes from one to two. It also reduces the impact of the personal unconscious, which therefore goes to zero. The total is now plus three – the person has become very collective.

The third column shows what happens after raising awareness of the collective unconscious, as illustrated by the example of the waiter's dream. There is a radical change in the conscious attitude, because the person develops an individual perspective that is different from the prevailing culture; it now has a score of zero. The collective unconscious has less impact than in earlier stages, so now it also has a score of zero. When added up, this column has a total collectivity score of zero, being a better balance between individuality and collectivity.

This model illustrates how raising awareness of the personal unconscious makes us more collective, but raising awareness of the collective unconscious makes us more individual. The model is admittedly very simplistic, which is for the purposes of illustration. We cannot become fully aware of the contents of the unconscious because it is so vast. On the contrary, the more we become aware of it, the bigger and more powerful it seems to become. Also, the personal and collective unconscious are not clearly delineated domains; they can be mixed up with each other. Raising awareness of the personal unconscious eventually leads to raising awareness of the collective unconscious (Jung 1928b, p. 158). Discovering the unconscious in ourselves is akin to an archaeological dig that starts out investigating what appears to be a small hut. As we dig down, we find streets and buildings that go on endlessly. Eventually, we reach a point when we realise we are dealing with a large town, city, or civilisation that is far bigger than we ever imagined. The archaeologist feels humbled by the scale and importance of this find, which becomes a major project for years to come. In a similar way, as we raise unconscious contents to consciousness, the scale of what we are dealing with seems to increase. As consciousness expands, the ego feels less and less powerful.

Relationships

In any relationship between two people, there are two egos, with two unconscious psyches. They share some attitudes, such as typology and archetypes, though they may have developed them differently due to their skills and life experiences. What makes the dynamics of a relationship very different from an individual's intrapersonal dynamics is that there is no single ego. The interaction of the conscious and unconscious aspects of each person can create complicated interpersonal dynamics. We saw an example of this in Chapter 2, in the relationship between Capulet and Montague. Figure 6.2 shows the dynamics between two people in any form of relationship (Jung 1946a, p. 221).

Relationship (a) is the direct, uncomplicated communication between the conscious egos of the two people. Relationships (b) and (c) are between the conscious and unconscious attitudes of each person, which we discussed in the last

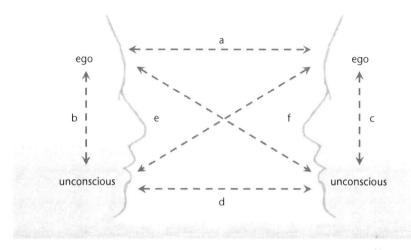

Figure 6.2 Interpersonal relations.

section. Relationship (d) is the interaction between the unconscious psyches of the two people. The unconscious holds many attitudes, including archetypes, repressed memories, experiences, and complexes. Complexes refer to things that are all mixed up or concreted together. For example, if we had a bad childhood experience with a dog that we have forgotten, we may have unconsciously mixed up the sight of a dog with the emotion of fear. This visual stimulus and inner emotion are concreted together in a complex that gives us an irrational fear of all dogs.

When two people interact, their unconscious complexes can interact without them realising. Something that one person says or does can inadvertently trigger a complex in the other person that causes an irrational response. We cannot see such unconscious interactions directly, but we can sometimes feel them viscerally, or infer their impact through other observations or experiences. They can be like two icebergs which appear to be some distance apart but collide beneath the surface of the water.

Relationships (e) and (f) represent the interaction of the unconscious in one person with the ego of the other. We can sometimes recognise something in the other person that they cannot see in themselves. Alternatively, we might project into them – assigning views, feelings, or characteristics which have their origins in ourselves to the other person. We might derive these projections from a past relationship, archetype, or both – such as taking the same attitude towards our boss as we had towards a parent. The projection is stronger if the other person has some characteristics that resonate with it. For example, Capulet was able to justify labelling Montague as aggressive because he sometimes acted aggressively.

78 Individuals, relationships, groups, society

In any relationship between two people, they each have their own attitudes, both conscious and unconscious. Where those attitudes are the same, they are a collective attitude – a form of collective consciousness and a collective unconscious. The term 'collective' in this context refers to the fact that they occur in parallel within the two people. When two people have opposing viewpoints, they often still share something in common. Opposites are rarely entirely different; there is usually some common element that defines their opposition. Hot and cold are opposites; they are both forms of temperature. High and low are opposites; they are both forms of altitude. Comparably, when two people have contrary views, there is usually something about their attitudes that they have in common. For example, they might both have an interest in politics, even though one is right wing and the other left wing. Or they might share some religious beliefs, although they interpret those beliefs differently.

Participation mystique

When two people share an unconscious attitude, they experience participation mystique, which means they (unconsciously) identify with each other. That is, they imitate each other without realising it, and adopt the same attitudes. Jung's version of participation mystique is an adaptation of a concept developed by the philosopher Lévy-Bruhl, and it has a significant impact on one-sidedness. In Lévy-Bruhl's version, a primitive mind identifies itself with an external object and is unable to distinguish itself from it; in contrast, the modern mind can make the distinction between self and object. However, Jung argued that participation mystique is still relevant today, albeit in a different form. It is an identification with other people rather than with objects. We do not make the distinction between ourselves and collective attitudes, so we think those attitudes are our own. We inadvertently imitate the conventional ways of thinking and behaving, and thereby change our personality to be the same as the norm (Jung 1921, p. 440). Such unconscious identification can underpin a romantic or social relationship. When two people fall in love, this is often the result of unconscious projections that have their origins in parental relationships (Jung 1925, p. 190). They identify with the similarities in their relations with their parents, which leads to a mutual attraction and imitation of each other.

Imitating others is an essential part of development in childhood, and it can sometimes be useful in adulthood. The main problem arises when it is unconscious and becomes a hindrance to the development of the individual attitude. Participation mystique is a form of projection so, when we share the same one-sidedness, we share the same projections. For example, if two people are unconsciously agitated and identify with each other, they might both ascribe that agitation to someone else, to the same third person. Other people can thereby become the scapegoats who carry the collective projections of two or more people (Jung 1931b, p. 65).

Groups

Although Jung did not distinguish between groups and society, these two categories can help reveal some different analyses that he offered about collective functioning. The difference, for the present discussion, is that a group is based on interpersonal dynamics, whilst society is based on culture. The two overlap but, in a group, one person joining or leaving can make a significant difference to the way the members of the group interact and to their relationships. In a society, it is the underlying culture and subcultures that drive the collective attitudes and how people behave.

The dynamics of groups are significantly more complicated than the dynamics of relationships. There are many more egos and unconscious psyches involved, creating a complex network of attitudes and projections that have individual, shared, and emergent aspects. Jung viewed the group's collective psychology as the accumulation of the common elements of the individual members' psychologies. What tend to be most common in members of a group are unconscious instincts. Therefore, the shared attitudes in a group tend to be inferior to those held by individuals. They can be more primitive, more violent, more extreme, and more suggestible (Jung 1936, pp. 570–71).

Projections play a significant role in the formation and functioning of groups, whether they be family, friends, work colleagues, or other groups with whom one has little direct contact. For the one-sided person to feel comfortable in daily life, they need to find carriers of unconscious projections (Jung 1954a, pp. 266–67). We keep the positive projections inside the group of intimate relations and push the negative ones outside that group (Jung 1916/1948, pp. 271–72). This creates intergroup tensions and conflicts. This aspect of Jung's analytical psychology has similarities with the ingroups and outgroups of social identity theory (Figure 6.3). We treat people in our ingroup favourably, and we disparage, belittle, or fear those in the outgroup. For example, Capulet's household carried his positive projections, and his negative projections were carried by Montague and his household. Other members of Capulet's family shared this split, which is why Juliet was horrified when she discovered that Romeo was a 'loathed enemy' (Shakespeare 1982, *Romeo and Juliet*, I.v.141).

Jung's various discussions of collective group psychology suggest he sees it as often reinforcing one-sidedness. Groups entice members into mutual imitation, through participation mystique and because group conformity is safer than confronting oppositions with other people or within oneself. In participation mystique, people can become so identified with the group that they lose sight of the difference between their uniqueness and the group psychology. Their individuality becomes submerged within the group as they think more collectively, and their suggestibility also makes them susceptible to primitive or even dangerous behaviours (Jung 1940/1950, pp. 125–27). The group can stimulate attitudes or responses in an individual that they would not use when alone (Jung 1959, pp. 470–71). Social psychological experiments have confirmed this group

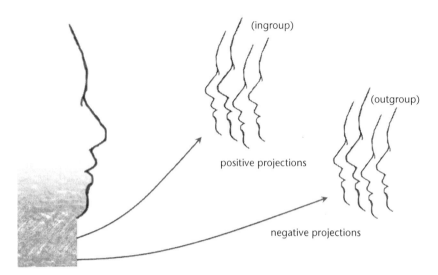

Figure 6.3 Split group projections.

tendency and shown it to be relevant to the problem of political one-sidedness (Bishop and Cushing 2008, pp. 58–78). We can see practical demonstrations in the partisan shouting during Prime Minister's Questions in the House of Commons. The government and opposition face each other in a physical expression of the split of projections. All the physical and psychological elements combine to encourage the expression of instinctual behaviours.

Jung suggests it is not possible to change collective attitudes by applying his methods at a group level (Jung 1955–56, p. 106fn). We can only bring about a change within the individual, within ourselves, which can affect the behaviour of the group in two ways. If enough people work on themselves, the diversity of conscious attitudes can begin to change the collective psychology. Alternatively, if the leaders set an example, the behaviour of the group can change through its collective suggestibility (Jung 1948, pp. 609–10).

Type as a collective psychology

Towards the end of chapter X of *Psychological Types*, Jung states that the type descriptions are not of individuals, they are 'Galtonesque family portraits' (Jung 1921, p. 405). Sir Francis Galton was a pioneer in various fields, including statistics and psychometrics, but Jung's reference is to his photographic work. He took multiple images of different individuals, centred on their eyes, and superimposed them. This removed their individual features and left an average face. A Galtonesque family portrait shows what is common to the group, and it removes their individuality. Comparably, Jung's descriptions of psychological types show the aspects of psychology that people with each form of one-sidedness share, and it removes their individuality. That is, typology is collective psychology, and the type descriptions are stereotypes.

The value of these stereotypes is that they act as '*points de repère*' (Jung 1957b, p. 304, original italics). The meaning of this phrase is 'landmark', which is a static reference point. Jung used a related analogy when describing the typological functions as 'somewhat like the four points of the compass' (Jung 1931a, p. 541). These geographical references show the difference between a psychological type and an individual. There is an infinite number of locations in the world, but there are only a few landmarks. When we are orienteering, we do not usually describe our location as being permanently at a landmark. Rather, we describe where we are by reference to the closest landmarks. Sometimes, in our journey, we might be close to one landmark, at other times we may be between two or more landmarks, and the nearest landmarks may change as our location changes. Similarly, our closest psychological type can change over time (Jung 1937, p. 230) as our individual personality changes. And the group of people who are in-between types are 'the most numerous' (Jung 1923, p. 516).

Because the types are stereotypes, and a typological function is a social function, it 'is as detrimental to the individual as it is valuable to society' (Jung 1921, p. 72). When we identify with a typological function, or group of functions, 'individuality falls into the unconscious' (ibid., p. 440), and it puts us into 'a collective state' (ibid., p. 100). A straightforward way to think of this is that there are 16 types and a world population of seven billion. Therefore, if we identify with a type, we are declaring our psychology to be the same as hundreds of millions of other people in the world. The problem of one-sided types serving a social purpose but damaging the individual is a key theme in chapter II of *Psychological Types.* In Jung's view, this problem had grown much worse in the century between Schiller first describing it and Jung writing about it (Jung 1921, p. 74).

Individuation is concerned with developing the individual as distinct from collective psychology. Hence, Jung is concerned when people identify with groups. He even expressed concern about people identifying with groups of Jungians – in his famous statement: 'thank God, I am Jung, and not a Jungian' (Hannah 1976, loc. 1483). Jung was reacting to many of his pupils turning his concepts into shared dogma and thereby overlooking the individual. He was rejecting the identification with a collective way of thinking and asserting that he was an individual. Although he acknowledged the value of collective functioning, he viewed the West as failing to get the balance right and not recognising the downsides of collectivisation:

> We need not stress the social advantages of living in a group, let alone the necessary and vital protection afforded by society. They are known to everyone. On the other hand, nobody likes or dares to mention in so many words the negative effects of group-existence.
>
> (Jung 1959, pp. 471–72)

Society

The main difference between groups and society, for the present discussion, is one of scale. There are so many people involved that the driver of behaviours is not interpersonal relations; it is the underlying shared culture or subculture, which can include a range of values, beliefs, myths, structures, processes, and norms. One person is unlikely to have a significant impact on culture, apart from exceptional cases of leadership such as Mahatma Gandhi or Nelson Mandela. Even then, these leaders were enabled and empowered by the culture. They helped to deliver what many people wanted. That is, the eras of change they ushered in were not due to their leadership alone, but due to the tide of change which made them symbolic spearheads. This aspect of leadership can be compared to a tidal bore, which may appear to be leading the flow of water but is a symptom of the opposition between the outflowing river and the incoming tide. The bore does not move the water; it is pushed along by powerful forces that it does not control.

If there had been no racial persecution in South Africa, Gandhi and Mandela would have had successful careers in the legal profession. The culture in South Africa made it difficult for them to pursue their chosen careers; it created the need for leaders to oppose prejudice and it motivated them to meet that need. Gandhi spent more than 20 years defending the cause of Indians in South Africa, before returning to India to campaign for home rule. The collective culture played a significant role, alongside their talents and motivations, in turning Gandhi and Mandela into political activists. They became symbolic spearheads for the movements they represented – though they fulfilled that role with aplomb because they were not one-sided in their main political attitudes.

Promoting world peace

When discussing changes in culture or society, Jung repeatedly returns to the individual relationship between the ego and the unconscious. His best opportunity to influence global international relations came shortly after the Second World War. UNESCO invited several leading psychologists to suggest ways of promoting world peace, as part of what was known as the Tensions project. Jung proposed a programme aimed at improving the relationship between the ego and the unconscious in people who played a leading role in society and education. His aim was to change the attitude of the mass indirectly through the example and influence of many people in leading positions, such as politicians and teachers (Jung 1948, p. 610).

Jung supported his proposal to UNESCO with three works, one of which was *Psychological Types.* However, when staff prepared a summary of expert contributions, they ignored Jung's ideas. They focused instead on submissions by various social scientists and Anna Freud. UNESCO described her proposals as 'one of the approaches to psychological methods of attitude change which will most need to be considered' (UNESCO 1948a, p. 6). The report produced after the conference (UNESCO 1948b) shows that Jung's theory ought to have been highly relevant. Half of the ten conclusions relate to the forms of intrapersonal and interpersonal tensions that analytical psychology addresses.

It seems that Anna Freud had succeeded, where Jung had not, because of the style and nature of her presentation. She described experiences with refugee children, explaining them from the perspective of psychoanalysis, and then made practical suggestions that UNESCO could take forward. Jung's presentation was very different because he took a theoretical approach, highlighted all the difficulties from the start, and used pejorative language about those who would be involved. For example, he implied that schoolteachers were patients who needed treatment, which they were unlikely to pursue anyway unless they were already 'absolutely convinced that his personal attitude is in need of revision' (Jung 1948, p. 610). UNESCO had already expressed an interest in Jung's theory, but he did not make it relevant and applicable to their concerns, nor did he provide evidence that it would have the impact they were looking for. He included a mass of reading material that, for this audience, was incomprehensible. The theory may have been good, but his presentation was poor, or a poor fit for the audience, so UNESCO ignored it.

Psychic epidemics

One recurring theme in Jung's work, which is very relevant to one-sidedness in society, is his analysis of psychic infections and epidemics. Jung drew a comparison between psychic and medical epidemics (Jung 1934a, p. 101). Whereas in the medical model there is an organism that invades the body, in the psychic model there is an unconscious complex that invades consciousness. A psychic infection is the transmission of an unconscious complex that destroys individuality (Jung 1958, p. 381). It can happen through face-to-face discussion between two people, including a therapist and a patient, or the transmission of images, ideas, or information through the media. A psychic epidemic occurs when the infection becomes contagious, triggering unconscious complexes in large numbers of people.

A complex consists of psychic contents that are joined (or concreted) together. It can include archetypes, emotions, images, beliefs, judgments, etc. It is like a spider's web, where vibrations on one part are transmitted to the rest of it. Triggering any one part of a complex triggers the whole of it. For example, suppose an individual has a 'father complex', which joins the father archetype with various memories. If the person sees someone behaving in a way that reminds them of the father, it will trigger all the thoughts and emotions in the complex. The individual then has similar feelings and makes similar judgments to those they had made about the real father. It is a 'transference'; they project emotions and thoughts associated with one person into another person. The individual regards the judgments as valid ways of reacting to that person because the transference is unconscious.

84 Individuals, relationships, groups, society

Psychic epidemics are the spread of complexes that create an unconscious uniformity within a section of society (see Figure 6.4). Parents can (unconsciously) pass complexes to their children (Jung 1927/1931b, p. 34), and politicians and journalists can pass them on to everyone (Jung 1929, p. 37). Jung mentions a wide range of complexes that can become infections and be spread through psychic epidemics:

- the example set by others (Jung 1928a, pp. 149–50; 2009, p. 249);
- way of life (1930a, p. 493);
- religious beliefs (1930b, p. 69);
- behaviour (1930c, p. 508);
- feelings of inferiority (1930c, p. 513);
- academic prejudices (1928/1931, p. 87);
- confusion (1933, p. 517);
- the psychic atmosphere (1935, p. 145);
- transference projections (1935, pp. 152–54);
- taking responsibility for others' problems (1945b, p. 596);
- psychic disturbance (1946a, p. 172fn);
- neurotic suffering (1926/1946, p. 78);
- ideas (1934/1950, p. 304);
- sadness and wretchedness (1911–12/1952, p. 71fn);
- political ideologies (1911–12/1952, p. 156);
- the spirit of the times (1957a, p. 264).

The contemporary triggers for a psychic epidemic can be a TV programme, a newspaper report, a tweet, or a Facebook post that 'goes viral', or any form of communication that reaches many people. However, mass media do not have to be involved. Just as a medical infection can be transferred from person to person

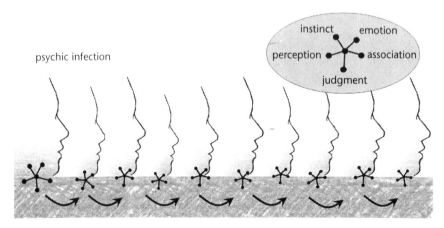

Figure 6.4 The spread of complexes.

Individuals, relationships, groups, society   85

and reach epidemic proportions, so too a psychic infection can be replicated through natural transmission between individuals so that it becomes a psychic epidemic. Some ideas are themselves so inherently infectious that they affect groups, communities, and nations without the need for the involvement of mass media.

At no time does Jung articulate a list of symptoms of psychic epidemics. He sprinkles his ideas about them throughout his work, without pulling them together or summarising them. We can infer many of the characteristics from his discussion of archetypes, because 'the driving forces of a psychological mass movement are essentially archetypal' (Jung 1946b, p. 237). Psychic epidemics tend to involve one-sidedness on a grand scale, with large groups of people being polarised or split between irreconcilable differences. We may defend our cause, or attack the other, using emotional judgments, distorted reasoning, and selective facts. The debate might focus intensely on a few individuals, describing them using extreme language, and associating what is right with one person and wrong with another. And these behaviours are unconscious, so we are unaware that a collective complex is sweeping us along and driving our thoughts and decisions. We believe our descriptions of the individuals are objectively accurate.

Psychic epidemics do not necessarily produce adverse consequences. In the medical model, there are many good viruses on which our ongoing physical health depends; so too, in analytical psychology, there are beneficial complexes. They are such a fundamental concept that, at one point, Jung considered renaming his theory 'complex psychology' (Samuels *et al.* 1986, p. 34). When bad medical viruses affect people they usually (though not always) realise they are infected. Their temperature goes up, and they feel unwell. In the psychic model, however, people usually do not realise what is happening because it is an unconscious process and there is little public awareness of the role of the unconscious in daily life. Psychic epidemics occur very frequently – for example, 'the political mass movements of our time are psychic epidemics' (Jung 1946b, p. 232).

An example of a political psychic epidemic was the 2016 US Presidential election. Political debates can sometimes be productive because they resolve issues in a constructive way. But psychic epidemics have their roots in one-sided attitudes and the reaction to them. The driving forces are therefore not the political issues but the underlying psychology. The 'so-called leaders are inevitable symptoms of [the] mass movement' (Jung 1933/1934, p. 154) and not the cause of it. Donald Trump was the spearhead of the psychic tidal bores. Each side saw the other candidate as immoral in some way – for example as racist or corrupt – and its own candidate as able to save the country from that evil. When there is a duality between two political leaders, it is often an aggregation of the one-sided projections of the supporters. It arises from the split between consciousness and the unconscious, and from archetypal influences (Jung 1943/1948, p. 246). That is, there is a direct relationship between the divisions that occur between major political parties and the split within the psyche of the people who take part in

86 Individuals, relationships, groups, society

those movements. The aggregation of individual attitudes leads to the division between countries (e.g. USA/Russia), religions (e.g. Christianity/Islam), beliefs (e.g. atheism/religion), common views of spiritual beings (e.g. God/devil), and many other forms of opposite.

Psychic epidemics tend to involve emotional reactions (Jung 1927/1931a, p. 41) where the affective temperature crosses a threshold and we replace reason with slogans (Jung 1957a, p. 248). A one-sided political attitude can seem very attractive because it can be a powerful carrier of projections. One side carries our good projections and the other side the bad ones. Trump's campaign slogans resonated strongly with a one-sided attitude. 'Make America Great Again' implied Trump would be the saviour of the USA. When his supporters chanted 'Lock Her Up', it reinforced the projections of immorality and criminality into Hillary Clinton. Although she also used slogans – such as 'Stronger Together', 'I'm With Her', or 'Love Trumps Hate' – they were based more on relationship, did not rely so much on projection, and were not as attractive because they did not align quite so powerfully with a one-sided view. They were more subtle and implicit. For example, the slogan 'love trumps hate' was ambiguous and let people project a variety of meanings into it.

What causes psychic epidemics?

Underpinning a psychic infection or epidemic is mutual unconsciousness (Jung 1937/1966, pp. 329–30). The infection spreads when there is a breakdown of conscious hopes and expectations (Jung 1920/1948, pp. 314–15). This may have been the most significant factor in the 2016 presidential election. This breakdown of expectations was identified long before the election in *The Unwinding: Thirty Years of American Decline* (Packer 2013). Through a series of individual anecdotal stories, Packer describes the deindustrialisation of the Rust Belt, the rise of inequality, and the lingering resentment at the continued increase in wealth of those who caused the 2007–8 crash. One of Jung's recommendations for mitigating psychic epidemics is to not lose sight of the individual behind the statistics (Jung 1957a, p. 253). Historical graphs of gross domestic product (GDP) growth or unemployment rates present a favourable view of the US economy. But the individual experiences suggested by Packer are very different. And some statistics support Packer's analysis. For example, before the presidential election, inequality was rising throughout the world, and the US had one of the highest rates (OECD 2015). Also, homeownership in the US had been falling steadily and, before the 2016 election, had reached its lowest level for half a century (tradingeconomics.com 2018). When Clinton opened her presidential campaign, she included inequality as one of her priorities. However, many people may have viewed her as part of the problem rather than the solution. The failure of the establishment to address the issue led to 'scalding hatred of the president [Obama] that had energized the resurgence in the Republican grassroots' (Packer 2013, p. 403). Whether this assessment of

Obama or Clinton is fair is not the point. In a psychic epidemic, the facts, truth, and reason are not as powerful as the widespread breakdown of expectations. If we want to understand a tidal bore, then we must examine the conflicting forces that are behind it, and not just look at the surface of the water. So too, if we're going to understand the election of President Trump, we need to look beyond his character and policies to examine the hopes and expectations of those who voted both for and against him.

Another factor in the spread of psychic epidemics is unconscious suggestibility (Jung 1945a, pp. 198–99). This concept has its roots in hypnosis, which is a technique to lower consciousness (Jung 1921, p. 202). At the time of Jung's training, many psychiatrists used hypnosis. Today, marketeers and others use suggestibility to change behaviours. For example, anchoring or nudging shift the individual's expectations about price or the best product. In the context of psychic epidemics, suggestibility gives prominence to statements, which may be true or false, that trigger and reinforce a one-sided attitude. An individual is more susceptible to suggestibility within a crowd (Jung 1940/1950, p. 126) such as a political rally. Psychic epidemics can also spread because of social pressure, especially in a large group (Jung 1935, p. 46). The individual 'begins to fear that if he doesn't join in, he will be considered a fool' (von Franz 1964, p. 175).

Whatever the cause – a breakdown of expectations, suggestibility, or social pressure – the result is that the unconscious complex has a hypnotic effect, 'drawing everyone under its spell' (Jung 1940/1950, p. 127), and it takes over the ego (Jung 1939, p. 278). Psychic infections are more likely to spread when people have an unreflecting belief, understand mythology too literally (Jung 1957a, p. 266), repress their projections (Jung 1917/1926/1943, pp. 95–96), or have a lack of self-knowledge (Jung 1957a, p. 249). If we do not take the unconscious into account, it can take us over and we can become 'the shuttle-cock of every wind that blows' (Jung 1945a, p. 201).

Psychic infections are also more likely to become an epidemic when various psychological states are widespread, including a split in the network of projections (Jung 1916/1948, pp. 271–72), participation mystique (Jung 1921, pp. 456–57), and concretism (ibid., pp. 420–21). The term concretism describes a state in which different ideas, identities, experiences, emotions, etc. are not seen as separate, but they are all mixed up together. Intelligence is no immunity to psychic infections because the factors that encourage them are psychological, not intellectual. As Jung pithily put it, 'a collection of a hundred Great Brains makes one big fathead' (Jung 1934b, p. 500). Jung himself felt infected at times, for example whilst on a trip to the Sahara (Jung 1963, p. 270).

Countering psychic epidemics

There are some natural conditions that counter psychic epidemics. One is a culture of mistrust and obstinacy (Jung 1941, pp. 586–87) which makes people less susceptible to suggestion. Another is the new interpretation of old myths (Jung 1940,

88 Individuals, relationships, groups, society

p. 157) or a new, more balanced faith that replaces a twisted faith (Jung 1957a, p. 264). One psychic infection can counter another (Jung 1930b, p. 69) so long as the second one restores wholeness, rather than increases the one-sidedness. Social norms can play a role in inhibiting psychic infections, on condition that they are not themselves part of the problem (Jung 1927/1931b, p. 47).

There is a role for rational argument in countering psychic infection, on condition that emotions are kept at a low level (Jung 1957a, p. 248). For example, people in positions of respect can counter psychic epidemics by disseminating relevant, factual information (Jung 1954b, p. 629). Also, some group rituals and symbols can help us to keep thinking more individually (Jung 1940/1950, p. 127). However, most of the active measures that Jung suggested for combatting psychic epidemics are related to the individual's work in overcoming their own intra-psychic split between the ego and the unconscious. Such work involves engaging in self-criticism, recognising the value of opposites, looking to reduce our personal one-sidedness, and creating the conditions in which the transcendent function can transform our conscious and unconscious attitudes.

The transcendent function

Jung repeatedly stresses that 'every individual needs revolution' (Jung 1917/1926/1943, p. 5) in order to achieve social and cultural improvement, because it enables us to discover the morality that is within each of our souls (ibid., p. 27). If societal norms are our only guide, and society is morally sick, then we will also become morally sick. If we each look to discover the morality within ourselves, whilst respecting collective norms, then the diversity of attitudes will restore a healthier balance between collective and individual morality. That is, the first task is for each of us to engage with opposites and allow the transcendent function to develop – and keep on redeveloping – new attitudes that bring greater wholeness and greater individuality. Discovering the deeper aspects of the unconscious requires 'profound reflection [and is] uncommonly difficult' (Jung 1928b, p. 155) because the culture exerts an intense pressure for social conformity (ibid., pp. 152–53).

This work in developing the transcendent function at an individual level can aggregate to have a significant impact on relationships, groups, and society. As illustrated by the barbershop quartet analogy, something systemic can emerge that overcomes one-sidedness at a collective level. We could view the peace processes in Northern Ireland and South Africa as being transcendent functions that exist in the 'imaginal world' (Samuels 1993, p. 283). Although there were no collective egos to be aware of what was happening, there was something happening in parallel in large swathes of society that bridged the individual's internal schism and the schism between political opponents. There was also an emergent aspect that embedded the change of attitudes into collective procedures and structures. These shared attitudes and new structures are the means by which the 'imaginal transcendent function' has an impact on society.

Individuals, relationships, groups, society 89

Changing collective attitudes is an area where Myers-Briggs typology can potentially make a significant contribution to the process of individuation in society. It is a popular model that encourages people to begin the process of self-development. It influences the way that people relate or work within groups. Myers-Briggs typology is therefore a form of collective transcendent function because it helps mediate between opposites. However, despite being an experiential example of reconciling opposites in groups, it omits the fifth function of typology from its theoretical presentation. As a result, individual development tends to stop at a stage of one-sidedness rather than transcend it. Society therefore misses out on the lessons about the transformation of collective attitude that Jung's solution brings. What is missing from Myers-Briggs typology is the stage beyond type that Isabel Briggs Myers acknowledged was possible (Myers 1980, p. 168) but saw no need for (Myers 1977, p. 21). The big question is, how do we restore the gravamen of Jung's theory?

References

Bishop, B., Cushing, R.G. (2008). *The Big Sort: Why the Clustering of Like-Minded America Is Tearing Us Apart.* New York: Houghton Mifflin.

Hannah, B. (1976). *Jung, His Life and Work: A Biographical Memoir.* Wilmette, IL: Chiron Publications, Kindle Edition.

Jacobi, J. (1958). 'The process of individuation'. *Journal of Analytical Psychology* 3(2): 95–114.

Jung, C.G. (1911–12/1952). *CW5.*

Jung, C.G. (1916/1948). 'General aspects of dream psychology'. In *CW8.*

Jung, C.G. (1917/1926/1943). 'On the psychology of the unconscious'. In *CW7.*

Jung, C.G. (1920/1948). 'The psychological foundation of belief in spirits'. In *CW8.*

Jung, C.G. (1921). *CW6.*

Jung, C.G. (1923). 'Psychological types'. In *CW6.*

Jung, C.G. (1925). 'Marriage as a psychological relationship'. In *CW17.*

Jung, C.G. (1926/1946). 'Analytical psychology and education: three lectures'. In *CW17.*

Jung, C.G. (1927/1931a). 'Introduction to Wickes's "Analyse der Kinderseele" '. In *CW17.*

Jung, C.G. (1927/1931b). 'Mind and earth'. In *CW10.*

Jung, C.G. (1928a). 'The significance of the unconscious in individual education'. In *CW17.*

Jung, C.G. (1928b). 'The relations between the ego and the unconscious'. In *CW7.*

Jung, C.G. (1928/1931). 'The spiritual problem of modern man'. In *CW10.*

Jung, C.G. (1929). 'Commentary on the secret of the golden flower'. In *CW13.*

Jung, C.G. (1930a). 'The rise of a new world'. In *CW10.*

Jung, C.G. (1930b). 'Richard Wilhelm: in memoriam'. In *CW15.*

Jung, C.G. (1930c). 'The complications of American psychology'. In *CW10.*

Jung, C.G. (1931a). 'A psychological theory of types'. In *CW6.*

Jung, C.G. (1931b). 'Archaic man'. In *CW10.*

Jung, C.G. (1933). 'Foreword to Adler: "Entdeckung der Seele" '. In *CW18.*

Jung, C.G. (1933/1934). 'The meaning of psychology for modern man'. In *CW10.*

Jung, C.G. (1934a). 'A review of the complex theory'. In *CW8.*

Jung, C.G. (1934b). 'La révolution mondiale'. In *CW10.*

90 Individuals, relationships, groups, society

Jung, C.G. (1934/1950). 'A study in the process of individuation'. In *CW9i*.

Jung, C.G. (1935). 'The Tavistock lectures'. In *CW18*.

Jung, C.G. (1936). 'Psychology and national problems'. In *CW18*.

Jung, C.G. (1937). 'Letter to Gerda Hipert, 20 March 1937'. In *Letters 1*.

Jung, C.G. (1937/1966). 'The realities of practical psychotherapy'. In *CW16*.

Jung, C.G. (1939). 'Conscious, unconscious, and individuation'. In *CW9i*.

Jung, C.G. (1940). 'The psychology of the child archetype'. In *CW9i*.

Jung, C.G. (1940/1950). 'Concerning rebirth'. In *CW9i*.

Jung, C.G. (1941). 'Return to the simple life'. In *CW18*.

Jung, C.G. (1943/1948). 'The spirit Mercurius'. In *CW13*.

Jung, C.G. (1945a). 'After the catastrophe'. In *CW10*.

Jung, C.G. (1945b). 'Marginalia on contemporary events'. In *CW18*.

Jung, C.G. (1946a). 'The psychology of the transference'. In *CW16*.

Jung, C.G. (1946b). 'Epilogue to "Essays on Contemporary Events"'. In *CW10*.

Jung, C.G. (1948). 'Techniques of attitude change conducive to world peace'. In *CW18*.

Jung, C.G. (1954a). 'On the psychology of the trickster figure'. In *CW9i*.

Jung, C.G. (1954b). 'On flying saucers'. In *CW18*.

Jung, C.G. (1955–56). *CW14*.

Jung, C.G. (1957a). 'The undiscovered self (present and future)'. In *CW10*.

Jung, C.G. (1957b). 'The Houston films'. In *C.G. Jung Speaking*. Princeton, NJ: Bollingen Paperbacks, 1977.

Jung, C.G. (1958). 'Flying saucers: a modern myth'. In *CW10*.

Jung, C.G. (1959). 'Introduction to Wolff's "Studies in Jungian Psychology"'. In *CW10*.

Jung, C.G. (1963). *Memories, Dreams, Reflections*. London: Harper Collins, 1995.

Jung, C.G. (2009). *The Red Book: Liber Novus*, edited by Sonu Shamdasani, trans. M. Kyburz, J. Peck, and S. Shamdasani. New York: W.W. Norton.

Lu, K. (2013). 'Can individual psychology explain social phenomena? An appraisal of the theory of cultural complexes'. *Psychoanalysis, Culture & Society* 18(4): 386–404.

Mattoon, M.A. (ed.) (1993). *Chicago 92: Proceedings of the Twelfth International Congress for Analytical Psychology: The Transcendent Function: Individual and Collective Aspects*, held August in Chicago, IL. Einsiedeln: Daimon.

Myers, I.B. (1977). *Conversations with Isabel*, transcript by Marcia Miller. Gainesville, FL: Center for the Applications of Psychological Type.

Myers, I.B. (1980). *Gifts Differing*. Palo Alto, CA: Davis Black, 1995.

OECD (2015). 'Inequality'. Organisation for Economic Co-operation and Development. Online at: www.oecd.org/social/inequality.htm, accessed 8-Feb-18.

Packer, G. (2013). *The Unwinding: Thirty Years of American Decline*. London: Faber and Faber.

Samuels, A. (1993). *The Political Psyche*. London: Routledge.

Samuels, A. (2010). 'The transcendent function and politics: NO!'. *Journal of Analytical Psychology* 55(2): 241–53.

Samuels, A., Shorter, B., Plaut, F. (1986). *A Critical Dictionary of Jungian Analysis*. Hove: Routledge.

Shakespeare, W. (1982). *Romeo and Juliet. The Illustrated Stratford Shakespeare*. London: Chancellor Press, 701–28.

Singer, T., Kimbles, L.K. (eds.) (2004). *The Cultural Complex: Contemporary Jungian Perspectives on Psyche and Society*. Hove: Brunner-Routledge.

Stein, M., Hollwitz, J. (eds.) (1992). *Psyche at Work: Workplace Applications of Jungian Analytical Psychology.* Wilmette, IL: Chiron Publications.

tradingeconomics.com (2018). 'United States home ownership rate 1965–2018'. Ieconomics, Inc. Online at: https://tradingeconomics.com/united-states/home-ownership-rate, accessed 8-Feb-18.

UNESCO (1948a). 'Methods of attitude change conducive to international understanding'. United Nations Educational, Scientific and Cultural Organization. Online at: http://unesdoc.unesco.org/images/0015/001582/158272eb.pdf, accessed 23-Aug-15.

UNESCO (1948b). 'Conference of delegates of national commissions on methods of attitude change conducive to international understanding'. United Nations Educational, Scientific and Cultural Organization. Online at: http://unesdoc.unesco.org/images/0015/001581/158154eb.pdf, accessed 23-Aug-15.

von Franz, M.L. (1964). 'The process of individuation'. In C.G. Jung (1964). *Man and His Symbols.* London: Picador, 1978.

Chapter 7

The caduceus

In Jung's writings from the 1930s onwards, he explains the process of psychological transformation primarily using the metaphor of alchemy. Alchemy is not a new theory; it is an ancient practice of working with metals that can be used as a psychological metaphor. It expresses the ideas in *Psychological Types* in a different, more complete, and better way. Jung brings together his early typological theory of individuation and his use of the alchemical metaphor in the image of the caduceus, a staff entwined by two snakes with wings at the top (Figure 7.1). In Greek mythology, the caduceus is the rod of Hermes, the messenger of the gods. The 'gods' represent the contents of the unconscious psyche, so Hermes and his staff stand for the process of communication between the opposites of consciousness and the unconscious.

Figure 7.1 The caduceus.

The crossings and separations of the snakes can represent various things. They can point to the reconciliation of a single pair of opposites, in alternating stages of progress and regress, or separation and joining. We saw that circular progress in the Northern Ireland peace process, with several attempts at power-sharing, and several collapses of the ceasefire and returns to violence. The weavings of the two snakes can also represent the reconciliation of different opposites. After we have overcome one opposition, we then focus on reconciling a different opposition or integrating more content from the unconscious. We saw examples of this in South Africa, which moved from reconciling different political agendas in the early 1990s to reconciling the perpetrators and victims of violence in the late 1990s. The caduceus can also represent a more complex form of development, in which the transformation of the personality goes through various stages, such as painful experiences, periods of deep reflection, discovering the true essence of oneself, making changes to our lifestyle, etc.

Before we start exploring the metaphor of alchemy in more depth, we first need to consider some sharp criticism of Jung's interpretation of alchemy from contemporary scholars, most notably the historian of science Lawrence Principe. We will then compare Principe's and Jung's views of alchemy using the distinction of *psychological* and *visionary*, which was developed by Jung for the analysis of art. These two categories will help us understand how to apply the metaphor of alchemy to contemporary psychological issues of one-sidedness and conflict.

A brief history of alchemy

In the last half-century, the understanding of alchemy and its history has changed radically (Principe 2013, p. 3). Alchemy emerged around two millennia ago and was initially concerned with making one metal appear superficially as another. The earliest surviving alchemical documents date from around the third century AD in Egypt. It then changed into an attempt to create the philosopher's stone, which can transform base metal into gold. Alchemy arrived in Europe via Arabic or Islamic sources, where it reached its heyday in the fifteenth to seventeenth centuries. The Greek, Arabic, and Latin writings of the alchemists are often difficult to understand because they are laden with mystical and religious terminology. Alchemists abandoned the goal of creating gold in the early eighteenth century, with the emergence of modern chemistry.

Principe describes three periods of revival of interest in alchemy. The first, in the late eighteenth century, revived the chemical practices and the attempt to create gold. The second, starting in the mid-nineteenth century, reinterpreted the alchemical work as psychological and cosmological. The third and current period is a critical re-examination of the history of alchemy. One of the reasons that we can interpret alchemy in such radically diverse ways – from chemistry to psychology – is the ambiguous nature of its language. It is a secret code, where fantastical creatures and mystical happenings stand for chemicals, instruments, techniques, and procedures.

Principe's critique of Jung

Jung recognised that the alchemists used a secret code (Jung 1942/1954, pp. 225–26) but he still interpreted their language as being psychological, as primarily concerned with self-transformation. In his view, alchemy was an irrational practice that became the vehicle for the expression of unconscious projections. In his view, it did not have a rational basis:

94 The caduceus

The real root of alchemy is ... in the projections of individual investigators
... Such projections [occur] whenever man tries to explore an empty darkness and involuntarily fills it with living form.

(Jung 1937, p. 245)

Jung developed his view of alchemy towards the end of the second period of
revival, drawing on a wide range of ancient and modern alchemical characters.
He gave particular credit to four writers (Jung 1937, p. 228) all of whom fall
within that second period – Silberer (1882–1923), Bernoulli (1880–1948), Evola
(1898–1974), and Reitzenstein (1861–1931). This era saw the development of a
collective attitude that 'attributed positive, self-transformative, and even grand
and cosmic designs to the earlier alchemists' (Principe 2013, p. 105). Principe
criticises Jung for looking back at alchemy through the lens of his milieu, and
for projecting the process of self-transformation into the historical facts:

Jung's ... formulations ... are simply not supported by the historical record,
and therefore – as influential as they were during the twentieth century in a
range of contexts – they are now rejected by historians of science as valid
descriptions of alchemy. An array of scholars approaching alchemy from
many different disciplinary perspectives have come to the same conclusion
... Accordingly, [Jung's formulations] need to be studied as products of
their own eras.

(Principe 2013, pp. 104–5)

Principe criticises Jung's portrayal of the alchemists as having poor chemical
or scientific knowledge, stumbling through their 'groping experiments and
speculations' (Jung 1937, p. 432), and as having nothing to offer chemistry
(Jung 1938/1954, p. 108). Principe affords the alchemists much more ration-
ality and understanding, and he claims support for his view from the works of
Basil Valentine. Both Principe and Jung (Jung 1937, p. 426) regard Valentine
as being a pseudonym. He was a composite of other authors from around the
late sixteenth century. In one text, *Of the Great Stone of the Ancients*,
Valentine describes introducing the eagle to the old dragon, setting them upon
a hellish seat, where Pluto will blow strongly, leading to a fight and then the
king having good fortune and health. The eagle stands for ammonium chloride,
and the dragon saltpetre. The rest of the text describes putting them in a
furnace and heating them until there is a reaction – represented by the fight
(Principe 2013, pp. 147–48).

In *The Triumphal Chariot of Antimony*, there is – what seems to be – an
impractical experiment, in which Valentine claims he can convert poisonous
antimony into a therapeutic medicine. The first step is to turn antimony into
glass. Principe tried it but, despite repeated attempts, he could not make the
instructions work. This failure might have led to the conclusion that the recipe
was not concerned with the transformation of antimony but was reflecting a

more profound secret of another kind. However, Valentine's text refers to 'Hungarian antimony', so Principe imported a sample from Eastern Europe. This time the procedure to produce glass was successful. Chemical analysis later showed there was an impurity in the imported ore which was crucial to the success of that stage. Further analysis revealed that Valentine's overall process worked, in a fashion. It removed all the antimony and left a non-poisonous substance that the process had extracted from the laboratory utensils. The experiment supports Principe's argument that there was a rational basis for the work of alchemists, and that they used religious and mystical language as an allegorical code.

Weak evidence

Principe's argument has itself been criticised as misrepresenting Jung due to translation issues (Hanegraff 2012, p. 290). However, Principe's criticism does raise some valid concerns, which are relevant to our use of the alchemical metaphor today. One of these is that Jung often cites very flimsy evidence to support his view. For example, to justify his interpretation of alchemy as primarily mystical, he points out that the title of an alchemical book has the word 'mystical' in it (Jung 1937, p. 242). He suggests this shows how the author, pseudo-Democritus, realised he was involved in a psychological rather than chemical work. The title of a book is a weak argument, but Principe also writes about it, and he debunks Jung's argument entirely:

> It carries the title *Physika kai mystika* ... The title, which may have been given to it much later, is often translated as *Physical and Mystical Things*. Although that might look like a reasonable rendering of the Greek, it is misleading. A better translation is *Natural and Secret Things*. The Greek word *mystika* did not refer in ancient times to what we today call mystical, that is, something having a special religious or spiritual meaning, or expressing a personal experience of the ineffable. Instead, it simply meant things to be kept secret ... For pseudo-Democritus, these processes are *mystika,* that is, *secret,* because they are lucrative artisanal processes – trade secrets, if you will.
>
> (Principe 2013, p. 12, original italics)

Jung not only cites flimsy evidence but sometimes he uses tortuous logic. For example, to show that the alchemists are projecting symbols of individuation into their experiments, he lays out the following argument (Jung 1937, pp. 243–45). He cites the alchemical principle of *tam ethice quam physice* (as much moral as physical). He equates the term *ethice* (moral) with psychological. He argues that this shows the alchemists are making a contradictory claim between physical and symbolic work (on the assumption that *ethice* not only means ethical and psychological but also symbolic). He claims physics cannot be the motivation for the work, because the alchemists had little to offer about the nature of chemistry. He also claims there was no philosophical basis for the work. Therefore, having eliminated all the other possibilities, he concludes that the work of the alchemists must be symbolic; the appeal of alchemy was not the mystery of matter, but the mystery of themselves that they projected into it. Each link in this argument is laden with assumptions and makes very tenuous inferences. To a modern, scientific mind, this line of argument is not sound, especially as Principe's research contradicts Jung's argument by showing the alchemists' experiments had a rational basis. Another example of flimsy evidence is that Jung refers to a sixteenth-century treatise by Theobald de Hoghelande, which includes the phrase 'it also seems as if a man with a head and all his limbs were seated upon a cathedra' (Jung 1937, p. 248). Jung then claims that such remarks 'prove that during the practical work certain events of an hallucinatory or visionary nature were perceived' (ibid., p. 250). Again, this argument is very tenuous, and it is such claims of hallucination that elicit the sharpest criticism from Principe.

Despite any flaws in Principe's critique, these weak links and inferences within Jung's evidence give credence to Principe's main criticism – that Jung's interpretation of alchemy says more about the collective attitude of his milieu than the historical nature of alchemy. Such dismissals of Jung's arguments from a scientific perspective are not new. For example, the *British Journal for the Philosophy of Science* reviewed Jung's contribution to *The Interpretation and Nature of the Psyche*, because the book also included an essay by Wolfgang Pauli. The reviewer was complimentary about Pauli's part of the book, but very dismissive of Jung's because it uses non-sequiturs. In the context of a scientific journal, it was thinly-veiled derision when the reviewer suggested it 'could scarcely have been written ... if Jung had paid more critical attention to the concept of causation' (Mundle 1957).

Principe's research points to at least three major fault lines in Jung's interpretation of alchemy. The first is Jung's inaccurate portrayal of the historical events, for example, that the alchemists' knowledge of materials was poor, or that the unconscious was the only justification for making certain statements. The second is Jung's interpretation of alchemy as being due more to the collective attitude of his milieu than to the nature of alchemy itself. Jung 'projected' the process of psychological transformation into the alchemists. The third is that his presentation and arguments are not robust and are easy for the contemporary scientifically minded reader to reject.

However, this does not necessarily invalidate the use of the metaphor of alchemy in contemporary psychological development. The second revival of interest in alchemy was an embryonic stage in the emergence of modern psychology. If it involved a misinterpretation of alchemy, this does not necessarily mean there was a misinterpretation of psychology. Jung's alchemical metaphor may still have relevance to the contemporary psychological problems of one-sidedness.

Zosimos

The similarities and differences between Principe's and Jung's perspectives become evident when we examine their analyses of the visions of Zosimos. Zosimos lived around 300 AD and wrote 28 books about alchemy, most of which are now lost (Principe 2013, p. 15). In the remnants of his work, there is a series of visions or dreams. Jung suggests that they are the same vision but presented in several variations:

> Psychologically at least, there is no ground for supposing that [Zosimos' dream is an] allegorical invention ... It was a highly significant experience which he wished to communicate to others. Although alchemical literature contains a number of allegories ... the vision of Zosimos may well have been an actual happening. This seems to be borne out by the manner in which Zosimos himself interprets it as a confirmation of his own preoccupation: 'Is not this the composition of the waters?'
>
> (Jung 1938/1954, p. 66)

Jung goes on to dismiss the potential counter-argument, that this vision is an allegorical code for an experiment. In Zosimos' visions he sees something different, because of the commentary notes that accompany Zosimos' dreams (Jung 1942/1954, p. 226) and from the similarity of the dreams' images to those that arise in other attempts to come to terms with the unconscious. In Jung's view, the vision was the description of an actual dream, which therefore makes it 'essentially a psychological problem ... a concretization, in projected and symbolic form, of the process of individuation' (Jung 1938/1954, p. 105). Jung provides an interpretation of Zosimos' text based on the images being produced spontaneously from the unconscious.

For Principe, however, these visions had a much more mundane explanation. Zosimos pursues a 'coherent program of research' (Principe 2013, p. 15) that advances the work of predecessors. He works in the context of earlier Greek philosophers and looks to advance their understanding of the nature of matter. Most of these philosophical predecessors saw a stable substrate in matter, which for Thales was water, for Democritus atoms, and for Aristotle prime matter. Empedocles was more pluralistic in suggesting four basic elements – earth, water, air, and fire – which later alchemists adopted. Zosimos had a dualistic theory about the nature of matter:

> Zosimos ... viewed the metals as composed of two parts: a non-volatile part that he calls the 'body' (*sōma*) and a volatile part that he calls the 'spirit' (*pneuma*). The spirit seems to carry the color and the other particular properties of the metal. The body seems to be the same substance in all metals ... Thus the identity of the metal is dependent on its spirit, not its body ... Zosimos uses fire – in distillation, sublimation, volatization, and so on – to separate the spirits from the bodies.
>
> (Principe 2013, p. 16, original italics)

98   The caduceus

Zosimos tried to make his theory work through his experiments. Although he was continuing the Greek philosophical investigation into the nature of the world, he was doing it with a more practical orientation. He was trying to separate the volatile part of the metal from the non-volatile. We now know, from texts discovered since Jung's analysis, that Zosimos used mystical language and imagery to disguise his alchemical procedures:

> To promote ... secrecy, Zosimos employs ... 'cover names' ... Zosimos himself tells us that [his dreams] are allegorical descriptions of practical transmutational processes ... Zosimos clearly states that his 'dreams' have a technical meaning in the context of the transmutation of metals.
>
> (Principe 2013, pp. 18–19)

The secrecy was necessary for a variety of reasons. Principe suggests that one may have been the collapse of the currency in the Roman Empire. Over many decades, the mints debased their coinage by using decreasing amounts of precious metal. They also made bronze coins look like silver by giving them a coating. Early alchemy was concerned with a closely related topic – how to make one metal appear as if it was another. The extent of their knowledge is shown in the papyri from the third century, which 'contain a series of tests to determine the purity of metals, both precious and common. [This shows they] understood the difference between genuine and imitation articles' (ibid., p. 10). Principe tested an alchemical process from around that period – using lime, sulphur, and urine – and he 'succeeded in making silver look astonishingly like gold' (ibid., p. 11).

The forgery of coins would itself be a significant incentive for secrecy, but there may have been an extra motivation because Emperor Diocletian tried to stabilise the currency by reissuing coinage of a higher quality. If the work of Zosimos and the other alchemists was undermining Roman currency, and therefore the stability of the Roman Empire, this could have put their lives at risk. Even after the currency crisis had ended, there were other reasons why alchemists needed to conduct their work in secret:

> The practical alchemists were well aware that if ... they succeeded in making gold artificially their lives might be in grave danger from the avaricious princes and other evilly disposed persons. Even the suspicion that they had discovered the secret was often sufficient to imperil them ... For reasons of safety, therefore, as well as from a cupidity that did not wish to share knowledge that might prove invaluable, the alchemists used to describe their theories, materials, and operations in enigmatical language, efflorescent with allegory, metaphor, allusion, and analogy.
>
> (Holmyard 1957, p. 16)

We can see the difference between Principe's and Jung's views of Zosimos in their interpretations of the phrase 'divine water'. For Jung, it is a psychological or spiritual reference that signifies the unconscious (Jung 1938/1954, p. 104). Principe points out that it also means 'water of sulfur' (Principe 2013, p. 17). That is, Zosimos exploits an ambiguity in the Greek language to hide the fact that he is describing a substance. Which explanation do we use, or can we use both? Let us return for a moment to Capulet in *Romeo and Juliet* to show how we can reconcile Principe's and Jung's analyses of Zosimos' dreams.

Capulet revisited

When Capulet enters the play for the first time, he calls for his sword. What motivates that action? One source of motivation is conscious. He hears a noise. He sees a fight. He knows that there is a history of conflict between the two households. He is aware that members of his family are in physical danger. He has an attitude that is ready to protect and preserve those for whom he feels responsible. But another source of motivation is unconscious. He is looking for a fight. He is unaware that he is aggressive and projects his own anger into Montague. He does not recognise that there are other options. It does not occur to him to calm the situation down or call for the fight to stop.

We do not have to choose between the two explanations because both sets of attitudes influence Capulet's action – both conscious and unconscious. His motivation is not a binary either/or question, but a question of the interplay between the two. When he calls for his sword, it is because he is conscious of the danger *and* has unconscious aggression. The two attitudes combine to produce a single, joint behaviour – they prompt him to call for his sword. The attitudes also influence each other. His unconscious aggression puts blinkers on his conscious viewpoint, and what he consciously sees triggers his unconscious aggression.

There was probably a similar dynamic at play in Zosimos, because – as far as we can tell – he was a real person. Like everyone else, he had a conscious attitude and an unconscious one. Although Jung came to an incorrect conclusion about the material nature of Zosimos' alchemical experiments, this does not invalidate all of his conclusions about Zosimos' psychology. When Zosimos practised alchemy, it was not solely an unconscious expression. But neither was it purely a conscious one. Both sides of his personality influenced his actions, and they had an impact on each other.

Principe and Jung have provided assessments of Zosimos' work that span both consciousness and the unconscious. Principe emphasises the former (consciousness). His research into the history of chemistry and alchemy sheds useful new light onto the conscious motivations of the early alchemists. He shows that Jung's historical analysis has overlooked some crucial elements, such as the philosophical attempt to understand the nature of matter. There was also a need to codify the experiments, for self-preservation, the protection of intellectual property, and other issues related to forgery, currency, and governance of the Roman Empire.

Principe also delves into some aspects of unconscious functioning. He notes that the mode of thinking in Zosimos' time was different. The modern mind separates philosophical, theological, and material notions as far as possible. Zosimos did not dissect topics into separate categories, so he mixed concepts in his understanding of the world (Principe 2013, pp. 21–22). He used philosophical and religious language to describe the alchemical procedures, instruments, and substances because they were all part of the same reality. Principe recognises the role that projection can play but applies it in a different way from Jung. He cautions against misunderstanding Zosimos by 'projecting our own knowledge and expectations onto the past' (ibid., p. 42).

Jung does acknowledge that alchemists used substances and procedures, but he emphasises the unconscious appeal (Jung 1955–56, p. 493). However, it is important to note that he wrote *Psychological Types* before he developed his interest in alchemy. He later realised that he could express his theory about the unconscious better using the alchemical metaphor. It was in the late 1920s that he began to notice many parallels between the imagery of alchemy and psychological development. That is, he developed his theory of transformation first. It did not originate from alchemy nor does it depend on his interpretation being historically correct.

Despite their different perspectives, there are some significant areas of agreement between Principe and Jung, such as the integrated nature of thinking throughout the time of the alchemists. For example, Principe points out that Thomas Aquinas, a thirteenth-century alchemist, viewed all knowledge as a gift from God – science and religion were not separate (Principe 2013, p. 194). Even when they were, in later centuries, alchemy acted as a metaphor to understand divinity. Sir Thomas Brown, a seventeenth-century alchemist, found that learning about the philosopher's stone taught him about God and his beliefs. Other natural studies also had a close connection with the divine because the mode of thought during the early modern period expected there to be multiple levels of meaning. In the later period of alchemy, enthusiasts began to read alchemy into everything – including Greek classics and the Bible (ibid., p. 180). For example, Michael Maier (1568–1622) used decorative images to link alchemy to various intellectual and aesthetic traditions. His aim was 'not simply to entertain readers but rather to ennoble a practice generally considered dirty and laborious by making it attractive' (Principe 2013, p. 178). Principe concludes that alchemy is 'a part of not only the history of science, medicine, and technology but also the history of art, literature, theology, philosophy, religion, and more' (ibid., p. 209).

There is no mention of psychology in Principe's list, even though it is at the centre of one of the three revivals of alchemy and underpins much of the current scholarship in the areas of theology, religion, and various other fields in the humanities. The errors in Jung's historical assessment and the over-exuberance of the second revival of interest do not mean that psychology has no relevance. If we correct the factual errors, we can then reassess the role of unconscious attitudes not only in the historical development of alchemy but also in contemporary equivalents.

The caduceus 101

There is a great deal of neurological research that shows the unconscious has a significant influence on conscious decision making, and is perhaps even the determinant of it. For example, researchers in brain-scanning (fMRI) experiments were able to predict a simple decision from unconscious brain activity up to ten seconds before the individual made the conscious choice (Soon *et al.* 2008). Therefore, although we believe we make our decisions consciously, such research suggests that the decision forms in the unconscious first. The ego then claims the decision as if it was its own. Jonathan Haidt illustrates this relationship between the ego and the unconscious (though using different terminology) with a rider and elephant analogy:

> The rider acts as the spokesman for the elephant, even though it doesn't necessarily know what the elephant is really thinking. The rider is skilled at fabricating post hoc explanations for whatever the elephant has just done, and it is good at finding reasons to justify whatever the elephant wants to do next.
>
> (Haidt 2012, p. 54)

Also, studies of consciousness are drawing attention to the significance of the unconscious. For example, scientific understanding can activate latent (initially unconscious) ways of knowing (Baruss 2007, p. 126). Some philosophers point to unconscious myths as structuring the way we think (Spector 2001). This can include contemporary science (Midgley 2004), a subject that we will return to in Chapter 11.

Although Principe criticises Jung for his misattribution of the source of the alchemists' language and images, he may be taking the argument too far, and not recognising the integral role of psychology in shaping both historical alchemy and contemporary science. The traditional view of alchemy is that it has an inherent 'twofold nature, an outward or exoteric and a hidden or esoteric' (Holmyard 1957, p. 15). The outward nature is the attempt to produce, for instance, the philosopher's stone – a substance that will transmute base metals such as lead, copper, iron, etc. into the precious metals of gold and silver. This aspect of alchemy is the forerunner of chemistry. Alchemists may not have recognised the inward nature of alchemy because they explored it through projection. The development of chemistry meant that this religious or psychological aspect of alchemy slipped away from public awareness until Jung restored its prominence (Craig 2005, p. 12).

Psychological vs visionary

One of the main differences between the two analyses is that Principe focuses on *psychological* sources for the alchemists' work and Jung focuses on *visionary* sources. Psychological art comes from a conscious source, either directly or cryptomnesically (i.e. indirectly through forgotten memories). It copies or imitates a work that someone else has already created, or develops that work using conscious thought processes such as logical deduction or by applying known techniques. Psychological sources for alchemy might include the work of predecessors, observations of changes in metals during experiments, the language and imagery that is available from religion, or any pre-existing system of codes that show how to keep things secret.

Visionary art is the product of spontaneous fantasy from the collective unconscious that reflects something of cultural or universal significance. It usually has numinous qualities, being mixed up with unconscious complexes, emotions, or convictions of truth. When artistic material comes from a deeper source, we can look at patterns that recur across many such works; they provide clues as to the structure of the part of the psyche from where those patterns came. Visionary sources are harder to identify, but their presence might be suggested by a sense of fascination or meaning, or a new powerful insight, such as Zosimos' idea that metals were comprised of two elements.

It can sometimes be challenging to work out whether an image or text has come from a psychological or visionary source. Art can often be a combination of the two – using material from a conscious source to express an otherwise ineffable meaning. Also, an image might have the outward appearance of being visionary (it seems to come directly from the unconscious), but it might only be psychological (it is a copy of a conscious source). Jung gives an even more complex example by suggesting that Dante and Wagner draw on old images that detract from the contemporary meaning in their work. Although their work is visionary, they are 'disguising the visionary experience in a cloak of historical or mythological events, which are then erroneously taken to be the real subject-matter' (Jung 1930/1950, p. 107).

A further complication is that the categories of psychological and visionary can be modes of reading, rather than creation (Rowland 2010, pp. 56–57). For example, an iron-age cooking pot, which was initially a psychological piece of work, can become the subject of visionary analysis, that is, the basis for imagination (ibid., p. 61). Another example is the famous Hollywood sign, which was originally a real-estate advertisement (a psychological work) but is now a fascinating symbol that reflects something of the film industry culture.

Zosimos revisited

The distinctions of psychological and visionary, when applied to artistic creation and reading, provide four ways to look at the analyses of Zosimos' work. Firstly, some material came from conscious sources for Zosimos. He drew on the writings of earlier alchemists, knowledge of smelting and other processes, earlier philosophers' ideas on the nature of matter, and religious images and language. He was also mindful of contemporaneous issues such as the collapse of the Roman currency, etc. These all provided conscious ideas and motivations for Zosimos' work with alchemy.

The second perspective considers the role of Zosimos' unconscious psyche in the experiments, including his creative ideas and living myths. He worked on the basis of assumptions about theology, philosophy, and the world, and his thinking was influenced by gnostic dualism. When Zosimos projected these unconscious contents into his experiments, they helped to shape his dualistic view of matter, as consisting of volatile and non-volatile parts. His persistence in trying to separate the two, and then reunite them again in new material, reflected a sense of purpose or meaning. His experiments were simultaneously an attempt to understand the nature of matter and a projection of his unconscious drive to develop himself. His proto-scientific alchemy was both an external and internal work, a philosophical and spiritual exercise, a conscious desire to separate the components of matter, and an unconscious desire to pursue his individuation.

The third perspective to consider is the conscious attitude of the reader or analyst. This refers to the conscious sources for Principe or Jung. When Jung looked at Zosimos' work, he had already developed his typological theory of transformation. He could see the parallels between Zosimos' dreams and the images in other myths, including stories such as *Prometheus and Epimetheus* or Goethe's *Faust I & II.* Principe's primary sources were different. He had seen recently discovered texts of Zosimos that shed new light on the nature of the experiments. He was also able to draw on recent historiographical criticism that highlighted some of the overenthusiastic psychological readings of alchemy in the nineteenth and twentieth centuries. Principe's perspective also drew on his extensive knowledge of the histories of chemistry and alchemy.

The final perspective is the analyst's unconscious, which draws on the imagination to fill the gaps in conscious knowledge. Both Principe and Jung take the evidence available to them and imagine what might explain that evidence. The milieu in which they work helps to shape their imaginative ideas. Jung worked in an era of radical new interpretations of alchemy. The more contemporary era of Principe gives more emphasis to the philosophy of materialism (that sees only matter as real).

In both Jung's and Principe's analysis of Zosimos' work, we can see evidence of all four sources – psychological and visionary sources in both Zosimos' writings and their analyses of it (see Figure 7.2). These are not discrete sources but overlap and influence each other. Jung attributes very little of Zosimos' work to conscious sources and thereby plays down the role of the philosophical investigation of matter. Principe affords the unconscious very little role, and thereby plays down the role of individuation in choosing and shaping the imagery and language that Zosimos uses. When we combine both perspectives, they give us a better picture of the nature of Zosimos' experiments, and the relevance of alchemy to contemporary psychology. The investigation of matter and the desire for psychological advancement both played a role.

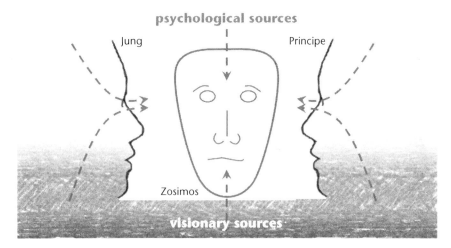

Figure 7.2 Psychological and visionary modes of creation and analysis.

Taking a symbolic attitude

There is a difference between the historical aims and practices of alchemy and the contemporary value it has as a metaphor for psychological transformation. Jung's portrayal of alchemy as 'not physical but psychological' (Jung 1952, p. 228) is untenable in the light of historical scholarship by Principe and others. However, having found physical explanations of some of the ancient texts, this does not mean we can conclude their work is 'not psychological but physical' and has no contemporary psychological value. Both perspectives are useful to a degree and when used for different purposes. Despite Jung's historical errors, alchemy still has value as a metaphor for psychological transformation.

The most basic principle of psychological alchemy is that, as we work with material in the outer world, we are simultaneously working with material in the inner world through projection. Our conscious and unconscious attitudes influence what we see and do, so what we see in the world reflects both sides of our own psyche. It is straightforward to see how our conscious viewpoint influences our dealings with other people and things. It is more difficult to spot the influence of our unconscious psyche. To do so involves taking a symbolic attitude, and recognising that our external work is, in part at least, a metaphor for our internal psychological development. It can also work the other way around. Jung felt he needed external work to understand himself better. He was aware of a split in his personality; he was 'two different persons' (Jung 1963, p. 50). In 1922 he bought a plot at Bollingen, a small village on the shore of Lake Zurich (Bair 2003, p. 322). He then started to build a tower that would become his retreat and provide a psychological metaphor for his own development. It helped him overcome his internal split by giving the neglected side of himself the opportunity for expression:

> The Tower [is] a concretisation of the individuation process ... I built it in a kind of dream. Only afterwards did I see how all the parts fitted together and that a meaningful form had resulted: a symbol of psychic wholeness ... Personality No. 2 ... comes to life again at Bollingen.
>
> (Jung 1963, p. 252)

The principle that this illustrates – of external work reflecting internal development – can apply to any form of activity. The environment we build around us reflects both our conscious and unconscious attitudes. Even science can be a spiritual exercise (Baruss 2007). A symbolic attitude recognises the inner–outer relationship and uses it to develop greater knowledge of our unconscious psyche.

References

Bair, D. (2003). *Jung: A Biography*. New York: Back Bay Books.
Baruss, I. (2007). *Science as a Spiritual Practice*. Exeter: Imprint Academic.
Craig, E. (ed.) (2005). *The Shorter Routledge Encyclopedia of Philosophy*. Abingdon: Routledge.
Haidt, J. (2012). *The Righteous Mind: Why Good People Are Divided by Politics and Religion*. London: Penguin Books, Kindle Edition.
Hanegraff, W. (2012). *Esotericism and the Academy: Rejected Knowledge in Western Culture*. Cambridge: Cambridge University Press.
Holmyard, E.J. (1957). *Alchemy*. New York: Dover Publications, 1990.
Jung, C.G. (1930/1950). 'Psychology and literature'. In *CW15*.
Jung, C.G. (1937). 'Religious ideas in alchemy'. In *CW12*.
Jung, C.G. (1938/1954). 'The visions of Zosimos'. In *CW13*.
Jung, C.G. (1942/1954). 'Transformation symbolism in the mass'. In *CW11*.
Jung, C.G. (1952). 'Eliade's interview for "Combat" '. In *C.G. Jung Speaking*. Princeton, NJ: Bollingen Paperbacks, 1977.
Jung, C.G. (1955–56). *CW14*.
Jung, C.G. (1963). *Memories, Dreams, Reflections*. London: Harper Collins, 1995.
Midgley, M. (2004). *The Myths We Live By*. London: Routledge, 2011.
Mundle, C.W.K. (1957). 'Review: the interpretation of nature and psyche'. *British Journal for the Philosophy of Science* 8(29): 73–76.
Principe, L.M. (2013). *The Secrets of Alchemy*. Chicago, IL: The University of Chicago Press.
Rowland, S. (2010). *C.G. Jung in the Humanities: Taking the Soul's Path*. New Orleans, LA: Spring Journal Books.
Soon, C.S., Brass, M., Heinze, H.J., Haynes, J.D. (2008). 'Unconscious determinants of free decisions in the human brain'. *Nature Neuroscience* 11: 543–45.
Spector, S.A. (2001). *Wonders Divine*. London: Associated University Presses.

Chapter 8

Two movements

Murray Stein, a Jungian analyst, summarises Jung's process of individuation as consisting primarily of two movements, the alchemical *separatio* and *coniunctio* – terms that describe the separation of psychological opposites and their reunion. They are related to one of the images on the caduceus – the snakes separating and coming together again at a higher stage. Stein shows how the idea of the two movements arose during Jung's work during the time of the First World War, for example in his personal notes published posthumously in *The Red Book* (Jung 2009). Jung identified links between alchemy and some of his early work when he revised his seminal book *Symbols of Transformation* (e.g. Jung 1911–12/1952, p. 76fn). There is no equivalent work that shows the links between typology and alchemy because he did not revise *Psychological Types*. Nevertheless, he drew the connection between typology and alchemy elsewhere, such as:

> The secret of alchemy was in fact the transcendent function, the transformation of personality through the blending and fusion of the noble with the base components, of the differentiated with the inferior functions, of the conscious with the unconscious.
>
> (Jung 1928, p. 220)

After developing his interest in alchemy, Jung wanted to revise *Psychological Types* but he did not do so because readers had failed to understand the basics of it (Jung 1937a, p. xii). We need to do further work, therefore, to draw the links between those early writings on typology and the alchemical metaphor that he used in his later work. In *Psychological Types*, Jung first points to the two movements of individuation in his discussion of Schiller's ideas, in chapter II. Schiller describes a fundamental division between two psychological functions within the individual (*separatio*) and then reconciles them through a third thing (*coniunctio*) which helps to form an individual who has a distinct psychology.

The story of *Prometheus and Epimetheus*, which is discussed in chapter V of *Psychological Types*, also points towards the two movements of *separatio* and *coniunctio*. Most of the story focuses on events during the first movement. The brothers go their separate ways, which represents the *separatio* of consciousness and the unconscious, different functions, conscience and soul, etc. For most of the story, the Epimethean group of attitudes is conscious and dominant. The Promethean attitudes stay out of sight, in the unconscious. The story describes, in metaphorical terms, a variety of psychological events that unfold after that separation.

The potential for the second movement, the *coniunctio*, appears in the Pandora interlude, but Epimetheus loses the opportunity. He does not realise that the jewel is a treasure with the power to reconcile. He does not see any need for reconciliation because he is content with his life. He does not realise he is one-sided, nor does he think symbolically, nor does he recognise the imbalance between the opposites. In the end, a disaster forces the *coniunctio* on him. He could have avoided that disaster – including the deaths of two sons of God – if he had taken a different attitude towards the opposites, recognised the importance of the symbol, and shown respect to it even though it seemed false and disgusting.

The *coniunctio* at the end of the story takes place in two dimensions of the caduceus. One is horizontal. Spitteler restores parity between the brothers, represented by the two snakes coming back together in one of the cycles. Neither of the brothers holds sway over the other, so they meet on equal terms to rebuild their relationship, and their conflict no longer dominates the people of Earth. Psychologically, this stands for a reconciliation of the two opposing attitudes, at which point neither dominates the personality. The second dimension is vertical. When the snakes reunite, they are higher up the caduceus than before, but the staff joins the top of the cycle to the bottom. In Spitteler's story, there is a new king who is also a divine heir. Messias is a symbol that stands at the meeting of the snakes. He symbolises a new function and a new attitude, which is an advancement of consciousness (upwards) whilst also building a better connection with the divinity in the unconscious (downwards).

We can find the two movements not only in Spitteler's story but also in other parts of *Psychological Types*, in the descriptions of the types and the definitions in chapters X and XI. Jung describes the conscious and unconscious characteristics of each kind of one-sidedness, which is the *separatio* of the two parts of the psyche. He describes the *coniunctio* in his definition of the constructive method – as a building up from a prospective function that forms in the unconscious towards a future psychological development that brings consciousness and the unconscious into harmony (Jung 1921, pp. 422–23). Also, in the definition of a symbol, he describes how the new attitude appears from between the tension of opposites. The symbol provides 'raw material' (Jung 1921, p. 480) which the transcendent function then shapes to become the new content that dominates consciousness.

The two movements in politics

The *separatio* not only creates a split within individuals, but it also has the effect of dividing people into groups. For example, political *separatio* often leads to

108 Two movements

the creation of two major parties, such as Democrats and Republicans, or Labour and Conservative. They have different sets of attitudes, based on different governing principles. For example, left-wing parties are often more concerned with social justice and right-wing parties with economic competence.

A *coniunctio* not only reconciles the division within the individual, but it also brings two groups of people together to overcome their differences and work collaboratively for a common purpose. For example, political parties operate within organisational frameworks such as the House of Representatives or the House of Commons, which bring the parties together to agree on legislation and budgets for the overall good of the country.

The problem of one-sidedness arises in individuals or society when there is too much emphasis on the first movement, and the second is neglected. As a result, the *separatio* only leads to a partial *coniunctio*, or none at all. We can see this in the perpetuation of political conflicts. Although the system of government brings the two sides together, in practice the political *separatio* is sometimes so strong that the *coniunctio* of these chambers does not work. Each side is more concerned with inflicting a defeat on the other. Therefore, one side tends to dominate the political agenda, until an election when the other party wins, and they change the government's policies to match their own one-sided values.

There are some forums, such as the UK's parliamentary committees, that tend towards a much more dialectical approach. They tend to be less partisan, less driven by the conflict between political opponents, and more focused on bringing different political views to bear on solving problems related to UK governance. These forums put a lot more emphasis on the *coniunctio* between the interests of opposing parties.

There have been some attempts to reconcile political opposites on a broader basis, such as Harold McMillan's middle way, or Bill Clinton's third way, which Tony Blair adopted in the UK. These were not purely centrist policies because political centrism can also be one-sided, albeit in a different way – by excluding or being intolerant of non-centrist views. The third way tried to be inclusive, reconciling the priorities of political opponents without eliminating them. The degree to which such initiatives succeeded is a matter of debate. From the perspective of Jung's typological solution, even if they had some success, they tended to reconcile the opposites in only the horizontal dimension on the caduceus – for example, between social justice and economic competence. They did not necessarily resolve the conflict in the vertical direction, which is the relationship between consciousness and the unconscious. As a result, the third way was a more temporary than permanent change of attitude. The political opponents continued to project into the other and portray them in pejorative terms.

The vertical aspect of political conflict – between consciousness and the unconscious – is more powerful than the horizontal aspect, which is more concerned with competing values or conflicting policies. Solutions that address the horizontal aspect but fail to deal with the unconscious are unlikely to last long because the psychological schism that led to the conflict is still there. This is why the Truth and Reconciliation Commission was a crucial factor in the longevity of South Africa's transformation of race relations. It extended the reconciliation process to interpersonal relationships, mutual projection, and the split between consciousness and the unconscious within individuals. What matters in the long term is not finding agreement on specific policies, but addressing the underlying psychological one-sidedness that keeps bringing society back to the same old conflicts.

Differentiation

There are a couple of definitions in *Psychological Types* where Jung confuses things by using the same word (differentiation) to refer to both *separatio* and *coniunctio*. Although he points this out, it is so subtle that it is easy to miss. His definition of the word is a page in length. He introduces it by describing differentiation as 'the development of differences, the separation of parts from a whole' (Jung 1921, p. 424). He clarifies his use of the term as being '*chiefly* with respect to the psychological functions' (ibid., emphasis added). He goes on to describe how the psychological functions start in an undeveloped state – that is, they are fused together. We cannot use them separately, so we mix up facts, possibilities, logic, and values.

Jung's first use of the word 'differentiation' applies to the *separatio* of one psychological function from the others, learning to use it independently. We can then pay attention to those things of concern to that function without other types of information clouding the issue. For example, if we differentiate the sensing function, we can look at facts separately from their implications (intuition), truth (thinking), or worth (feeling). This is a simplistic portrayal of the process, because differentiation of a psychological function is not a one-off activity; it is an ongoing process. The more we differentiate a function, the more we can use it in a nuanced and sophisticated way. For example, we can recognise when some things are more real or tangible than others.

This type of differentiation tends to lead to greater one-sidedness and specialisation. Much of the literature on type development tends to describe how the sensation function changes with greater degrees of differentiation. However, when considering one-sidedness and polarisation, what is more significant is the state of the other functions.

If we differentiate sensation, and continue differentiating it, then it becomes an increasingly important and sophisticated part of the conscious attitude. However, the other functions stay fused together and unconscious, so the ego does not notice the subtle issues concerned with truth, values, and possibilities. Even when it does, they tend to be mixed up (concreted together) with themselves and with other unconscious contents, such as emotions, fears, defences, and archetypal instincts. We then project these characteristics into other people, whom we might see as unrealistic dreamers, or getting upset over nothing, or fearful of things that are unlikely ever to happen, or too emotionally involved (see Figure 8.1).

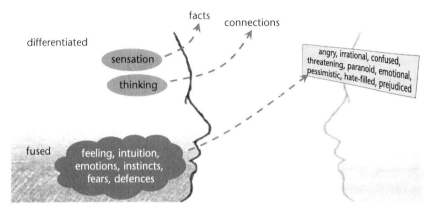

Figure 8.1 Projection of unconscious and fused typological functions.

The differentiation of a typological function is therefore both an advantage and a drawback at the same time. It is an advantage because it means we develop a specialised and sophisticated approach to a particular type of information – facts, possibilities, logic, or values. It is a disadvantage because it creates an intrapersonal split between consciousness and the unconscious. Also, by repressing and projecting the other functions, we see other people in a very distorted way. This can create interpersonal difficulties or, when aggregated, exacerbate the polarisation between groups.

Differentiation in coniunctio

In the definition of differentiation, the word 'chiefly' is the only clue that Jung puts the word to a different use elsewhere. We can find this alternative use in his definition of the term individuation, 'the process by which individual beings are formed and differentiated ... the development of the psychological individual as a being distinct from the general, collective psychology' (Jung 1921, p. 448). This is not the *separatio* of a function from the rest of the psyche; it is the separation of the individual from collective psychology, which is a consequence of the *coniunctio* of functions.

Jung drew the term individuation from the writings of Nietzsche (Jung 1921, p. 507), who in turn quoted Schopenhauer's *principium individuationis* (Nietzsche 1886, p. 17). It denotes the background of time and space which enables something to appear as different. The process of 'differentiation' therefore involves making something distinct from everything else. In Jung's two uses of the term, the backgrounds are different, and what we separate is different. Also, in one case it is a direct act; in the other, it is a consequence. The first movement of *separatio* involves the differentiation of a psychological function from the unconscious (the background). This leads to greater one-sidedness. In the *coniunctio*, we reconcile the opposites through a third thing and thereby build greater wholeness of the personality. As a result, the individual develops a unique attitude that is distinct from collective psychology (the background).

A jigsaw puzzle analogy

We can illustrate the two forms of differentiation that occur in *separatio* and *coniunctio* with the analogy of a jigsaw puzzle (see Figure 8.2). Alchemy uses many strange terms which refer to something practical and mundane. For example, the word *circumambulatio* denotes our concentration within an enclosed space (Jung 1929, p. 25) or on a centre (Jung 1936, p. 145). When we start a jigsaw puzzle, we open the box, and tip everything onto a large tray or table, and start looking at the pieces. We are then circumambulating the jigsaw pieces that are in front of us. That is all that *circumambulatio* means. Similarly, the terms *separatio* and *coniunctio* have straightforward and practical meanings.

Separatio

In the jigsaw analogy, *separatio* is the separation of certain types of pieces from the pile. When we start inspecting them, they all look very similar, and the overall pile has the same appearance as any other puzzle. The pieces are undifferentiated from each other, and the jigsaw is undifferentiated from other jigsaws. Our first action might be to separate out the edge pieces, pulling them into the foreground, and leaving all the others in the background. We are using the operation of *separatio* to create a small pile of jigsaw pieces that are different from all the rest. There is still nothing unique about this picture. All puzzles have edge pieces, so an edge is a collective characteristic. Therefore, the jigsaw still looks the same as any other puzzle that is at the same stage of development.

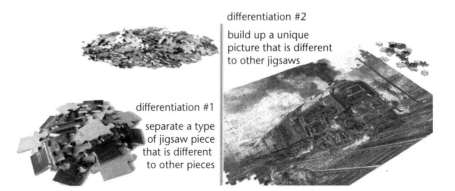

Figure 8.2 Two types of differentiation.

We can then continue working on the edge pieces by doing more *separatio*. For example, we can differentiate the sky edges from other edges due to their light blue colour, or buildings because of their brick or plaster colour. We can take the *separatio* of the edge pieces to further levels of refinement to produce several, small piles of edge pieces. There may now be a hint that there is something unique about this picture. The piles may look slightly different from those in other puzzles that are at the same stage of development.

Coniunctio

The next stage is to start putting some of the edge pieces together, which involves inspecting one of the small piles. For a piece to fit next to another one, they must each have a side that is opposite to the other. Matching them in this way is the beginning of the building phase – the *coniunctio* – because it involves reconciling opposites. The *coniunctio* of the edge pieces means that the jigsaw is starting to take shape. There may now be more hints, around the edges, that the picture is different from other puzzles.

Once we have assembled the edge pieces, we then focus on the large, undifferentiated pile in the background. At this stage, we know nothing about this shadowy pile. It is mysterious, unknown, disorganised, and jumbled up. So, we return to the interplay of *separatio* and *coniunctio*. In *separatio*, we differentiate pieces based on their characteristics. In *coniunctio*, we put opposites together and integrate them into the overall picture.

As we make progress in developing the central part of the jigsaw, a picture starts to appear that is unique. It is this picture that differentiates it from other puzzles, which is the second kind of differentiation. At the beginning of the process, it had the same appearance as any other puzzle. It was a pile of pieces on the table. The role of *separatio* was to differentiate one type of piece from another. The first type of differentiation created separate piles. The purpose of *coniunctio* was to put the opposites back together again. The second type of differentiation is a consequence of joining pieces together; it leads to the development of an individual picture that is different from other puzzles.

The jigsaw as the self

Becoming a personality type is an act of *separatio* with minor acts of *coniunctio*. We differentiate one psychological piece of ourselves from the rest, bringing it into conscious awareness. We might then differentiate a second or even a third piece from the rest. At this stage, the parts we have separated are aspects of collective psychology. These differentiated functions do not represent our uniqueness. They give us a one-sided and primarily collective *Weltanschauung*. If we individuate – which tends to happen in the second half of life if at all – we turn to focus on those aspects of our psychology that we have previously neglected. Both halves of life involve the combination of *separatio* and *coniunctio* but each half tends to have one of the processes as a major theme. In the first half of life (before midlife) we tend to focus on the *separatio* – which is akin to building up the edges of the jigsaw. In the second half of life, we place the emphasis more on the *coniunctio* – which is similar to turning towards the hitherto-untouched pile of pieces in the middle and starting to build up the main body of the unique picture.

The first form of differentiation (*separatio*) can include not only typological functions but also many other forms of attitude, which might be governed by specific ideas, or religious beliefs, or political views, or emotional experiences, or practical skills, etc. As we differentiate (*separatio*) our view or interpretations of things in the world, we simultaneously differentiate parts of ourselves. For example, if we ask increasingly complex questions about how the world works, we are separating the psychological functions that seek evidence and explanations. The same is true in reverse. If we ask more profound questions to understand our mental functioning, such as how we investigate and explain things, and the influence of our emotions, complexes, or myths, then it also changes the way we see the world.

The second movement

What does a *coniunctio* involve? What does it mean to 'integrate the opposite' or 'integrate the unconscious' into consciousness? It involves coming to terms with those things that we find 'despicable and odious' (Jung 1917/1926/1943, p. 35). We must look beyond what we already believe to be good, true, or right, to discover what is good, true, or right about those things we condemn, and learn how to reconcile them within ourselves. This movement starts with 'the withdrawal of all the projections we can lay our hands on' (Jung 1938/1940, p. 85). That is, we recognise how those things that we dislike most are reflections, at least in part, of our unconscious attitudes. It is a challenging task because we cannot see the unconscious in ourselves, and we usually do not want to see it.

The Jungian analyst Murray Stein gives some practical guidelines to withdrawing projections (Stein 2006). He suggests that we need to develop an attitude of being curious, listening to small clues, paying attention to the numinous, looking to expand knowledge, etc. The approach is embodied in a saying attributed to Abraham Lincoln: 'I do not like that man. I must get to know him better'. We avoid condemning people we do not like or who stir strong emotions in us; we take an interest in them. This does not mean we have to submit to their wishes, nor do we have to accept they are right and we are wrong. But we need to respect their point of view and treat it as seriously as our own.

We can find the 'other' in individuals, political or religious groups, national cultures, God, fictional characters, animals, and anything else to which we can ascribe anthropomorphised characteristics. Individuation involves discovering what it is about them that triggers intense feelings or reactions in ourselves. The stronger that we condemn someone, the more likely it is that they reflect something about ourselves that we won't accept. This can also work the other

114 Two movements

way. If someone is doing something that is patently wrong but we just accept it, our lack of reaction may also point to something that we have repressed in ourselves. The other can take many forms and be manifest in many different ways. Acknowledging and respecting the opposite in this way can be an uncomfortable experience because it challenges all the certainties we take for granted.

It is through reconciling the two sides that we develop a third attitude. In the jigsaw analogy, when we turn our attention from the edge pieces to the unknown pile in the middle, it is at first a difficult task. There are so many pieces that we cannot make sense of them. But as we work out how to fit them into the jigsaw, a new picture starts to emerge. In a comparable way, when we withdraw projections and see ourselves as involved in both opposites rather than just one, a third attitude starts to emerge, from the unconscious, that resolves the contradictions and conflicts between them.

The withdrawal of projections is not only difficult but can also sometimes be dangerous. Projections serve a useful purpose by protecting the individual from truths about him- or herself that are unpalatable and could be injurious to mental health. Asking people to withdraw projections is akin to 'expecting the average respectable citizen to recognize himself as a criminal' (Jung 1951, p. 19). It runs the risk of developing neuroses or experiencing an 'inflation' (Jung 1944, p. 479), which is when the individual becomes disoriented by the contents of the unconscious. We are not even capable of incorporating all the projections withdrawn from the world (Jung 1938/1940, p. 88). They are part of our psychological defences that protect our self-esteem and prevent us from being overwhelmed by too much information, which is too difficult to digest. Also, relationships depend on projection, and becoming conscious of those projections can sometimes become an obstacle to our relations with others (Jung 1916/1948, p. 272). Such problems raise a profound doubt as to whether we should pursue the withdrawal of projections at all (Jung 1951, pp. 17–18). On the other hand, unconscious projections can be 'dangerously illusory. War psychology has made this abundantly clear' (Jung 1916/1948, p. 271). On balance, Jung took the view that there is a need to raise awareness of the unconscious and develop a culture of integrating it into consciousness:

> Man's worst sin is unconsciousness ... and in all seriousness [we need to] seek ways and means to exorcize him, to rescue him from possession and unconsciousness, and make this the most vital task of civilisation.
>
> (Jung 1945/1948, pp. 253–54)

> If even the smallest and most personal stirrings of the individual psyche – so insignificant in themselves – remain as unconscious and unrecognized as they have hitherto, they will go on accumulating and produce mass groupings and mass movements which cannot be subjected to reasonable control or manipulated to a good end ... The crux of the matter is man's own dualism, to which he knows no answer.
>
> (Jung 1957a, p. 299)

There is a paradox here. On the one hand, the withdrawal of projections is potentially harmful to the individual because it removes some of our psychological defences. On the other hand, it can help overcome the one-sidedness that creates problems for the individual and society. Jung resolves the paradox by suggesting that we encourage the *natural* process of individuation within the individual (Jung 1934/1950, p. 349). The risks to individuals arise when they are *forced* to withdraw their projections, which normally happens only in a therapeutic context. Jungian analysts have the skill not only to help clients recognise their projections but also to deal with any problems that might arise. There is no such safety net outside the therapy room. Therefore, the most we can do is to highlight the need and create the conditions where individuals can voluntarily withdraw projections. The 'urge to a higher and more comprehensive consciousness fosters civilization and culture, but must fall short of the goal unless man voluntarily places himself in its service' (Jung 1946, p. 263). To be able to choose voluntarily, we must know there is a choice, why that choice is worth making, and how to make it. Jung's hope was that *Psychological Types* would do all of those things.

Myers-Briggs typology vs Jungian individuation

Having established that the process of individuation is based around the two movements of *separatio* and *coniunctio*, we are now in a position to examine some of the main similarities and differences between Myers-Briggs typology and Jungian individuation. We can make the comparison using the image of the caduceus and Spitteler's story of *Prometheus and Epimetheus.*

Jung saw the type problem as being twofold: the conflicts between opposing attitudes, which correspond to horizontal differences on the caduceus; and the schism between consciousness and the unconscious, which corresponds to the vertical axis. The movements of the snakes on the caduceus illustrate the two movements of individuation. The horizontal movements – outwards then inwards – represent the *separatio* and then *coniunctio* of opposing functions or attitudes. The move up the caduceus represents the ongoing development of new attitudes that emerge from the unconscious. The staff connecting the top to the bottom represents the bridge between consciousness and the unconscious, or the ego and the self.

Isabel Briggs Myers saw the type problem as being the need for balance between two sides of consciousness – between introversion and extraversion, and between a judging function and a perceptive one. Her solution was to develop a dominant and auxiliary function, and to retain that hierarchy throughout all future development:

> Good type development ... demands two conditions: first, adequate but by no means equal development of a judging process and a perceptive process, one of which predominates; and second, adequate but by no means equal facility in using both the extraverted and introverted attitudes, with one predominating.

When both conditions are met, the person's type development is *well balanced*. In type theory, *balance* does not refer to equality of two processes or of two attitudes; instead, it means superior skill in one, supplemented by a helpful but not competitive skill in the other.

(Myers 1980, p. 174, original italics)

In disallowing the opposites to become equal, Myers-Briggs typology focuses on the *separatio* of functions but only allows a partial reconciliation; there is no substantial *coniunctio*. On the caduceus, the snakes separate but never fully come back together again, because the inferior function is never given full parity. Therefore, the dominant attitude does not change and the inferior function is developed to only a small degree. If we express this in terms of Spitteler's story, then Epimetheus retains his position of king no matter what happens. Prometheus is encouraged to live in the land, but only as an ordinary citizen and on condition that he does not cause too much trouble. Messias never gets the opportunity to become king himself. This means there is no new attitude and no bridge between consciousness and the unconscious.

The vertical dimension is an important aspect of the gravamen of *Psychological Types*. In Jung's view, most readers do not recognise there are two poles in psychic life that need to be bridged. In Jung's correspondence with Hans Schmid-Guisan, when forming his ideas on typology during the First World War, he saw the essence of the type problem as being 'the existence of two poles between which psychic development occurs' (Jung and Schmid-Guisan 2013, p. 48). Half a century later, he lamented his failure to get this message adopted by the general population:

> The contemporary cultural consciousness has not yet absorbed into its general philosophy the idea of the unconscious and all that it means, despite the fact that modern man has been confronted with this idea for more than half a century. The assimilation of the fundamental insight that psychic life has two poles still remains a task for the future.
>
> (Jung 1963, p. 193)

The unconscious

Isabel Briggs Myers acknowledges the existence of the unconscious, but only as the source of perceptions for the function of intuition (Myers 1980, p. 131) or as the shadow side of each personality type (ibid., p. 84). Although there are some overlaps between these concepts – the source of intuition, the shadow, and the personal and collective unconscious – the scope of each is very different. Intuition draws on the unconscious to adapt to the outer world. The shadow is the part of the unconscious that is opposite to the conscious attitude. And the personal and collective unconscious are much more extensive domains.

Myers recognises the potential to transcend one's type (Myers 1980, p. 168) but she sees no need for it (Myers 1977, p. 21). This sets a limit on the scope of any attempts to integrate the unconscious. For example, when looking at midlife processes the dominant function remains as the dominant attitude (Corlett and Millner 1993, p. 235). Similarly, when various ego development models are applied to type, one's 'actual psychological type does not change' (Bennet 2010, p. 220). In ego development, the transcendent function is only something to be 'accessed' (ibid., p. 42) or 'come into play' (ibid., p. 80). This would mean, in the Myers-Briggs alternative version of Spitteler's story, that Messias is given only a cameo role; he is brought out as and when needed to serve the king. These models stop short of personality transformation.

In Jungian individuation, type can change – for example, 'the function-type is subject to all manner of changes in the course of life' (Jung 1937b, p. 230) and 'type is nothing static. It changes' (Jung 1959, p. 435). Also, the transcendent function is not a momentary phenomenon; it is a function that facilitates a permanent change in personality. It displaces a basic typological function as the dominant function and ushers in a new attitude, as shown by the emergence of Messias as king in Spitteler's story. In this form of development, we do not merely access the inferior function but we reconcile it with the dominant function to transform our conscious and unconscious attitudes. And thereafter, we continue transforming the personality by experiencing the dialectic between various other forms of opposite. It is from between these opposites that the unique self emerges.

We can illustrate the different forms of development in Myers-Briggs Typology and Jungian individuation with the analogy of a building site. Jungian individuation is akin to excavating the sewers, to expose potential problems before (or as) we lay the foundations for the construction of a new building. In the Myers-Briggs version of the encounter with the unconscious, we lift the lid on the sewer, we inspect the visible part of the tunnel, but then we replace the lid. The landscape remains in the same state as it was before. This represents more of a peek at the unconscious than the integration of it. Although we gain some understanding of what lies beneath and learn how to use part of it more effectively, there is a limited degree of change, both above and below the surface.

The inferior function

One of the reasons for the divergence of Myers-Briggs Typology and Jungian individuation is that Myers believed Jung's interest lay primarily in psychopathology, in the treatment of people who had clinical need. She saw Jung's negative, one-sided portrayals of the types as being due to his lack of interest in the healthy population. Her son and collaborator wrote that Jung 'was not particularly interested in the aspects of psychological type displayed by healthy people' (Myers 1995, p. xii). However, this does not accurately represent Jung's view.

He was very interested in normal psychology (Myers 2013), and he wanted his ideas and experiences in *Psychological Types* to be used by lay readers (Jung 1920, p. xi).

It may also be that Myers thought Jung overlooked the auxiliary function because he frequently talks about one differentiated function. However, his points apply equally well whether we differentiate one, two, or even three functions. We are still one-sided in each case, there is still a split between the two main parts of the psyche, and individuation begins only when we try to differentiate the inferior function:

> Most people use one function (or its modification), more complicated people use two functions, and a very highly differentiated personality would make use of three functions. The inclusion of the fourth function belongs to what Jung has called the individuation process, and the reconciliation of the opposing trends of one's nature.
>
> (Fordham 1953, pp. 45–46)

Jung recommended Frieda Fordham's book as a good introduction to the unconscious (Jung 1957b, p. 402). Other writers also suggest that individuation starts with the differentiation of the fourth (inferior) function. For example, as the Jungian analyst John Beebe points out (Beebe 2006, p. 141), Marie-Louise von Franz related it to the transcendent function. She was also a Jungian analyst and close associate of Jung, and pointed out that differentiating the inferior leads to an entirely new attitude:

> When the fourth function comes up … the whole [conscious] structure collapses … This, then, produces a stage … where everything is neither thinking nor feeling nor sensation nor intuition. Something new comes up, namely, a completely different and new attitude toward life in which one uses all and none of the functions all the time.
>
> (von Franz 1971/1986, pp. 27–28)

In Jungian individuation, we give the inferior full parity with the dominant and, as a result, consciousness collapses into the unconscious. That is, we lose the certainties that had previously held our life together and we confront some of the contents of our unconscious psyche. It is in the midst of this difficulty that the transcendent function emerges to usher in a new attitude towards life. Another associate of Jung, Erich Neumann, describes this new attitude as the personality embarking on a third direction, which is neither extraversion nor introversion but 'centroversion' (Neumann 1954, p. 219). This is his own term for a new direction that is equivalent to individuation.

The difference between Myers and Jung is illustrated by the number of types they describe. Myers expands Jung's eight types to sixteen by completing the list of typical dominant/auxiliary combinations that he began at the end of chapter X

(Jung 1921, p. 406). On the surface, this increase to 16 might seem a minor change – especially as Jung acknowledged that 'one could increase this number at will' (Jung 1923, p. 523). However, it reflects a fundamentally different approach to the type problem. Jung did not finish his list of 16 types because he did not see it as necessary. He viewed all forms of type as a problem, whether based on a single function or a group of functions, because they are all forms of one-sidedness.

When Isabel Briggs Myers introduced the auxiliary function, to define her 16 types, she believed she was going 'beyond the point where Jung was content to stop' (Myers 1980, p. 24). However, Jung had gone further than she had. He saw the auxiliary function as still part of the first movement, as being part of a one-sided consciousness. Isabel Briggs Myers accused Jung of overlooking an aspect of his own theory – the balancing role of the auxiliary. But it was she who overlooked the more wide-ranging aspects of his theory, particularly the transcendent function. The omission of the fifth function underpins one of the long-standing criticisms of typological questionnaires, that they are 'contrary to the basic Jungian idea that opposites can be transcended' (Samuels 1985, p. 85).

Quaternities

One area of agreement between Myers and Jung is the typological sequence of personal development. Although Jung's analysis of *Prometheus and Epimetheus* focuses on the reconciliation of a dominant function and its opposite (the inferior), it is more practical to go through a sequence of development that involves all four functions. Differentiating the inferior function straight after the differentiation of the dominant is too much of a violation of our conscious attitude, or too great a leap. It is better to differentiate the other functions first and then the inferior (Meier 1995, pp. 57–58). This makes it easier and more acceptable to come to terms with the inferior function (Jung 1921, p. 407).

The relationship between the four typological functions and the transcendent function, which von Franz described, is mirrored in the metaphor of alchemy. Quaternities (fourfold structures) often occur in the psyche (Jung 1951), and the alchemists viewed the world as consisting of four elements – earth, water, air, and fire. Jung drew a direct comparison between these elements and the typological functions (Jung 1942, p. 167). Just as all other elements are formed out of the basic ones, so too all psychological attitudes are formed out of the basic attitudes that deal with facts, possibilities, logic, and values. The processes of alchemy describe how to transform elements from one form into another, and how to combine base elements into a higher, fifth element. The fifth element is the philosopher's stone, which is both the result of transformation and itself has the power to transform. This means that *Psychological Types* and Jung's writings on alchemy have a common foundation. They both aim to develop a function that is the means of transformation and the result of transformation – the fifth element or transcendent function.

120   Two movements

Whereas Isabel Briggs Myers looked to develop a hierarchy of typological functions, the emphasis in alchemy is on a much larger work. 'In general, the alchemists strove for a *total* union of opposites' (Jung 1955–56, p. 475, original italics). They aimed to unify everything, within themselves and the world. Alchemy is not a different theory from that in *Psychological Types*. They are different ways of explaining the same underlying principles, each with different strengths and weaknesses. *Psychological Types* provides a good analysis of the problem of opposites, such as how it arises from the discrimination of consciousness, the typical examples that occur (i.e. the types), and how it relates to collective psychology. Where the argument of the book is weak is in the clarity of the solution. Jung summarises it by suggesting there needs to be a 'differentiation of the self from the opposites' (Jung 1921, p. 114). He illustrates it with the story of *Prometheus and Epimetheus*, but that chapter makes difficult reading. Jung makes a better job of describing his solution elsewhere, in works such as 'On the psychology of the unconscious' (Jung 1917/1926/1943) or 'The transcendent function' (Jung 1916/1957). The strength of alchemy lies in its description of the solution. Alchemy complements *Psychological Types* because it 'endeavours to fill in the gaps left open by the ... tension of opposites' (Jung 1944, p. 23).

References

Beebe, J. (2006). 'Psychological types'. In *The Handbook of Jungian Psychology*, edited by Renos Papadopoulos. Hove: Routledge.

Bennet, A. (2010). *The Shadows of Type: Psychological Type Through Seven Levels of Development.* Morrisville, NC: Lulu Enterprises.

Corlett, E.S., Millner, N.B. (1993). *Navigating Midlife: Using Typology as a Guide*. Palo Alto, CA: CPP Books.

Fordham, F. (1953). *An Introduction to Jung's Psychology: An Exposition for the General Reader of the Theories and Technique of the Foremost Living Medical Psychologist.* London: Penguin Books.

Jung, C.G. (1911–12/1952). *CW5.*

Jung, C.G. (1916/1948). 'General aspects of dream psychology'. In *CW8.*

Jung, C.G. (1916/1957). 'The transcendent function'. In *CW8.*

Jung, C.G. (1917/1926/1943). 'On the psychology of the unconscious'. In *CW7.*

Jung, C.G. (1920). 'Foreword to the first Swiss edition'. In *CW6.*

Jung, C.G. (1921). *CW6.*

Jung, C.G. (1923). 'Psychological types'. In *CW6.*

Jung, C.G. (1928). 'The relations between the ego and the unconscious'. In *CW7.*

Jung, C.G. (1929). 'Commentary on the secret of the golden flower'. In *CW13.*

Jung, C.G. (1934/1950). 'A study in the process of individuation'. In *CW9i.*

Jung, C.G. (1936). 'Individual dream symbolism in relation to alchemy'. In *CW12.*

Jung, C.G. (1937a). 'Foreword to the seventh Swiss edition'. In *CW6.*

Jung, C.G. (1937b). 'Letter to Gerda Hipert, 20 March 1937'. In *Letters 1.*

Jung, C.G. (1938/1940). 'Psychology and religion'. In *CW11.*

Jung, C.G. (1942). 'Paracelsus as a spiritual phenomenon'. In *CW13.*

Jung, C.G. (1944). 'Introduction to the religious and psychological problems of alchemy'. In *CW12*.

Jung, C.G. (1945/1948). 'The phenomenology of the spirit in fairy tales'. In *CW9i*.

Jung, C.G. (1946). 'The psychology of the transference'. In *CW16*.

Jung, C.G. (1951). *CW9ii*.

Jung, C.G. (1955–56). *CW14*.

Jung, C.G. (1957a). 'The undiscovered self (present and future)'. In *CW10*.

Jung, C.G. (1957b). 'Letter to Dr N., 12 November 1957'. In *Letters 2*.

Jung, C.G. (1959). 'The "Face to Face" interview'. In *C.G. Jung Speaking*. Princeton, NJ: Bollingen Paperbacks, 1977.

Jung, C.G. (1963). *Memories, Dreams, Reflections*. London: Harper Collins, 1995.

Jung, C.G. (2009). *The Red Book: Liber Novus*, edited by Sonu Shamdasani, trans. M. Kyburz, J. Peck, and S. Shamdasani. New York: W.W. Norton.

Jung, C.G., Schmid-Guisan, H. (2013). *The Question of Psychological Types*, edited by John Beebe and Ernst Falzeder. Princeton, NJ: Princeton University Press.

Meier, C.A. (1995). *Personality: The Individuation Process in Light of C.G. Jung's Typology*. Einsiedeln: Daimon.

Myers, I.B. (1977). *Conversations with Isabel*, transcript by Marcia Miller. Gainesville, FL: Center for the Applications of Psychological Type.

Myers, I.B. (1980). *Gifts Differing*. Palo Alto, CA: Davis Black, 1995.

Myers, P.B. (1995). 'Preface'. In Myers 1980.

Myers, S. (2013). 'Normality in analytical psychology'. *Journal of Behavioral Sciences* 3(4): 647–61.

Neumann, E. (1954). *The Origins and History of Consciousness*. Princeton, NJ: Bollingen Paperbacks, 1970.

Nietzsche, F.W. (1886). *The Birth of Tragedy and Other Writings*, edited by Raymond Geuss and Ronald Speirs, trans. R. Speirs. Cambridge: Cambridge University Press, 1999.

Samuels, A. (1985). *Jung and the Post-Jungians*. London: Routledge, 1986.

Stein, M. (2006). *The Principle of Individuation: Toward the Development of Human Consciousness*. Wilmette, IL: Chiron Publications.

von Franz, M.L. (1971/1986). 'The inferior function'. In *Lectures on Jung's Typology*. Putnam, CT: Spring Publications, 2013.

Chapter 9

Axiom of Maria

Maria Judea lived around the third century AD and was one of the earliest authorities on alchemy. Zosimos credits her with a range of apparatus and techniques, some of which are still influential today – such as the *bain-marie* of French cooking (Principe 2013, pp. 15–16). Jung uses her axiom to summarise the process of individuation. There are several variations and interpretations. The one that relates most clearly to the process of individuation in *Psychological Types* is:

> One becomes two, two becomes three, and out of the third comes the one as the fourth.
>
> (Jung 1944, p. 23)

The meaning of the axiom

The axiom of Maria is a cryptic alchemical principle (Jung 1952, p. 513) that Jung believed even the alchemists struggled to understand (Jung 1955–56, p. 67). When applied to analytical psychology, it expands on the theme of two movements and relates them to typology and the caduceus. It describes four main stages that our conscious attitude goes through during the process of transformation.

One

In the axiom of Maria, the number one stands for the initial, undifferentiated state of unconsciousness. In *Romeo and Juliet*, it refers to the time before the Capulets and Montagues became distinct households. In Northern Ireland, it relates to the time before the distinctions between Protestants and Catholics, and before English or British rule in Ireland. In South Africa, it corresponds to the period before colonialism, before white settlers introduced systems of slavery and other forms of racial division. In *Prometheus and Epimetheus*, stage one occurs at the start of the story, when the brothers are living together in harmony. In the jigsaw, it is when all the pieces are jumbled up in the box. In typology, stage one occurs before any development, before any of the psychological functions have been differentiated. They are all fused together; a function is 'unable to operate on its own' (Jung 1921, p. 424). As a result, the person mixes up facts, possibilities, logic, and values, and experiences a lot of ambivalence, such as loving and hating at the same time.

One becomes two

The second stage in the axiom of Maria is the first movement described by Stein that we examined in Chapter 8. It involves the differentiation of a one-sided conscious standpoint. In the jigsaw analogy, it is the *separatio* that creates a distinct pile of edge pieces that is separate from those that are jumbled up in the background. In *Prometheus and Epimetheus*, the stage of 'one becomes two' occupies most of the story. It begins with the appointment of Epimetheus to be king, which results in him becoming separated from Prometheus. At first, Epimetheus knows little of what being a king involves. As the story unfolds, he develops a better understanding of his purpose, what powers he has, the decisions he needs to make, the key people for him to deal with, etc. Prometheus disappears into the background for much of the story, which represents the split with the unconscious. Although we follow his story as well, for most of the time he is of no significance to the people of Earth. In *Romeo and Juliet*, this stage of 'one becomes two' occurs long before the start of the play. Capulet had differentiated an attitude towards his own household that sees it as good, and the Montague household as bad.

In the apartheid system, this stage involved the white colonisation of South Africa in the seventeenth century and the introduction of slavery. Despite the abolition of slavery in the nineteenth century, the dominance of whites continued – for example, through policies of segregation. Non-whites were disenfranchised and, despite having higher numbers in the population, they had diminishing political influence. This stage culminated in the formal adoption of the system of apartheid by the South African government after the Second World War. There was a similar dynamic at play in Northern Ireland. Over several centuries, Protestant and unionist views became dominant, and they repressed the interests of Catholics and nationalists.

In typological terms, this stage involves the differentiation of one, two, or even three psychological functions. The conscious attitude pays attention to things that are relevant to those differentiated functions and ignores or discounts the type of information that is relevant to the other(s). For example, if we differentiate the typological function of thinking, then we develop a conscious attitude that pays attention to logical structure, explanations, truths, etc. The thinking function 'abstracts' (Jung 1921, p. 409) into consciousness what is relevant to itself.

Abstraction is a form of selective recognition. All four typological functions, when differentiated, abstract information. Each one notices, or draws out, what

124   Axiom of Maria

is relevant and ignores everything else. Sensation abstracts or notices facts or reality, intuition notices possibilities or potential, thinking notices logic or connections, and feeling abstracts inherent value or worth. The more they are differentiated, the more nuanced and sophisticated those observations become. Also, when we differentiate functions more, they go from being passive (observing or reacting) to being more active (creating and initiating).

For optimum decision making, all four functions 'should contribute equally' (Jung 1921, p. 518). The notion of equality does not mean we spend an equal amount of time using each function separately. Rather, all four attitudes should be 'equally at our disposal' (ibid.); they are given the same weight in our decision making so that we have a complete picture. If we use some functions more than others, it is because that is the best way to think or behave in the situation.

One way that we can avoid the challenging work of becoming psychologically whole is to live and work in an environment that values our particular form of one-sidedness. Society is tending to divide itself more, as we migrate to live alongside like-minded people. We can feel comfortable in our one-sided attitude because the people we interact with every day value our perspective. If we keep those with the opposite attitude at the right distance – not too close but close enough to carry our projections – then our attitude is strengthened by seeing how deluded or horrible the other is. However, living and work in such cultural silos can create problems for society, because the aggregation of the one-sided attitudes leads to conflict between the separate groups. Also, it can create problems for the individual if circumstances change and we are no longer able to live in the environment that values our one-sidedness. Jung gives the example of an American who devoted his life to his business. His one-sidedness meant that he was only able to adapt to the world of work. When he retired, he could not cope with the new lifestyle. By that age, his attitude was too entrenched to change:

> Until then he had lived entirely for his business ... with the incredible intensity and one-sidedness peculiar to successful American business men ... He had a complete nervous collapse ... He had differentiated one side of his being ... [After retirement] he would have needed [the] other side to 'live' ... A case so far advanced can only be cared for until death; it can hardly be cured.
>
> (Jung 1917/1926/1943, pp. 51–52)

This gentleman was an extreme case, but he shows that it is possible for an individual to remain one-sided and be content, so long as the social and working environment is conducive to that form of one-sidedness. The problem of opposites might only rise to the surface when the individual's circumstances change. However, for the benefit of society, and for an individual's long-term well-being, it is preferable to progress to the next stage of development at a natural pace.

Two becomes three

The next stage in the axiom of Maria is the beginning of the second movement. It involves differentiating the attitude that is opposite to our dominant standpoint, making it conscious and giving it parity of respect and seriousness. We withdraw the projections that we have invested in others and recognise the corresponding unconscious part of our psyche. The result is a paradox or conflict within us, which suggests we are something different from what we have believed ourselves to be. It presents a serious challenge to our view of what is right and wrong, or good and evil. It requires that we recognise and accept the regressive side of our personality and learn to value it.

This stage can be a tough one to move to because there are several hurdles to overcome. Our natural attitude towards the opposite is to dislike, fear, condemn, or avoid it. We support our tendentious standpoint using cognitive biases, which we do not recognise. They convince us beyond doubt that our perspective is much better than the other. We live and move in echo chambers that support the message that our beliefs are valid and well-balanced. Where we encounter opposition, it merely confirms that the opposite is irrational. The psychological influence of social and group norms makes it seem as if we need to avoid the other because it is extreme. In reality, we need to encounter the other to avoid our own view becoming extreme (Myers and Lamm 1976). Showing respect to the opposite attitude can also challenge our most fundamental sense of identity and meaning. Our self-esteem may depend on the repression of specific ideas that seem evil and on other people carrying our projections. To enter this stage of the axiom of Maria is a psychologically heroic task. It involves overcoming all those psychological barriers that warn it is evil territory which, if entered, are a threat to us and our relationships.

There is another major obstacle. It is easy to mislead ourselves as to the nature of what is genuinely 'opposite' or 'other'. There is a selective attention test that illustrates this difficulty. It consists of a video of two teams of basketball players, one wearing white shirts and the other black shirts (Simons and Chabris 1999). The video asks the viewer to count the number of times a player in a white shirt passes the basketball to another player in a white shirt. The task is encouraging viewers to adopt a particular attitude, to notice certain types of information and ignore others. The more the viewer concentrates on that task, observing the white shirts, the more likely they will count the passes correctly. However, this focused concentration means that many viewers do not see the black gorilla that walks through the field of play.

The designers of the video wanted to show that perception is selective. But it also shows the difficulty of recognising what is opposite or other. The logical opposite to the team in white might seem to be the team in black. However, the most crucial opposite in Jung's theory of individuation is the unconscious. Although the players in black are not the focus of attention, the viewer is conscious of their presence. The more significant opposite is what the viewer does not see – the gorilla.

126   Axiom of Maria

For those viewers who did not notice the gorilla, they might have been confident that they had a good understanding of the opposites. But these would have been opposites that are already within their field of consciousness. There are many opposites in life, some of which are superficial, akin to the behaviour of the players in black. Other opposites can be more difficult to recognise, and we can easily miss the fact that they are there. We can easily convince ourselves that we are well-balanced, and we do not see the gorilla that is deeper within the unconscious. The video illustrates the difficulty of discovering what is genuinely other to our dominant attitude.

Out of the third comes the one as the fourth

The final stage of the axiom of Maria is the most complex. The first stage was unconsciousness – a lack of awareness of the difference between the opposites. In the second stage, the ego differentiated a one-sided attitude, repressed the opposite, and projected it into other people. In the third stage, the ego engaged with the opposite that is unconscious, with the other. It withdrew projections and brought the opposite into conscious awareness, which created a paradox or tension between the two sides of the personality. If Capulet were to reach this stage, for example, he would recognise that, alongside being a caring head of the household, he does not listen well to his family. Being caring and not listening seem incompatible.

The final phase of the axiom of Maria has three parts: out of the third/comes the one/as the fourth. The first part – out of the third – shows that the ego plays a limited role in this stage. It must hold the tension of opposites from stage three and wait. What happens next is not something that the ego can itself produce; it emerges from between the tension of opposites. Any attempt to solve the conflict consciously will draw on existing attitudes, which have created the conflict and therefore do not hold the solution. Also, the creative imagination is fragile, so any conscious activity that seeks to impose an existing solution will prevent fantasy from developing or being expressed.

The second part of the phrase – comes the one – shows the source of the solution. In the axiom of Maria, the first stage is unconsciousness, so 'one' stands for something that is unconscious. This one is the unconscious imagination or fantasy, and it will eventually produce a transcendent function or symbol to reconcile the opposites, so long as the ego can hold the tension. This is akin to a firefighter rescuing people trapped in an elevator between floors. The firefighter forces open the doors, keeps them open against the pressure to close, and waits for the occupants to climb out. Psychologically, this stage of the axiom of Maria involves recognising the opposites, treating them both with parity, holding that tension, and waiting for a resolution to emerge. The pressure of withstanding the conflict can feel very uncomfortable, and there is a natural temptation to resolve it by choosing one side or the other, or by trying to walk away.

The final part of the phrase – as the fourth – refers to a new attitude. When a reconciling symbol first appears, it can seem mysterious, shocking, nonsensical, or fascinating. These are indications that it has an unconscious aspect – a meaning or significance that we cannot yet see. If we pay attention to the symbol and avoid the temptation to reject it or choose one side over the other, then its mysterious nature will start to fade. Over time, a more conscious or rational meaning begins to unfold, and we become aware of something that was previously unconscious. In the wording of the axiom, this is the fourth, a new attitude that takes a dominant position and has the most significant influence on the *Weltanschauung*. In Spitteler's *Prometheus and Epimetheus*, this new attitude is represented by Messias who, in Jung's informal epilogue, assumes the place of king.

We can see this interaction of symbol and attitude in Northern Ireland. After the initial shock caused by the image of the 'Chuckle Brothers', it quickly became apparent that Ian Paisley and Martin McGuinness wanted to make a success of power-sharing. They were prepared to put the violence and rhetoric of the past behind them. They had a new attitude of cooperation that was to dominate Northern Ireland's politics for many years to come. In South Africa, the image of the *Springboks* singing the new national anthem had an immediate impact. It forged a new political collaboration and created a fusion of black and white culture. These countries still had difficulties to overcome, and there would be many times when they regressed. But these symbols were indicators of progression, and they ushered in a new era of individual and collective attitudes.

The phrase 'out of the third comes the one as the fourth' therefore has a practical meaning (see Figure 9.1). From holding the tension of opposites (the third) comes a transcendent function and symbol that is initially unconscious (the one) which eventually takes the form of a new, conscious attitude (the fourth).

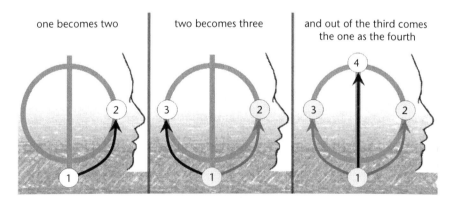

Figure 9.1 The axiom of Maria.

128   Axiom of Maria

The axiom of Maria in film

Spitteler's *Prometheus and Epimetheus* was an epic poem that reflected the psychological principles Jung was describing in *Psychological Types*. Many other creative works also illustrate the axiom of Maria. One of these is the oeuvre of Clint Eastwood, where we can see the four stages develop for the opposites of Western and Eastern culture, from his early work as an actor to his later work as a director (Myers 2018, pp. 166–71). He began his career as an unknown actor, with an undifferentiated (stage one) on-screen persona. He developed a heroic persona (two) through productions such as *Rawhide* (1958–66), the 'Man with No Name' spaghetti westerns, and *Dirty Harry* (1971). These heroes are a form of one-sided consciousness because they are good defeating evil. Although Eastwood's characters became increasingly sophisticated and morally ambiguous, they remained one-sided for half a century.

The turning point (beginning of stage three) was *Mystic River* (2003), which for the first time pointed to evil in the heart of good people (Edelstein 2003). Eastwood then engaged with both opposites on an equal basis in *Flags of Our Fathers* (2006) and *Letters from Iwo Jima* (2006). He had initially planned to produce one film, telling the story of the iconic photograph of soldiers raising a flag on Iwo Jima. During production, Eastwood grew curious about the respect shown by the Americans to a Japanese general (Eastwood 2013, pp. 206–7). He commissioned a script for a second film, showing the Japanese perspective. The latter was hailed as 'a feat of empathetic cross-cultural connection' (Turan 2006). Eastwood developed – and portrayed – equal respect for both sides and acknowledged the good and bad of both.

Eastwood moves towards the reconciliation of Western and Eastern cultural opposites (stage four) in his next film, *Gran Torino* (2008). He plays a veteran of the Korean War (Walt) who, at the start, has a poor view of his Hmong neighbours, one of whom (Thao) is a boy who tries to steal his car. Through various incidents, Walt's attitude changes, he withdraws projections, and he holds the tension of opposites by accepting help from the would-be thief. Walt begins to recognise the good side of the Hmong, he learns more about their culture, they develop mutual respect, and they become friends.

Towards the end of *Gran Torino*, a contradiction develops. In earlier films, Eastwood resolved such problems by choosing one of the options. For example, in the love story *The Bridges of Madison County* (1995), Francesca must choose between two men and, in *Million Dollar Baby* (2004), the choice is between Maggie living or dying. But in *Gran Torino*, Eastwood resolves the contradiction in a different way. Thao is faced with a dilemma. A gang is persecuting the Hmong, and one of them rapes Thao's sister. As no one will help the police through fear of the gang, Thao has to choose between accepting the violence or shooting the gang member.

Up to this point, the plot may seem to be heading towards a conventional ending because it presents a simple choice. But then Walt, who discovers he has a terminal illness, comes up with a creative solution that makes the gang face justice without Thao having to go to prison. Walt goes to the gang's house, makes a lot of noise so all the neighbours come out to watch, and has an argument on the doorstep. As tempers start to flare, Walt puts his hand in his pocket. It seems as if he is drawing a gun, so one of the gang shoots him. As all the neighbours run forward, Walt falls to the ground dead and a cigarette lighter falls out of his hand. The gang have shot an unarmed man in front of many witnesses. The police arrest the gang, who then face lengthy prison sentences for murder because of the number of witnesses, and Thao is free to continue his life without persecution. This solution was a 'third thing' that arose from between a clash of cultures and between two options that were both unpalatable. Thao was being forced to choose between remaining as a victim or becoming a persecutor himself. Walt's solution went beyond the limits of both – it was a transcendent solution.

In resolving Eastern and Western culture, Eastwood changed the nature of the heroism that he portrayed. Although the final heroic act of his character in *Gran Torino* was a physical one, for most of the film Walt's heroism was psychological. He was prepared to engage with a very different culture, to respect people he did not trust, and to develop a friendship with someone who was a criminal. Eastwood's next film – *Invictus* (2009) – takes this theme to a more sophisticated level by examining the nature of Nelson Mandela's psychological heroism in reconciling opposites. It portrays Mandela as a psychological hero who, rather than achieving victory at the expense of the opposite, overcomes obstacles and opposition on both sides to bring them together.

A biography of Eastwood has revealed two very different sides to his character (McGilligan 1999) and in the last two decades he has been reconciling some of his inner conflicts through his work on screen. His work has become more alchemical, not only for himself but also for others. We can see an example of this in the reactions to *American Sniper* (2014). Some critics misunderstood the film as jingoism rather than as a re-examination of the American hero, but the film won an award for its normal depiction of veterans and the lead actor (Bradley Cooper) described it as a life-changing experience. He has since been visiting military hospitals with the widow of Chris Kyle (the sniper), which has enabled the veterans to discuss their experiences in a new and beneficial way (Myers 2018, p. 171).

It is the psychological form of heroism and alchemy that Jung values in his process of individuation. Psychological heroes differentiate themselves from the opposites and treat both sides with equal respect. They look into their own psyches to discover the source of their one-sided and tendentious portrayal of the other. Rather than seeing their own viewpoint as good and projecting evil into others, they seek to reconcile the two sides by first coming to terms with the evil in themselves. In stage three of the axiom of Maria, the psychological hero holds the tension of opposites (Samuels *et al.* 1986, p. 66). In stage four, the ego obtains from the unconscious the knowledge that is transformational.

130   Axiom of Maria

The psychological hero 'does not seek to change the world ... but to transform the personality. Self-transformation is his true aim' (Neumann 1954, p. 220). In Mandela's case, he not only transformed himself, but he also helped change his country. Blacks and whites realised that there was both kindness and cruelty on both sides, and that – with the right attitude – the two could live together as equals. This was not a step change; it was a gradual process that took many decades. The axiom of Maria is not a one-off process; it is an iterative process. The term 'iterative' means to repeat something again and again with the aim of improving it. Individuation is a form of improvement of consciousness, of quantity and quality. Therefore, the process of individuation involves repeating the axiom of Maria for many different types of opposite and, in some cases, many times for the same opposites. This combination of repeated cycles combined with progress is illustrated by the image of the caduceus.

Alternative interpretations

The remainder of this chapter examines some theoretical issues that compare the above portrayal of the axiom of Maria with other interpretations and with ego development models. Schwartz-Salant (1998) and Sharp (1991) view the numbers two to four in a slightly different way. They see stage two as splitting into opposites, and the transcendent function as forming part of stage three. The use of numbers in Jung's writing is confusing because he uses them fluidly. For example, he describes the transcendent function as a third thing that emerges to reconcile two opposites. But he expresses wholeness not only using the third (Jung 1921, p. 58), but also other numbers, such as the fourth (Jung 1951, p. 184), the fifth (ibid., p. 225), or the ninth (Jung 1942, p. 151). Numbers denote different things in Jung's writing, depending on the context in which he uses them. The case for the interpretation of the axiom of Maria in the present book has been detailed elsewhere (Myers 2016). In summary, the description above is not definitive, but it fits better with other writings on achieving psychological wholeness, such as:

> The number three is not a natural expression of wholeness, since four represents the minimum number of determinants in a whole judgment ... Side by side with the distinct leanings of alchemy (and of the unconscious) towards quaternity there is always a vacillation between three and four ... Even in the axiom of Maria ... the quaternity is muffled and alembicated.
>
> (Jung 1944, p. 26)

The description provided in this chapter also fits better with other writings on alchemy, with the caduceus, and with typology. The transformation of four elements into something higher is a succinct summary of the alchemical process (Jung 1942, p. 150). Each cycle on the caduceus is one cycle of the axiom of

Maria, or one set of two movements, or the overcoming of the opposition between a pair of political, religious, or cultural opposites. It can also represent overcoming the schism between the dominant and inferior function. We can make progress up the caduceus even if we do not transcend the typological split though, as a result, 'the process of [typological] division will be repeated later on a higher plane' (Jung 1921, p. 480) – that is, higher up the caduceus. In fact, the division between opposites is rarely bridged in one attempt; they usually only ease off gradually (Jung 1946, p. 200).

Ego development

There are some similarities between Jungian individuation and some models of ego development, such as those developed by Loevinger (1976) and Kegan (1982). These models are 'fairly similar in nature; it is mainly the names given to each of the stages and the number of stages in each theory that differ' (Bennet 2010, p. 61). The relation of ego development to Jungian individuation has been examined by Hall and Young-Eisendrath (1991). They are Jungian analysts with a clinical interest who compare and contrast a variety of models for use in a therapeutic context. They note some difficulties with Jung's concepts of self and individuation (ibid., p. 155) but still give the transcendent function a central role in the dialectic between opposites, which occurs at the higher levels of ego development. The relation of such models to typology has been examined by Angelina Bennet (2010), an occupational psychologist with a professional coaching interest. Her analysis coincides with one of Jung's frustrations with the popular interpretation of typology. Ego development models provide something that Myers-Briggs typology lacks – the 'vertical development [which] is concerned with changing how we see the world' (Bennet 2010, p. 32). Bennet adapts Loevinger's model – because it is one of the earlier and more influential – for use in typological coaching. She then relates the transcendent function to that process at the highest level of ego development. Both sets of research identify problems with the theory they are using – Myers-Briggs typology for Bennet, and Jungian individuation for Hall and Young-Eisendrath. They then use the models of ego development to help clarify and enhance their work.

However, there are also some potential pitfalls of using ego development alongside Jung's version of typology or individuation. For example, Bennet's starting point is Myers-Briggs typology, so she works within the constraints that the theory imposes. This means that the typological structure of the psyche stays the same. Even at the higher levels, the person is the same type and has the same dominant and inferior functions, albeit with 'greater and more natural access to the non-preferred functions' (Bennet 2010, p. 80). That is, the overall attitude is the same just a bit more balanced. Also, Bennet portrays the highest level as having characteristics that are associated with spiritual or mystical experiences – for example, the individual can observe their own ego objectively, they no longer

132 Axiom of Maria

see opposites as separate but as parts of each other, and they 'have frequent transpersonal peak experiences' (ibid.). The linking of peak experiences or mysticism with the highest level of development is problematic.

Mystical experience

Although there can be a place for mystical experience in individuation, it is not the goal of the process, nor *Psychological Types*, nor individuation as described in the axiom of Maria. On the contrary, mysticism is a 'regression to the psychic conditions of prehistory' (Jung 1921, p. 255) and it involves sinking back into the unconscious. This can be a helpful temporary state if it raises symbols of transformation from the unconscious into conscious awareness; it plays a similar role to dreaming. But it is only a stage to go through and, in the axiom of Maria, it is followed by progression to a new attitude that is conscious, not mystical. Peak experiences can connect us to the unconscious, to the 'one' in the axiom of Maria. But, to be of value in transforming the personality, it must lead to a post-mystical experience in which a new conscious attitude emerges, the 'fourth'.

There are risks if we overvalue the unconscious mystical experience. If we make it part of the goal or see it as the end point of development, the risk is that we slip back into one-sidedness or a state of unconsciousness. Abraham Maslow, who coined the phrase peak experience and associated it with mysticism, also saw dangers in making it the aim. He acknowledged in one of his final writings that he had not provided enough warning about its potential for one-sidedness. Although it is a wonderful subjective experience, if it becomes the aim it can make people become self-absorbed and potentially even evil (Maslow 1970, loc. 51). This is illustrated by the case of David Koresh. He was a form of mystic who led a cult that died in a siege at Waco (Jenkins 2000, pp. 217–22). For comparison, Nelson Mandela reconciled racial opposites in South Africa but he did not report having any peak or mystical experiences.

Jung studied the alchemists' mystical experiences because they projected the individuation process from the unconscious (Jung 1938/1954, p. 105). Studying these projections can potentially help us understand the structure of the individuation process in the unconscious psyche because they are mythological reflections of it. But they are not the process itself. This is analogous to using a pinhole projector to see a solar eclipse. By studying the shadow projections created by the pinhole, we can understand the processes that take place in the eclipse. But the pinhole images are not the eclipse – and mystical experiences are not individuation.

Maturity vs wholeness

Another potential issue is the focus of ego development models on maturity. This term has different meanings and in analytical psychology conventional maturity can have some downsides. It can inhibit the creativity that comes from the unconscious and it can take us away from the roots of the psyche (Jung 1943, pp. 140–45). Jung did not use Spitteler's *Prometheus and Epimetheus* to show that the transcendent function develops maturity but that it helps a mature person to reconnect with the unconscious part of the psyche (Jung 1921, p. 272). Epimetheus seemed to be a mature king who was respected by the people of Earth but he was one-sided and separated from Soul.

Also, conventional maturity can make us more collective whereas the goal of individuation is to develop the individual as distinct from (as well as in relation to) the collective. For example, the highest level of ego development deals with primitive impulses by using 'mature defences such as sublimation and non-hostile humour' (Bennet 2010, p. 80). However, although sublimation can have significant value, it is primarily a Freudian concept that depends too much on social attitudes and works against individuation – 'The development of individuality is ... impossible [through] sublimations ... since these are in their essence collective' (Jung 1928, pp. 58–59). Another way that ego development can make us more collective is if it focuses on the personal unconscious and not the collective unconscious. As explained in Chapter 6, raising awareness of the personal unconscious encourages us to conform to the existing culture.

Ego-based vs opposites-based

Another potential issue is that the two approaches – ego development and the axiom of Maria – each carry different assumptions about the basis of development. Ego development implies that progress is related to the ego. Therefore, all opposites are at the same stage of one-sidedness or reconciliation, depending on the 'maturity' of the ego. It is a single journey that can potentially lead to a final state of transcendence. However, Jung's theory places the opposites at the centre of the development process, which implies it is possible for an individual to transcend pairs of opposites separately. Whereas the ego development model can imply that we have developed in all areas, the Jungian model implies that we make progress in some areas but remain undifferentiated or one-sided in others. Also, the collectivity of ego development means that we only focus on those opposites where both poles are culturally acceptable.

Figure 9.2 provides a simplistic but illustrative comparison of the implied development of the ego-based model (left) and the opposites-based model (right). The horizontal axis represents a range of opposites. For example, one point on the axis might stand for a pair of racial opposites, seeing people differently because of their skin colour. On the vertical axis, each dark bar shows how far the person has reconciled that pair of opposites. If there is no bar, or a very short one, it means those opposites are unconscious or there is a degree of one-sidedness. An example of this is Robert Mugabe's attitude towards race, because he took a one-sided view in which he wanted to inflict defeat on the former white rulers. When the bar extends right to the top, it means those opposites have been transcended. An example of this is Nelson Mandela's attitude towards race,

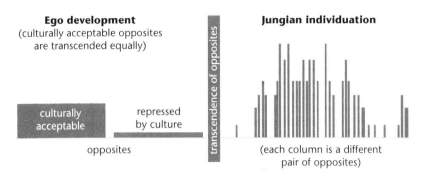

Figure 9.2 Ego development vs Jungian individuation.

because he respected and valued both communities, and sought to reconcile blacks, whites, and other ethnicities.

The model on the right allows the possibility of transcending some opposites but not others. For example, although Mugabe was very one-sided in some respects, he may have transcended some opposites that Mandela had not. In his early life, Mugabe was a talented teacher, keen to continue learning, and he developed a good awareness of different political philosophies (Meredith 2007, pp. 22–24). In Mandela's case, despite transcending racial opposites, there were some areas where his attitude was so limited that he was repeatedly criticised by the African National Congress – such as his lack of consultation over policy issues (Meredith 2010, p. 439). The ability to see the opposites and bring them together can vary according to the nature of the opposite.

In ego development, progress is related to the ego and not the opposites. This logically implies that as a person develops they transcend all the opposites to the same degree. However, this will only occur in areas where both poles are culturally acceptable. For example, in some Western cultures, it is acceptable to transcend competing philosophies but not peace vs aggression. Aggression is often viewed as something to be avoided or condemned, which means that it is more likely to be repressed than integrated. Therefore, the ego development diagram on the left of Figure 9.2 splits the opposites into two categories. Development takes place at the same pace for opposites that are culturally acceptable. In other areas, where at least one pole is unacceptable, such as aggression, reconciliation of the opposites does not take place at all. Those instincts are not integrated but repressed or sublimated in subordination to a social conscience.

Individuation does not necessarily mean that any one individual is more 'mature' or developed than another. Such a judgment depends on perspective. This can be illustrated by thinking of the model diagram on the right of Figure 9.2 as a cityscape, with some low buildings and some skyscrapers. Each person's cityscape will have a unique shape, as they make progress in different areas or in relation to various opposites. If the cityscape is viewed in three dimensions from different angles, it might sometimes appear to be built up more on the left, some-times on the right, or sometimes in a random pattern. Whether someone appears 'mature' to other people can depend on the perspective taken and how well their cityscape meets the expectations of a particular culture or context.

It may be that some people develop a greater tolerance for the opposites overall, so have more skyscrapers in their cityscape. However, there is no ceiling, so there is always more to build. The unconscious is unlimited and con-sciousness can only integrate a limited amount of information. Therefore, we all need to continue working on our individuation. It is a task that can never be completed but progress is nevertheless of great value to ourselves and, indirectly, to society.

Attitudes towards the opposites

A final problem that potentially might arise with ego development models is a collapse of the opposites into sameness. People at the highest ego level 'no longer see opposites' (Bennet 2010, p. 80). For example, 'being able to let go of dualities, they will see that Thinking is part of the same concept as Feeling, and that Intuition is part of the same concept as Sensing' (ibid., p. 161). This is similar to Schiller's solution to the problem of opposites, which Jung found raised complex problems. Although viewing the opposites as the same can be an aspect of individuation, the axiom of Maria implies a more pluralistic attitude. Collapsing the opposites into sameness can potentially be a reversion to stage one or stage two of the axiom of Maria, where there is no discrimination or everything is viewed from the same standpoint.

In chapter II of *Psychological Types*, Jung gave Schiller credit for being the first to explore how opposite psychological functions can be reconciled within the individual. He also credited Schiller with the idea of producing a third thing that bridges between the two. However, Schiller's solution needed modi-fication, for a few reasons. It was too oriented towards his own type and he tried to solve the problem of opposites too rationally. Schiller 'reverted to the intellect and thus allied himself to one side only' (Jung 1921, p. 116). Although Jung did not have the metaphor of alchemy at his disposal when he made his criticism, it is nevertheless directly transferable into the terminology of the axiom of Maria – Schiller got 'stuck at an early stage in his attempt at a solution' (ibid., p. 127).

At stage four of the axiom of Maria, we have separated the opposites and can see their differences and conflicts as well as any aspect they share. We continue to see the opposites as ever-present, even if they have been transcended. We don't lose sight of the oppositions; on the contrary, our awareness of them is heightened, and we carry the opposites with us all the time:

> Once you become familiar with the phenomenon of the opposites, once you've really got it, then you'll see them operating everywhere, because

136 Axiom of Maria

> they're the very core of the psyche ... Whenever you fall into an identification with one of a pair of warring groups or factions of any kind, then you have momentarily – so far as you are identified anyway – lost the possibility of being a carrier of the opposites.
>
> (Edinger 1995, pp. 322–23)

There are therefore two potential development paths when confronted by opposites. One is to return to a previous stage of one-sidedness or lack of discrimination between the opposite viewpoints; this is the return to stage two or stage one of the axiom of Maria. The other path is to invest ourselves equally in both viewpoints to make the experience of the separation more vivid. To achieve such a balance and give full parity to the opposites, this may require the temporary sacrifice of our initial one-sided attitude. But it means that, when we reach stage four of the axiom, we have developed respect for both sides. We are acutely aware of the opposites, standing between them, and mediating between them. As a result, we don't just stand back from any conflict or discount it as no longer substantial; we recognise the depth of it, and we take a conscious decision on whether or how to get involved.

The Jungian analyst Andrew Samuels warns against seeing the transcendent function as advocating triangulation – standing outside a dispute, only being a mediator, and seeing arguments from a disinterested standpoint (Samuels 2010, p. 243). His argument could be extended even further to suggest that, if we always take the middle standpoint, it raises the question as to whether we've actually slipped back to stage one rather than advanced to stage four. Although we may be able to recognise the opposites conceptually, our experience of them has become mired in sameness.

An example of this return to sameness in politics might be loyal supporters of a right-wing or left-wing party who decide to abstain from voting because they don't see any substantial difference between the parties any more. However, if we were to progress to stage three, then we would for a time embrace the views of the party opposite to our original preferences, to gain an understanding of their attitude and learn to value it. Then, at stage four, we would have a much better appreciation of the opposing attitudes and be able to cast our vote in a much more informed and considered way.

The highest culture in *Psychological Types* is not the capacity to avoid getting drawn into a dispute; it is the capacity for voluntary one-sidedness (Jung 1921, p. 207) – to get actively involved in a dispute with the aim of resolving it through holding the tension of opposites. Nelson Mandela has given us a clear example of how to do this. He was acutely aware of the racial conflict, yet he took a voluntarily one-sided and violent approach as a result of carrying the opposites within himself. The final stage of the axiom of Maria is a state of heightened awareness that enables us to get actively involved in a much more informed way; it sometimes means that we take sides.

References

Bennet, A. (2010). *The Shadows of Type: Psychological Type Through Seven Levels of Development.* Morrisville, NC: Lulu Enterprises.

Eastwood, C. (2013). *Clint Eastwood Interviews*, revised and updated. Jackson, MS: University Press of Mississippi.

Edelstein, D. (2003). 'Dirty Harry wants to say he's sorry (again)'. *The New York Times.* Online at: www.nytimes.com/2003/09/28/movies/dirty-harry-wants-to-say-he-s-sorry-again.html, accessed 8-Feb-18.

Edinger, E.F. (1995). *The Mysterium Lectures: A Journey through C.G. Jung's Mysterium Coniunctionis.* Toronto, ON: Inner City Books.

Hall, J.A., Young-Eisendrath, P. (1991). *Jung's Self Psychology: A Constructivist Perspective.* New York: The Guildford Press.

Jenkins, P. (2000). *Mystics and Messiahs: Cults and New Religions in American History.* Oxford: Oxford University Press.

Jung, C.G. (1917/1926/1943). 'On the psychology of the unconscious'. In *CW7.*

Jung, C.G. (1921). *CW6.*

Jung, C.G. (1928). 'On psychic energy'. In *CW8.*

Jung, C.G. (1938/1954). 'The visions of Zosimos'. In *CW13.*

Jung, C.G. (1942). 'Paracelsus as a spiritual phenomenon'. In *CW13.*

Jung, C.G. (1943). 'The gifted child'. In *CW17.*

Jung, C.G. (1944). 'Introduction to the religious and psychological problems of alchemy'. In *CW12.*

Jung, C.G. (1946). 'The psychology of the transference'. In *CW16.*

Jung, C.G. (1951). *CW9ii.*

Jung, C.G. (1952). 'Synchronicity: an acausal connecting principle'. In *CW8.*

Jung, C.G. (1955–56). *CW14.*

Kegan, R. (1982). *The Evolving Self: Problems and Process in Human Development.* London: Harvard University Press.

Loevinger, J. (1976). *Ego Development: Conceptions and Theories.* San Francisco, CA: Jossey-Bass, 1987.

McGilligan, P. (1999). *Clint: The Life and Legend.* London: HarperCollins.

Maslow, A. (1970). 'Preface'. In A. Maslow (1964). *Religions, Values, and Peak Experiences.* Seattle, WA: Stellar Classics, Kindle Edition, 1970.

Meredith, M. (2007). *Mugabe: Power, Plunder, and the Struggle for Zimbabwe.* New York: PublicAffairs.

Meredith, M. (2010). *Mandela: A Biography.* London: Simon & Schuster.

Myers, D., Lamm, H. (1976). 'The group polarization phenomenon'. *Psychological Bulletin* 4: 602–3.

Myers, S. (2016). 'Myers-Briggs typology and Jungian individuation'. *Journal of Analytical Psychology* 61(3): 289–308.

Myers, S. (2018). 'Beyond the male hero myth in Clint Eastwood films'. In *The Routledge International Handbook of Jungian Film Studies*, edited by Luke Hockley. Abingdon: Routledge.

Neumann, E. (1954). *The Origins and History of Consciousness.* Princeton, NJ: Bollingen Paperbacks, 1970.

Principe, L.M. (2013). *The Secrets of Alchemy.* Chicago, IL: The University of Chicago Press.

Samuels, A. (2010). 'The transcendent function and politics: NO!'. *Journal of Analytical Psychology* 55(2): 241–53.

Samuels, A., Shorter, B., Plaut, F. (1986). *A Critical Dictionary of Jungian Analysis*. Hove: Routledge.

Schwartz-Salant, N. (1998). *The Mystery of Human Relationship: Alchemy and the Transformation of the Self*. London: Routledge.

Sharp, D. (1991). *C.G. Jung Lexicon*. Toronto, ON: Inner City Books.

Simons, D., Chabris, C. (1999). 'Selective attention test'. The website of Daniel Simons. Online at: www.dansimons.com/videos.html, accessed 8-Feb-18.

Turan, K. (2006). 'Know thy enemy'. *Los Angeles Times*. Online at: http://articles. latimes.com/2006/dec/20/entertainment/et-letters20, accessed 8-Feb-18.

Chapter 10

Four perspectives

When the symbol and transcendent function have helped to transform our conscious attitude, the conflict between opposites does not go away, but it does have less impact on our personality. Instead of being riven by the battle between the opposites, we become more aware of the two sides and have more conscious choice over our action and thought. Instead of being dominated by a one-sided attitude, we can now see things from four points of view which correspond to the stages of the axiom of Maria. We can see how the opposites are the same or what they have in common (stage one). We recognise the argument of each side, how those attitudes dominate their thinking and actions, and how each side regards itself better than the other (two). We can see how they conflict (three). And we can see either the potential for reconciliation or the actual solution (four). When we reach this point for any particular set of opposites, we then have the flexibility to use the attitudes of any of the four perspectives, as illustrated by Jung's analogy of the army ego commander. We do not have to take the fourth, transcendent perspective all the time because, sometimes, one of the other three may be more suitable in the context. The ability to be consciously one-sided is a sign of the highest culture; it is only involuntary one-sidedness that is barbarism.

We have seen an example of this flexibility in Nelson Mandela. He transcended the differences between black and white in himself before setting up the *uMkhonto we Sizwe* (MK). He recognised the common humanity of the different races and that they had some shared interests as fellow citizens of South Africa (perspective one). He understood not only the values of the blacks and other ethnicities but also those of the whites (two). He could see how the two sides were conflicting (three), and he had the vision for their ultimate reconciliation in a democratic South Africa (four). But, to achieve that reconciliation, he took a one-sided approach and used violence to restore parity between black and white. He was not excessively one-sided but restricted the MK to sabotage to make it easier to bring the two sides together. Sabotage was a conscious choice, aimed at ending the dominance of whites over blacks whilst building a foundation for future reconciliation. For a time, the whites viewed him as a terrorist, an evil other. Eventually, their attitude towards Mandela changed but, if he had chosen other forms of violence, the task of reconciliation could have been much harder.

140   Four perspectives

From the very earliest days of resistance to apartheid, Mandela was trying to move South Africa from stage two to stage three of the axiom of Maria, whilst also having an eye on stage four. His ability to see all four perspectives enabled him to make better judgments about how to end apartheid and build a peaceful and united country.

Another example, in whom the flexibility of perspective played a significant role, was George Mitchell, the US senator who facilitated the negotiations that led to Northern Ireland's Good Friday Agreement. He was not only a skilled mediator, but he understood the local issues and was able to appreciate the perspectives of the different communities. Unlike Mandela, who was deeply involved in the conflict, Mitchell had an independent role. His detailed understanding of the various perspectives enabled him to bring most of the main parties to the negotiating table and keep them there. Mitchell afforded equal respect to the political and religious opposites, for example acknowledging that 'the conflict in Northern Ireland was fueled and conducted by paramilitary organizations on both sides – Catholics and Protestants, Nationalists and Unionists' (Mitchell 2017). He created an environment, based on six principles, in which he could chair the negotiations between the parties. He did not know what the ultimate solution would be, for that only emerged through the negotiations. Mitchell was a modern-day alchemist who helped transform the attitudes of the protagonists by holding the tension between them. This parallels the alchemist's use of a vessel to hold the materials that he seeks to transform. The Good Friday Agreement was not the final stage in Northern Ireland's transformation, but it was an important one.

Science and religion

This flexibility of perspective can help us discover which opposites we have transcended and which we have not. For example, science (as a collective attitude) has transcended many opposites, and Jung both praises and criticises it. He praises it for having withdrawn projections from the material world (Jung 1938/1940, p. 83). He criticises it for not taking enough account of other forms of knowledge and reality (Jung 1947/1954, p. 220; 1926, p. 328). In that respect, it is still a form of one-sidedness. Nevertheless, many scientists demonstrate a great deal of flexibility within their field. Although the standpoints of individual scientists vary, many can compare different theories and know how to reconcile them. Paradoxes within science are usually welcome because they help us discover more about the nature of the material world. Scientists are often able to understand the perspective of someone who is at stage one, to the extent that they can help them understand the different theoretical perspectives. For example, in the BBC's annual *Royal Institution Christmas Lectures*, eminent scientists explain intricate theories to an audience of children using fun experiments.

There have been similar developments within various religions and in the teaching of comparative religion. As in science, religious leaders are often able to explain conflicting beliefs to a young audience. However, the reconciliation of opposites is not so advanced in religion as in science. The viewpoints of different people can vary, but there is still a great deal of conflict and prejudice expressed between different faiths, and between those who are religious and those who are not. Religious intolerance can take many forms, such as fundamentalism, anti-Semitism, Islamophobia, persecution of Christians, or attempts to exclude religion from involvement in public life.

One of Jung's criticisms of Western culture is concerned with the relationship between science and religion. They are opposites where there is often a lack of understanding of the other perspective. Science invests too much in the philosophy of materialism (that the only reality is matter). It does not (in the main) recognise the other forms of existence in the world, such as psychic or spiritual facts, or the importance of meaning as well as truth. On the other hand, religion invests too much in unquestioning faith. It does not (in the main) embrace the notion of reflective criticism and apply it to its own beliefs. Through these attitudes, 'the West ... developed a new disease: the conflict between science and religion' (Jung 1939/1954, p. 477). Another area, where there has been polarised conflict, is politics. One prominent example is the UK's referendum in 2016 on leaving the European Union. In the remainder of this chapter, we will take an in-depth look at the various attitudes involved in Brexit, how complex considerations on both sides were galvanised into simplistic one-sidedness, and why there is very little manifestation of stage four of the axiom of Maria.

Brexit

The UK became a member of the European Economic Community (EEC) in 1973 which, for a variety of reasons, was controversial. In 1974, the Labour Party won an election with a manifesto that promised a renegotiation of the UK's terms of entry to the EEC and then a referendum on whether to remain or leave. They won the election, renegotiated the UK's membership, and then the UK voted in the referendum to remain by a clear margin of two to one (Miller 2015).

In 1992, the EEC became the European Union (EU) when member states signed the *Maastricht Treaty*. This was again controversial because of the loss of some national powers. Some member states held a referendum, but not the UK. In 1993, a new political party formed with the aim of withdrawing the UK from the EU – the United Kingdom Independence Party (UKIP), led by Nigel Farage. As UKIP grew in popularity and began to pose an electoral threat, the leader of the Conservative Party (Michael Howard) tried to denounce UKIP as extremists (Watt 2004). Tony Blair, then prime minister, also recognised the threat and promised a referendum in a manifesto (Labour Party 2005), though it never materialised. David Cameron became the leader of the Conservative Party soon after and described UKIP members as being fruitcakes, loonies, and closet

142 Four perspectives

racists (Carlin 2006). That did not prevent their ascendency, and they officially became a major political party in 2014, after winning the most votes in elections to the European Parliament.

In the 2015 UK general election, in another defensive move against the rise of UKIP, the Conservative manifesto pledged to renegotiate the UK's relationship with Europe and then hold a referendum. This strategy echoed the successful Labour manifesto of the 1974 general election. The Conservatives won the election, achieving their best result for a quarter of a century. Although Cameron then renegotiated the UK's relationship with the EU, many people viewed the concessions he gained as minimal and inadequate (Clarke *et al.* 2017, p. 26). In 2016, the UK voted to leave the EU by 52 percent to 48 percent.

Complex attitudes

Research into the reasons for Brexit suggests that there were many sophisticated and complex attitudes on both sides, at both conscious and unconscious levels, that contributed to the voting decision. For example, in an exit poll (Ashcroft 2016) Remain voters cited concerns about the economic risks of leaving, keeping access to the single market, or a feeling that the UK would become more isolated. Leave voters cited the desire to bring back decision making from Brussels, wanting to regain control over immigration, or being concerned by the UK's lack of influence over the EU's future membership and powers. Various other analyses point to more unconscious reasons for voting. One uses a threefold model that Hooghe and Marks (2005) developed after the 1975 referendum, based on calculations, community, and cues.

The attitude of 'calculations' looks at the costs and benefits of membership of the EU. This might seem to be a conscious decision, but being a winner or loser can affect unconscious attitudes towards the EU and exacerbate one-sidedness. Those who work in high status occupations are winners; they tend to see immigration from the EU as bringing various benefits to the UK economy. Those in low-status, poorly paid jobs that require little education lose out because they have to compete more with similar immigrant workers from other EU countries; for them, the associations with immigration are more negative because they feel the impact of competition (Clarke *et al.* 2017, p. 63).

One-sidedness can use calculations in a tendentious way. For example, a pro-Remain online newspaper reported a study by the London School of Economics (LSE) that showed immigration had no impact on wages (Fenton 2016). There was an element of truth in this, because overall there is no effect. However, other research confirms that 'low-wage workers lose while medium and high-paid workers gain' (fullfact.org 2017). Nevertheless, many people used research such as the LSE's to blame Brexit on the poor level of education in those who voted to leave (e.g. Stone 2017). This is a fundamental attribution error – attributing an undesirable outcome to the characteristics of the person rather than the circumstances or context.

The one-sidedness of attitude occurred on both sides, though it took different forms. For example, prior to the referendum, those involved in the Leave campaign argued that agreeing a future trade agreement between the UK and EU would be simple (Gove 2016). However, at the time of completing this book (April 2018) the negotiations have proven very difficult. Also, when those who voted Remain have expressed concerns, they have often been labelled as 'Remoaners' – a term that disparages the opposition. The term implies (unfairly) that the concerns of Remain voters are not valid but are due to a moaning attitude.

The second collective attitude, in Hooghe and Marks' analysis, refers to the 'community' with whom we identify. In the EU referendum, we might see our identity as primarily nationalist, British, European, or include all of these in different measures. The structure of our identity engenders different attitudes towards the EU, depending on whether we see the EU as a threat to our identity or as a protector of it. Concerns about loss of identity can create a corresponding 'fear of the other' through unconscious projection. Those who see themselves primarily as British may regard a Remain vote as threatening their British identity; the other that they fear is someone from a different culture who, through immigration, is destroying their British culture. Those who see themselves as being European, or as having a multilayered identity that includes Europe, may see the Leave vote as a threat to their European identity; the other that they fear is the nationalist who, through narrow-mindedness, is threatening their freedom to work and travel throughout Europe.

The third collective attitude was 'cues'. When there are complicated political issues involved, some people rely on the signals provided by leaders to decide which way to vote. The voter regards a signal as significant because of their unconscious identification (participation mystique) with the leader who is giving that signal. The tendency to rely on leaders has reduced since the *Maastricht Treaty* because the public has become more sceptical of political elites. Nevertheless, in the EU referendum, there were popular leaders on both sides, so the different cues they gave increased further the degree of polarisation in the voting population.

Over the next few years, further research may reveal other attitudes that have had a significant influence on the Brexit vote. For example, in the decade or so before the referendum, the UK population had grown at a rate comparable with the post-war baby boom (ONS 2016a) but the number of homes being built declined, which pushed up house prices (ONS 2016b). Some voters may have been attracted by the Chancellor of the Exchequer's forecast that house prices would fall by 18 percent in the case of a Leave vote (Mason and Osborne 2016). Another factor could have been local infrastructure spending. Prior to the referendum, London was receiving 50 percent of the UK's spending on transport (IPPR 2017), despite having only 12 percent of the UK population. Most of the London regions voted to Remain. There may also have been other material or psychological factors that had an unconscious influence on the voting decision.

144 Four perspectives

Simplification into opposites

The evidence suggests, therefore, that the decision to remain or leave was complex, influenced by a wide variety of attitudes that were both conscious and unconscious. However, there was very little concrete information as to what would happen in each of these areas, so the gaps in knowledge were filled by one-sided opinions and unconscious projections. As a result, the campaigns tended to focus on high level and largely unsubstantiated claims, many of which were demonstrably false. For example, the Chancellor of the Exchequer claimed that Brexit 'would cost British households £4,300 per year' (Osborne 2016) and the Leave campaign bus claimed Brexit would yield an extra '£350 million a week' (Chu 2016) to spend on the NHS. Both numbers were distortions – about three times bigger than they should have been – and they earned a sharp rebuke from the UK government's Treasury Committee (parliament.uk 2016).

At times, the debate reached an absurdly simplistic level. This is illustrated by a question posed by a TV interviewer to the Prime Minister, David Cameron: 'Which comes first: World War Three or the global Brexit recession?' (Rentoul 2016). The question itself received a round of applause from the audience. Many in the electorate recognised the dishonesty of the two campaigns (Clarke *et al.* 2017, p. 42). One-sidedness meant there was a tendency to point only to the dishonesty on the other side but, as some independent fact-checking organisations highlighted, the dishonesty was on both sides:

> Claim: Campaigners on both sides of the EU referendum made false claims. Conclusion: That's correct. Sometimes they even made false claims about the false claims made by each other.
>
> (fullfact.org 2016)

The debate became grossly simplified and exaggerated. Clarke *et al.* (2017) explain this in a theory of valence politics. Valence issues are those where there is a broad consensus amongst a large section of the electorate on what the policy should be. Voters tended to align themselves and their various views with the side that has the same standpoint on the valence issue. The two issues of most significance in the EU referendum were the economy and immigration. Many people had taken firm positions on these issues long before the referendum campaigns. Voters then tended to align all their other views around these two issues. This led to an overall simplification of the debate, which became focused on two main viewpoints known as Project Fear and Project Fantasy. Project Fear tried to frighten people into voting Remain by engendering an excessive fear of economic meltdown. Project Fantasy incited people to vote Leave by promising an unrealistic amount of extra money and resources.

The valency of the opposing issues is an example of participation mystique. People identify with one of the campaigns, and then unconsciously imitate the collective attitudes, behaviours, and views on that side. Hence, people on each side start to express the same views on most things. These shared beliefs tend to be more primitive than the outlook of the individuals, so they lose sight of the various complex or subtle arguments, and exaggerate the collective, simplified attitudes.

Four attitudes

When an attitude has been differentiated, it then *abstracts* information that is relevant to it and ignores everything else (Jung 1921, pp. 409–10). We can see the process of abstraction on the two sides of the Brexit debate in some of the reactions to Nigel Farage, one of the most controversial people in the lead up to the referendum. He was not involved in the official Leave campaign but, as leader of UKIP for two decades, he had been a prominent campaigner to leave the EU. One of Farage's main arguments is illustrated by an article he wrote in the *Daily Express*. He pointed to the forecasted growth in population and highlighted the impact this would have on the UK infrastructure, including housing, schools, hospitals, roads, etc. He then drew a link between population growth and immigration:

> We've always welcomed those from outside but the rate at which our population is growing is unlike anything we have ever experienced. Mass migration is, of course, driving much of this with 68 per cent of the increase down to immigration directly and resulting birth rates.
>
> (Farage 2015)

The two sides of the debate interpreted Farage's statements in radically different ways. They abstracted different types of information or meaning according to what was relevant to their own attitude. The Remain side saw Farage's argument as having no rational substance so dismissed it as normalising xenophobia (e.g. Cooper 2016). From this perspective, Farage had imagined a problem, exaggerated it, and then placed the blame for it solely on immigrants. The other attitude tended to abstract or notice a different aspect of Farage's argument. From the Leave perspective, he highlighted the problems of population growth and its impact on the UK infrastructure. This attitude tended to notice what it regarded as a valid problem and Farage's message resonated with those who could feel the impact in their daily lives.

These polarised attitudes, which abstracted certain types of information and ignored others, were at stage two of the axiom of Maria. The two groups had differentiated a one-sided viewpoint, which they wanted to prevail over the opposite. However, these were not the only attitudes that were in evidence in the referendum debate. In 2015, two Remain strategists (Coetzee and Cooper) carried out some research using focus groups to segment the electorate. They found six groups of voters, two of whom were staunchly committed to Remain

146　Four perspectives

and two staunchly committed to Leave. Two other groups did not fall into either of these camps – the 'Disengaged Middle' and 'Hearts vs Heads' (Clarke *et al.* 2017, pp. 32–33).

When an attitude falls between the opposites, it can be at any of the stages of the axiom of Maria apart from stage two. If we are at stage one, we see everything as the same; there is no difference because there is no discrimination between the opposites. At stage three, we recognise the differences between them, but we are unable to reconcile them. They are in conflict, and the tension in that conflict may be difficult to bear. At stage four, we not only recognise the differences between the opposites and how they conflict, but also how they can be reconciled.

In the Coetzee and Cooper research, the Disengaged Middle had not differentiated either standpoint. This is associated with stage one of the axiom of Maria. The second group, Hearts vs Heads, represented about a quarter of voters who were struggling with the two sides of the argument. They can be associated with stage three of the axiom of Maria, recognising and valuing aspects of both sides, but not yet being able to reconcile the two.

There was very little evidence of stage four of the axiom of Maria. The Prime Minister, David Cameron, recognised the need to deal with the opposition to EU membership. However, his solution was different from that outlined in *Psychological Types*; his actions did not follow the pattern of the axiom of Maria. He renegotiated the UK's relationship with the EU before holding the referendum. Although Cameron was seeking a compromise, he kept the sides apart. He tried to impose a solution, excluding UKIP and other Eurosceptics from the negotiations, and making modest requests of the EU. This strategy may have been based on polls at the time which suggested that less than a quarter of the population would want to leave the EU if it had reduced powers.

If we imagine a world in which Cameron followed the axiom of Maria, then his approach would have been very different. He would have set up a framework for negotiations. Both sides would have been given equal respect. Neither side would have been allowed to win outright, for example by being stubborn and refusing to give ground. Any settlement would have to be jointly agreed. Jung's theory suggests that, in these conditions, the unconscious imagination eventually finds a solution. However, Cameron did not have the political power or opportunity to create that form of negotiation, so he resorted to imposing his own solution, one drawn from a conscious source. It was a repeat of the strategy used by the Labour government in 1974 in which, after renegotiating the terms of membership, there was an overwhelming vote to Remain.

When Cameron decided to repeat the approach that succeeded in the 1970s, he made the same error for which Jung criticised Goethe in his solution to the conflict between Prometheus and Epimetheus. He sought to impose a conscious solution that had been successful in a previous time and culture. Cameron's strategy led to a temporary success because it enabled him to win the 2015 General Election outright. But it did not solve the greater conflict, which has been evident in the UK since the formation of the EEC – the tension between membership of a European body and the UK's relations with other parts of the world, including the Commonwealth.

A one-sided approach can achieve short-term success, but it will rarely resolve a psychological conflict in the long term. At some point, in whatever context the conflict takes place, the defeated opposite will return, in a stronger, more vociferous, or more dangerous form. Or, if it does not return, it displaces the conflict elsewhere, which may not happen straight away. The fact that the UK has voted to leave the EU does not end the matter; it only provides a temporary reprieve. There is a deeper, more fundamental conflict within the collective British psyche that we have not yet identified and resolved. Perhaps the act of leaving might provide the opportunity for that cultural schism to surface and be resolved. It is possible that, in the remaining time for Brexit negotiations (after April 2018), a 'third thing' might emerge – such as a form of customs union that meets most of the aspirations of the two sides. However, in view of our failure so far to reach stage four of the axiom of Maria, the conflict may remain under the surface. It may start to re-emerge in a different form over the next decade or so.

References

Ashcroft, M. (2016). 'How the United Kingdom voted on Thursday … and why'. Lord Ashcroft Polls. Online at: https://lordashcroftpolls.com/2016/06/how-the-united-kingdom-voted-and-why/, accessed 8-Feb-18.

Carlin, B. (2006). 'Off-the-cuff Cameron accuses UKIP of being "fruitcakes and closet racists"'. *The Telegraph*. Online at: www.telegraph.co.uk/news/uknews/1514830/Off-the-cuff-Cameron-accuses-Ukip-of-being-fruitcakes-and-closet-racists.html, accessed 9-Feb-18.

Chu, B. (2016). 'EU referendum: statistics regulator loses patience with Leave campaign over "£350m a week" EU cost figure'. *The Independent*. Online at: www.independent.co.uk/news/business/news/eu-referendum-statistics-regulator-loses-patience-with-leave-campaign-over-350m-a-week-eu-cost-a7051756.html, accessed 8-Feb-18.

Clarke, H.D., Goodwin, M., Whiteley, P. (2017). *Brexit: Why Britain Voted to Leave the European Union*. Cambridge: Cambridge University Press.

Cooper, C. (2016). 'Xenophobia has become the new normal – and these poisonous ideas won't go away after the referendum'. *The Independent*. Online at: www.independent.co.uk/voices/eu-referendum-brexit-immigration-xenophobia-new-normal-debate-nigel-farage-david-cameron-a7095371.html, accessed 8-Feb-18.

Farage, N. (2015). 'Nigel Farage: It's official … Britain's population is totally out of control'. *The Daily Express*. Online at: www.express.co.uk/comment/expresscomment/615678/Nigel-Farage-Ukip-Britain-immigration-figures-soar-uncontrolled, accessed 8-Feb-18.

Fenton, S. (2016). 'EU immigration has no negative impact on British wages, jobs or public services, LSE research finds'. *The Independent*. Online at: www.independent.co.uk/news/uk/home-news/eu-immigration-has-no-negative-impact-on-british-wages-jobs-or-public-services-research-finds-a7026796.html, accessed 8-Feb-18.

148 Four perspectives

fullfact.org (2016). 'False claims, forecasts, and the EU referendum'. Full Fact (fact-checking charity). Online at: https://fullfact.org/europe/false-claims-forecasts-eu-referendum/, accessed 8-Feb-18.

fullfact.org (2017). 'How immigrants affect jobs and wages'. Full Fact (fact-checking charity). Online at: https://fullfact.org/immigration/immigration-and-jobs-labour-market-effects-immigration/, accessed 8-Feb-18.

Gove, M. (2016). 'The facts of life say leave: why Britain and Europe will be better off after we vote leave'. *The Huffington Post*. Online at: www.huffingtonpost.co.uk/michael-gove/michael-gove-vote-leave_b_9728548.html, accessed 8-Feb-18.

Hooghe, L., Marks, G. (2005). 'Calculations, community and cues: public opinion on European integration'. *European Union Politics* 6(4): 419–43.

IPPR (2017). 'New transport figures reveal London gets £1,500 per head more than the North – but North West powerhouse "catching up"'. Institute for Public Policy Research. Online at: www.ippr.org/news-and-media/press-releases/new-transport-figures-reveal-london-gets-1-500-per-head-more-than-the-north-but-north-west-powerhouse-catching-up, accessed 8-Feb-18.

Jung, C.G. (1921). *CW6*.

Jung, C.G. (1926). 'Spirit and life'. In *CW8*.

Jung, C.G. (1938/1940). 'Psychology and religion'. In *CW11*.

Jung, C.G. (1939/1954). 'Psychological commentary on "The Tibetan Book of the Great Liberation"'. In *CW11*.

Jung, C.G. (1947/1954). 'On the nature of the psyche'. In *CW8*.

Labour Party (2005). *Britain Forward Not Back: Labour Party Manifesto 2005.* London: The Labour Party.

Mason, R., Osborne, H. (2016). 'House prices could fall by 18% if Britain quits EU, says George Osborne'. *The Guardian*. Online at: www.theguardian.com/politics/2016/may/20/eu-referendum-george-osborne-house-prices-brexit, accessed 8-Feb-18.

Miller, V. (2015). 'The 1974–75 UK renegotiation of EEC membership and referendum'. The House of Commons Library. Online at: http://researchbriefings.files.parliament.uk/documents/CBP-7253/CBP-7253.pdf, accessed 9-Feb-18.

Mitchell, G. (2017). 'George Mitchell transcript'. United States Institute of Peace. Online at: www.usip.org/public-education/educators/george-mitchell-transcript, accessed 24-Sep-17.

ONS (2016a). 'Population estimates for UK, England and Wales, Scotland and Northern Ireland: mid-2016'. Office for National Statistics. Online at: www.ons.gov.uk/peoplepopulationandcommunity/populationandmigration/populationestimates/bulletins/annualmidyearpopulationestimates/latest, accessed 8-Feb-18.

ONS (2016b). 'UK perspectives 2016: housing and home ownership in the UK'. Office for National Statistics. Online at: www.ons.gov.uk/peoplepopulationandcommunity/housing/articles/ukperspectives2016housingandhomeownershipintheuk/2016-05-25, accessed 10-Apr-18.

Osborne, G. (2016). 'HM Treasury analysis shows leaving EU would cost British households £4,300 per year'. Her Majesty's Treasury. Online at: www.gov.uk/government/news/hm-treasury-analysis-shows-leaving-eu-would-cost-british-households-4300-per-year, accessed 8-Feb-18.

parliament.uk (2016). 'The economic and financial costs and benefits of the UK's EU membership'. UK Parliament. Online at: https://publications.parliament.uk/pa/cm201617/cmselect/cmtreasy/122/12204.htm, accessed 8-Feb-18.

Rentoul, J. (2016). 'EU referendum: David Cameron challenged over "hypocrisy and scaremongering" in Sky News special'. *The Independent*. Online at: www.independent. co.uk/voices/eu-referendum-david-cameron-challenged-over-hypocrisy-and-scare-mongering-in-sky-news-special-a7062521.html, accessed 8-Feb-18.

Stone, J. (2017). 'Brexit caused by low levels of education, study finds'. *The Independent*. Online at: www.independent.co.uk/news/uk/politics/brexit-education-higher-university-study-university-leave-eu-remain-voters-educated-a7881441.html, accessed 8-Feb-18.

Watt, N. (2004). 'Howard denounces "extreme" UKIP'. *The Guardian*. Online at: www.theguardian.com/politics/2004/jun/02/uk.eu, accessed 9-Feb-18.

Chapter 11

One-sidedness and analytical psychology

Typology is not a discrete theory that stands alone from the rest of analytical psychology; it is part of the foundation. All of Jung's theories relate in some way to the central message of transformation in *Psychological Types.* They are all related through the fulcrum of the transcendent function:

> The transcendent function is Jung's root metaphor for psyche itself ... [It] is Jung's attempt to describe the most fundamental depth psychological activity, the interchange of information and images between consciousness and the unconscious, and everything else that Jung proposed represented merely a refinement or differentiation of that phenomenon ... [It is] the concept and practice of a dialogue between consciousness and the unconscious through which the psyche transforms itself ... This is why we see the transcendent function emerge in the development and discussion of each of the other key concepts in Jung's writings.
>
> (Miller 2004, p. 78)

We have already seen how the transcendent function lies at the heart of Jung's solution to the type problem of one-sidedness. The gravamen of *Psychological Types* is how to overcome one-sidedness in self and society through the transformation of oneself. We have seen that Jung equated the transcendent function with the alchemical metaphor, which is concerned with the same psychological process of transformation. Most of Jung's other works deal with the same theme, of developing the personality through raising awareness of unconscious contents, in which the transcendent function plays a central role.

Integrating the unconscious is an inherently tricky subject to deal with because, by definition, we cannot see it; we can only infer its presence. Contemporary research has provided us with plenty of evidence that it exists, and that it has a considerable influence on conscious decisions – such as the brain scanning (fMRI) experiments referred to in Chapter 7. Jung also conducted tests early in his career, which involved suggesting trigger words to the participant, and timing and recording the response. The delays in responding to each question, and the replies, tended to occur in thematic patterns. These results

One-sidedness and analytical psychology 151

supported the emerging notion of a complex which, though often credited to Jung, was first mooted in the late nineteenth century by Joseph Breuer and Pierre Janet (Myers 2009). Nevertheless, there is an enormous difference between knowing that the unconscious exists and working out how to bring its contents into consciousness. The latter problem is the focus of most of Jung's theories.

Raising awareness of the unconscious

Jung discussed a wide variety of techniques to raise awareness of the unconscious. Although he studied mysticism, he did not advocate it as a way of overcoming one-sidedness. Mystical experiences, or other forms of altered states of consciousness (for example, brought about by drugs), involve a diminution of the ego (Velmans and Schneider 2007, pp. 168–69). Although experiencing the unconscious in this way can play a part in helping symbols of transformation to emerge from the unconscious, individuation needs 'a sturdy, responsible and ethical ego' (Edinger 2002, p. 28). Also, the qualities involved in altered states of consciousness, mystical experiences, etc. are often feelings of harmony and unity. Although such feelings may sometimes go along with individuation, there are other attributes that Jung associates with the process, such as the development of the unique individual or greater awareness of the conflict of opposites.

Jung devoted some of his research and writing to related areas, such as the spiritual exercises of Ignatius or yoga, which he saw as 'directly comparable' (Jung 1935, p. 197). However, he did not advocate their use in the West as a means of overcoming one-sidedness. For example, he felt that the spiritual exercises of Ignatius only work up to a point because they impose certain fixed ideas on consciousness (Jung 1936a, p. 127) and need a corrective to enable a genuine transformation. However, it has been argued that this view is due to Jung's misunderstanding of the exercises (Becker 2001, p. 7).

Psychological Types describes yoga as a method for liberating the individual from the opposites, and for creating a mediatory condition (Jung 1921, p. 119). But Jung only advocates its study, not its use, because 'a European can only imitate it and what he acquires by this is of no real interest' (Jung 1938–40, p. xxx). The oriental mind is radically different from the occidental one because of its history (Jung 1923, p. 39). Jung does not address the question of other benefits of yoga but he dismisses it as a solution to the problem of Western one-sidedness:

> If I remain so critically averse to yoga, it does not mean that I do not regard this spiritual achievement of the East as one of the greatest things the human mind has ever created ... My criticism is directed solely against the application of yoga to the peoples of the West. The spiritual development of the West has been along entirely different lines from that of the East ... Western civilisation is scarcely a thousand years old and must first of all free itself

152 One-sidedness and analytical psychology

from its barbarous one-sidedness ... The West will produce its own yoga, and it will be on the basis laid down by Christianity.

(Jung 1936b, p. 537)

This view has also been criticised, by the author of *Jung and Yoga* (Nardi 2017), that it reflects Jung's milieu. There has been a subsequent change in Western culture that makes it more relevant (D. Nardi, personal communication, 16 Feb 2018). Nevertheless, even though both cultures are one-sided, Jung regarded the West as more consciously differentiated than the East (Jung 1939/1954, pp. 493, 499), and there is some data from my PhD research that suggests this is still the case. The research included gathering data on typological one-sidedness by country through an online self-report questionnaire. It produces a one-sidedness score based on the degree of difference between the emotional reactions to each of the typological opposites (Myers 2017).

The results of this research, shown in Figure 11.1, suggest that the degree of one-sidedness in childhood and old age tends to be the same in East and West, with both showing greater one-sidedness in later years. However, they take different routes to get there. In the West, one-sidedness tends to develop in early life, in the East it develops in later life. The graphs in the figure – based on responses from 48,000 people, 2,400 of whom are from Eastern countries – compare one-sidedness with age, in the West and the East.

These are only averages. It is likely that, due to the variety of human personality, spiritual exercises and yoga will work for some people in the West and not others. When considering psychological development, therefore, we need to consider the relevance of Jung's arguments to the individual paths taken in our own lives. For example, he saw the West and the East as, on average, presenting different problems. Yoga is a solution to Eastern problems, in which the psyche tends to be more balanced. It is not a solution to the Western problem of one-sidedness. 'The Western man has to develop that connection with his unconscious first [otherwise] yoga exercises ... only procure a conscious thrill' (Jung 1932, pp. 96–97). Nevertheless, even if yoga does not solve the problem in Western culture, there is value in its study, because of the insights it provides.

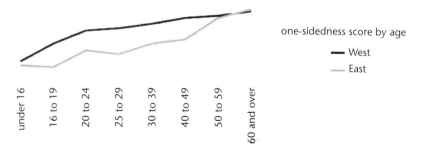

Figure 11.1 One-sidedness score by age – East vs West.

Jung pointed to Christianity as the basis for future spiritual development in the West because it is a one-sided religion. Western culture and Christianity have evolved together; they have both developed in a one-sided way. Therefore, he saw the spiritual growth that will overcome the one-sidedness in the West as linked to the overcoming of one-sidedness in Christianity. The relevance of this argument has changed in the last century, depending on where in the West we live. The number of Christians in the world quadrupled between 1910 and 2010, though the percentage of Christians in Europe dropped (Pew Research 2011). Nevertheless, many of those who were once Christian, or live in a country that has Christian traditions, have inherited a form of thinking shaped by the historical one-sidedness of Christianity. And that form of one-sidedness is spreading to other regions of the world.

To overcome the one-sidedness of the West, Jung promoted awareness of other subjects that he saw as more relevant and potentially more impactful – such as archetypes, dreams, and mythology, which we will examine in this chapter. We will also look at Jung's philosophy, and particularly his epistemology or theory of knowledge, which he called *esse in anima*. Although it tends to receive very little attention in analyses of his works, Jung positioned it in *Psychological Types* as a solution to a pair of philosophical opposites. Also, he concludes his final and most substantial work – *Mysterium Coniunctionis* – by returning to epistemology, in a discussion of 'the self and the bounds of knowledge' (Jung 1955–56, pp. 544–53). As we shall see, his philosophical standpoint lays the foundation for the way that we view and experience the individuation process.

Archetypes

One of the doorways into the unconscious is archetypes. At its most basic level, an archetype is 'an inherited organization of psychic energy, an ingrained system' (Jung 1921, p. 447). It has an evolutionary basis, being the result of 'ever-recurring psychic experiences' (ibid., p. 444). For example, the action of parenting is a fundamental psychic behaviour that appeared in the earliest forms of life and is repeated, reinforced, and developed in every evolutionary era. As a result, there are parenting instincts in the human psyche that are part of our phylogenetic inheritance (Jung 1927/1931, pp. 29–49).

There has been some research to substantiate the theory of archetypes, for example using memory associations. Words associated with archetypal themes are easier to remember (Rosen *et al.* 1991; Brown and Hannigan 2006). Archetypes – as an organisation of psychic energy – are not fixed but can change under the influence of other conscious and unconscious factors. Also, the archetypes can have different content or forms in different cultures (Roy 2004, p. 67). Therefore, when we think about archetypes, we are considering those aspects of the psyche that are common either to a specific society or to humanity.

If we know about archetypes, it can help us recognise our projections of them, which then points back to our unconscious psyche. The characteristics we see in other people have an *objective* aspect and a *subjective* one. The objective element belongs to the other person; the subjective element belongs to ourselves. For example, when Capulet saw Montague as starting the fight, the objective aspect was Montague's aggression, the subjective aspect was Capulet's own aggression that he projected into Montague. If we interpret what we see subjectively, then we recognise it as reflecting something of ourselves. Knowledge of archetypes can also help us to understand some of our own behaviours. For example, when we interact with someone who acts like a parent, it can trigger or activate the parental archetype in our unconscious. We therefore treat them as if they were a real parent. The father and mother are particularly important archetypes that we need to recognise; Jung suggests we need to overcome our parent complexes before we can embark on the process of individuation (Jung 1917/1926/1943, pp. 73–74).

Archetypal projections are not always carried by other people. Sometimes, they can be carried by groups, fictional characters, animals, or even objects. Also, the projected characteristics can be good or bad. We project good qualities into heroes and bad qualities into villains. Often, it is our projections that make the difference as to whether someone is a hero or villain (through the psychological process of projective identification, in which the person becomes what we expect them to be). However, our intense emotional reactions to people we idealise or demonise usually point back to the source of the projection, the one-sidedness within ourselves.

The Jungian analyst John Beebe has developed a model that enables us to relate the hero and villain archetypes to typology. He suggests there are eight archetypes, including heroic and demonic characters, and each one carries a Jungian function-attitude – for example, the hero archetype carries the dominant function-attitude (Beebe 2017, p. 45). Beebe's model uses typology to raise awareness of, and integrate, the unconscious. That is, by 'integrating one's typology, the issues associated with each archetypal complex must be faced, exactly as in classical individuation' (Beebe 2006, p. 144). He developed the model based on his own experience, in which he associated heroic and demonic qualities with psychological functions in himself. He found this helped him discover aspects of himself that were otherwise hard to recognise. For example, by coming to terms with the function that he associated with evil, he found he was experiencing the problem of evil in himself (Beebe 2017, p. 43).

Beebe's post-Jungian model introduces the second movement, or *coniunctio*, into the framework of Myers-Briggs typology whilst staying within the constraints that the Myers-Briggs framework imposes. For example, he presents the relationship between the dominant and inferior functions as the 'spine' (ibid., p. 27) of consciousness. In classical Jungian theory, however, the spine of the personality is the ego-self axis (Edinger 1992, pp. 1–7).

The self, which represents both the unconscious core and the entirety of the individual psyche (Jung 1921, pp. 460–61), can act as if it were an independent person, out of the control of the ego:

> The unconscious [is] a real autonomous factor capable of independent action ... We have a counter-actor in our unconscious ... that can interfere with consciousness any time it pleases ... Now this is very uncomfortable, because I think I am the only master in my house. But I must admit there is another somebody in that house that can play tricks.
>
> (Jung 1957, pp. 339–40)

Working out what the self is, and what the ego-self axis looks like in practical terms, can be difficult because – as with other Jungian concepts – it is nebulous. Some post-Myers-Briggs writers acknowledge the ego-self axis, but they make it coincident with the dominant–inferior relationship (Corlett and Millner 1993, p. 51) and then lay the emphasis on the latter as being the core of the personality (ibid., p. 235). This has some benefits, such as preserving identity during a midlife crisis that involves unsettling change. However, the ego-self axis has a much broader significance than the dominant–inferior relationship.

The Jungian psychotherapist Angelo Spoto has mapped out a different relationship between the typological functions and the ego-self axis (Spoto 1989, p. 128). As shown in Figure 11.2, he does not place them on the ego-self axis, as Corlett and Millner do, but he relates them primarily to the ego, which is at the centre of the conscious part of the psyche; he places the inferior function at the border with the unconscious. The archetype of the self is at the centre of the whole personality, which includes both consciousness and the unconscious. Spoto notes that the balance of power between the ego and the self is crucial for psychological well-being. In an individual's development, the differentiation of the typological functions is a stage to go through in order to begin the process of individuation beyond type (Spoto 1989, p. 154).

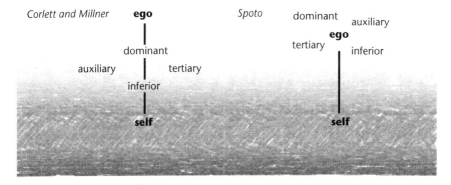

Figure 11.2 Different views of the spine of the personality.

There can be a relationship between the two views of the spine. If we identify ourselves with a type then, at that point in time, the dominant–inferior relationship appears to be the spine of the personality, but this is only a veneer. Behind it, there is a lot more to the psyche that is out of the reach of consciousness. As development progresses, then other forms of psychology will move to the fore, and we begin to recognise that it is the ego-self axis that defines the personality.

When we differentiate ourselves from the typological opposites, we look beyond the basic psychological functions to develop a relationship with the unconscious, and particularly with the archetype of the self. The typological functions then seem to move to the side, away from the ego-self axis. Spitteler portrays this process in his poem. The dominant–inferior spine, represented by Prometheus and Epimetheus, defines the personality for most of the story. In the end, they both withdraw and allow a new function and attitude to become dominant, represented by Messias. He also bridges the people of Earth to the divine realm, which stands for the relationship between consciousness and the unconscious – that is, the ego-self axis. Our unique potential is realised through symbols, functions, or attitudes that emerge from between the interplay of various opposites.

The present book extends Spoto's model by applying the process of individuation on a much broader basis, to include a vast range of opposites and not just typology. If we transcend typological opposites, the process of individuation is far from complete. There are very many opposites in the psyche – political, religious, cultural, scientific, and of various other forms. The task of individuation can never be finished because we can never reconcile all those opposites, we can never raise the entire unconscious to conscious awareness. Typological functions are just one set of opposites amongst many, albeit a significant set.

Beebe's dominant–inferior spine refers to typological attitudes only. By making that spine central to his model, and linking it to archetypes, he introduces the unconscious to those who work within the Myers-Briggs paradigm. However, the present book has laid aside the constraints of that paradigm to examine Jung's typological theory in the broader context of his complaints about the interpretation of *Psychological Types*. Where both approaches agree is in seeing typology as a stepping stone to a more extensive process of integration that involves many other opposites:

> As I have found myself, connecting deeply to the typological opposites within us is a necessary step to opening up the dialogical self to the full creative range of its positions.

> (Beebe 2017, p. 219)

Dreams

Another way to integrate contents from the unconscious is to pay attention to dreams. When we are dreaming the conscious mind is inactive, so the unconscious has more opportunity to shape images and bring them to the attention of

One-sidedness and analytical psychology   157

the ego at the point when we awake. Dreams are a spontaneous expression of contents of the unconscious, and they are central to the psychotherapeutic process of Jungian analysis (Jung 1928–30, p. 3). In normal psychology, they do not have quite such a significant role, but they are still closely related to the process of individuation (Jung 1921, p. 138). They compensate naturally for some of the one-sidedness of ordinary life. The dreamer does not have to understand their meaning but understanding them can increase their efficacy (Jung 1945/1948, p. 294).

The value of dreams is that – if approached in the right way – they are a safe way to resolve conflicts between consciousness and the unconscious. In the story of *Prometheus and Epimetheus*, dreams are akin to Pandora's jewel. They present themselves to us, and there is no compulsion to respond. We can ignore them, or we can pay attention to them, value them, and try to understand them. Although the unconscious is often trying to communicate something of importance through dreams, they are symbolic, so need careful interpretation to get the most benefit. The more we learn to interpret dreams symbolically, the more progress we will make in our individuation, and the less likely we are to experience the disaster of enantiodromia. Some dreams have an objective meaning; they are telling us something about our external circumstances. Others have a subjective meaning; they reflect aspects of our own psyche. The dreams may include people that we know, such as public figures or famous people, or objects or situations. In a subjective dream, these contents each represent various parts of ourselves. The way that the elements of a dream interact can also convey meanings that help us in our individuation.

There are many techniques to help understand the meaning of a dream. It can be useful, for example, to keep a *dream diary*, writing it down before we forget it. Articulating the dream, whether orally or on paper, can help give it a tangible form and translate its meaning into our conscious life. *Artwork* can also help understand dream images – such as painting, writing a story, playing with sand, carving objects, etc. Through the development of the art, and reflection on it, we can explore its significance. The technique of *amplification* involves drawing on the meaning of images or characters from other sources, such as myth, film, or literature. There are several symbol dictionaries, which are a useful source of information, but they are not always right. The same dream can mean different things to different people. A dream interpretation is likely to be meaningful if it feels right, seems compelling, or is very memorable. The technique of *association* involves allowing free thought to link other images to the dream. This approach tends to produce more personal interpretations than amplification because it enables the unconscious imagination to present ideas spontaneously. *Active imagination* is a more advanced technique that involves re-entering the dream whilst awake and seeing how it develops:

Letting the unconscious come up is only the first half of the work. The second half … consists in *coming to terms with the unconscious* … You

158   One-sidedness and analytical psychology

> must step into the fantasy yourself and compel the figures to give you an answer. Only in this way is the unconscious integrated with consciousness by means of a dialectical procedure, a dialogue between yourself and the unconscious figures.
>
> (Jung 1950, p. 561, original italics)

There are some risks with this approach because it can sometimes be unproductive, mislead into further one-sidedness rather than confronting the opposite, or become disturbing (Samuels *et al.* 1986, p. 10). Jungian analysts are trained in dream interpretation and can help clients make the best use of the various techniques.

Mythology

Another way to discover the contents of our unconscious psyche is through myth. For Jung, as well as many other theorists of myth, the term does not have the colloquial meaning of falsehood but can mean various things. It is a form of narrative that has its roots in the human imagination. It can be fictional or explain how something works. It can have elements of truth and falsity. We can view myth literally (e.g. God created the world in seven days) or symbolically (the Genesis story represents the evolutionary development of consciousness out of the unconscious). And it can be shared widely, or it can be a personal myth. Mythology includes not only archaic myths, such as Homer's *Odyssey* or the Sumerian account of the flood, but also contemporary myths, such as film, television, or modern literature. When a myth has significance for our unconscious psyche, there is often an associated emotion, visceral reaction, or certainty about truth. If we feel gripped, enthralled, or repulsed by a story then it probably reflects something that we do not recognise in ourselves.

Contemporary writers often use mythic principles when writing films, books, or computer games. Their aim is not to tackle one-sidedness, nor to develop greater conscious awareness, but to make a commercial gain. Theirs is a psychological rather than visionary use of myth – using a known mythological formula rather than expressing the contemporary contents of the unconscious. This has its origins in the work of the mythographer Joseph Campbell. He argued that, in different myths, 'all we find in the end is ... a series of standard metamorphoses' (Campbell 1949, p. 13). On this basis, he developed the monomyth – the universal story of the hero – that can be used to analyse all forms of myth, including film. In Jung's theory this is a psychological use of myth because it imposes an existing interpretation. Jung's interest was more in using visionary analysis to draw out what new meaning a story can reveal for the individual or contemporary culture:

> To interpret a myth, Campbell simply identifies the archetypes in it. An interpretation of the *Odyssey*, for example, would show how Odysseus's life

conforms to a heroic pattern. Jung, by contrast, considers the identification of archetypes merely the first step in the interpretation of a myth. One must also determine the meaning of those archetypes in the specific myth in which they appear and the meaning of that myth in the life of the specific person who is stirred by it. One must analyze the person, not just the myth.

(Segal 1999, p. 140, original italics)

The writer and director George Lucas was the first to use Campbell's formula in film, in *Star Wars IV: A New Hope*. He consulted Campbell when constructing the plot and characters (Lucas 2004). Following the success of Star Wars, Campbell's structure was adapted to help screenwriters increase the popular appeal and commercial success of subsequent artistic works (Vogler 1992). It succeeds because archetypal characters build an unconscious resonance between the screen and viewer.

Jung acknowledged that film can provide an outlet for the excitement, passion, and fantasy that is repressed in everyday life (Jung 1928/1931b, p. 93) but much film analysis done in the name of Jung takes a Campbellian rather than Jungian approach. It engages in archetype spotting rather than drawing out contemporary significance. This can be a circular exercise because modern writers are likely to have used those archetypes or that mythic structure when producing the script. It can even be misleading because, by imposing a psychological interpretation on a myth, it leads us down the path of starting to see everything as being the same and we run the risk of missing contemporary visionary meaning (Jung 1930/1950, p. 107).

The culmination of Jung's work was to produce his own, personal, unique myth (Jung 1963, p. 17). He also came to recognise religion, science, and psychology as all being myth – each one is a 'living and lived myth' (Jung 1940, p. 180). The culmination of Campbell's work was to produce a single, collective myth, based on his belief that psychology was true. He failed to recognise psychology as myth:

Campbell ... does not regard the psychological approach to life and the anthropocentric perspective implicit in it as mythical. His perspective is true, and accurate, and absolute. He sees things as they are, in contrast to the naïveté of people who took their myths seriously. But this sense of having direct access to reality is precisely what myth involves ... In identifying myth with reflections of psychic impulses, Campbell does not recognize the mythic nature of his own basic perspective.

(Grant 1998, p. 165)

It is sometimes difficult to recognise psychology and science as being myth because we are convinced of their truth and they 'approximate to the unconscious conditions of our own time, our own culture, and our own personality' (Neumann 1954, p. 267). Nevertheless, they are explanations, of the phenomena

160 One-sidedness and analytical psychology

we see or experience, which have their origins in the imagination. They provide the raw material that we use to build our *Weltanschauung* (Jung 1928/1931a, p. 380). Mythology is an attempt by the creative imagination to explain things we cannot see or understand. Psychology and science therefore contain reflections of the structures deep within the psyche.

Myth as scientific explanation

Recognising religion, psychology, and science as being forms of myth can help us come to terms with the role that the unconscious plays in everyday life. Karl Popper, the philosopher of science, has described the relationship between myth and scientific knowledge. He uses his terms, atypically for a scientist, in a very broad sense (Popper 1963a, pp. 156–57). For example, he uses the words 'myth', 'theory', and 'conjecture' interchangeably. Scientific theories are 'in the main, the products of myth-making and of tests [which] challenge us to produce new myths, new theories which may stand up to these observational tests' (Popper 1963b, p. 172).

Popper uses the term myth to signify an explanatory story without prescribing the nature of that story, what it contains, or the structure it has. In his description of the advancement of scientific knowledge, there are two sequential and iterative components in the process of developing scientific myths. The first is 'poetic inventiveness, that is, story-telling or myth-making: the invention of stories that explain the world' (Popper 1963a, p. 40). The second is 'critical discussion of the various explanatory myths – with the aim of consciously improving upon them' (ibid., pp. 40–41). The improvement of a scientific myth does not change it into something else – it does not become a theory. Although scientific progress leads to the improvement of the myth, it is still myth: a 'theory always remains hypothetical, or conjectural. It always remains guesswork' (ibid., p. 157).

Popper sees the origin of myth as being the creative imagination and its function as being to explain the world. He sees both science and religion as forms of mythology that have their origin in the imagination's attempt to solve experiential problems. What distinguishes science from religion is that the myths of science are refined through critical discussion and testing, whilst those of religion are not:

> According to the view of science which I am trying to defend here ... scientists have dared ... to create myths, or conjectures, or theories.
>
> (Popper 1963b, p. 137)

> My thesis is that what we call 'science' is differentiated from the older myths not by being something distinct from a myth, but by being accompanied by a second-order tradition – that of critically discussing the myth ... In other words, under the pressure of criticism the myths are forced to adapt themselves to the task of giving us an adequate and a more detailed

One-sidedness and analytical psychology 161

picture of the world in which we live. This explains why scientific myths, under the pressure of criticism, become so different from religious myths. I think, however, we should be quite clear that in their origin they remain myths or inventions, just like the others.

(Ibid., pp. 170–72)

The advancement of science is an iterative process of myth making and myth criticism. Progress depends on 'man's power to grow, to transcend himself, not only by the imaginative invention of myths ... but also by the rational criticism of his own imaginative inventions' (ibid., p. 515).

Alchemy as myth

The alchemists were proto-scientists, in the sense that they mythologised about the nature of matter and then tried to make that mythology work through their experiments. The creative imagination was not only the source of ideas to explain the nature of matter, but it was also the root of their religion, philosophy, psychology, and their unconscious projections into other people and things. These were all mixed up together, which is why the attempts to explain the components of metals also reflected aspects of their religion and psychology.

Just as the alchemists had a view of matter that was distorted by their projections from the imagination, our unconscious projections can give us a distorted impression of people, things, and truth (Jung 1921, p. 129). When we mythologise or fantasise, we cannot easily separate all the material that comes up from the unconscious into discrete categories, as it is all mixed up (or concreted together) with other forms of knowledge, such as ideas, perceptions, or experiences. We can never see things wholly objectively, but we can develop a *better* understanding of someone or something by withdrawing projections as much as possible.

Science has withdrawn many of its projections from the world (Jung 1938/1940, p. 83), which puts it in a much better position than alchemy to explain the nature of matter. However, science focuses on material reality whilst tending to reject or repress spiritual reality. This leaves a gap of knowledge for non-material reality because religion does not tend to reflect critically on its myths. Although some theological thinkers have reflected on religious beliefs as myth – such as Paul Tillich, Dietrich Bonhoeffer, and Rudolf Bultmann – knowledge in this area is not so advanced, and many religious differences are still unreconciled. Marie-Louise von Franz suggested a solution – that alchemy could become a modern religious myth:

The Christian myth, on which we have lived, has degenerated and become one-sided ... Alchemy is the complete myth. If our Western civilization has a possibility of survival, it would be by accepting the alchemical myth ... The Christian myth is deficient in not including enough of the feminine ...

162   One-sidedness and analytical psychology

> Christianity treats matter as dead and does not face the problem of the opposites – of evil. Alchemy faces the problem of the opposites, faces the problem of matter, and faces the problem of the feminine.
>
> (von Franz 1977)

However, just as Jung projected too much into the history of alchemy, von Franz projects too much into its future. The challenges from alchemical scholarship, such as Principe's, undermine its truth as a religious myth, which would make alchemy unacceptable as a living myth for most people. On the other hand, psychology is a living myth because most people regard it as being true. It is the best explanation we have at present for how the human mind works. If alchemy is still to have a value, it can only be as a *psychological metaphor* for Jung's process of transformation and the reconciliation of opposites. The fact that it is not 'true' does not undermine its value as a metaphor. On the contrary, there is a line of argument presented by two mythographers (Thury and Devinney 2005) that, if we accept a myth as fictional, it can become more effective. It becomes easier to recognise the important messages it conveys about our human nature because we are not distracted by debates about its veracity. Just as fictional film or literature can make us reflect on our nature, so too Jung's portrayal of alchemy can help us reflect on how we can overcome one-sidedness, reconcile opposites, and individuate.

Mythology and one-sidedness

The relationship between myth and one-sidedness is described in *The Origins and History of Consciousness* (Neumann 1954). Erich Neumann was a friend and collaborator of Jung, and Jung was 'deeply impressed by Neumann's study' (Jung and Neumann 2015, p. xxxviii). He endorsed the book by writing a foreword for it, and later amended one of his own works, *Symbols of Transformation*, to suggest Neumann's work 'carries forward' (Jung 1911–12/1952, p. 6) the ideas it contains. Jung saw drafts of Neumann's book and thought it was an impressive work. There was only one point of disagreement between them – the portrayal of the archetype of sacrifice (Jung and Neumann 2015, p. xxxviii). Otherwise, Jung viewed Neumann's book as giving a 'clearer … picture [and] a comprehensive structure' (Jung 1954, pp. xiii–xiv). Five years after publication, the University of Hamburg accepted the book as Neumann's doctoral thesis (Jung and Neumann 2015, p. xii–xiiifn).

Neumann's book has two parts. In the first, Neumann describes three essential myths – the creation, hero, and transformation myths. He interprets them symbolically, as reflecting processes that take place deep in the psyche. He does not mention the axiom of Maria ('one becomes two, two becomes three, and out of the third comes the one as the fourth'), but the three myths relate to the three clauses in the axiom. The creation myth corresponds to *one becomes two* and describes how opposites emerge from unconscious wholeness. In the hero myth, the ego recognises, confronts, and battles with the opposite in the unconscious *(two becomes three)*. The transformation myth describes the discovery and recovery of the treasure, and how it transforms the attitude of consciousness (*out of the third comes the one as the fourth*).

The second part of the book describes four stages in the development of consciousness, which coincide with the numbers one to four in the axiom of Maria. Neumann sequences them using letters rather than numbers. Stage A is 'the original unity' (Neumann 1954, p. 259), which corresponds to the unconsciousness of stage one in the axiom. Stage B is 'the separation of the systems' (ibid., p. 313) which, in the axiom, is the *separatio* that occurs in stage two, the differentiation of a one-sidedness consciousness. Neumann describes stage C as 'the balance and crisis of consciousness' (ibid., p. 361), which is the encounter with the opposite, or the beginning of the *coniunctio*, the second movement of individuation. Neumann's stage D is 'centroversion and the stages of life' (ibid., p. 395), which corresponds to the emergence of the symbol, the transcendent function, and a new attitude in consciousness. The term centroversion describes not only a balance between extraversion and introversion but also a new direction in life, of individuation. Neumann's work shows the close relationship between mythology and individuation, as expressed in the axiom of Maria.

Neumann's description of the hero myth is very different from the myth of *Prometheus and Epimetheus.* Although there is a treasure in both stories, the attitudes towards it are very different. In Spitteler's story, Epimetheus rejects Pandora's jewel, as do social conscience, and various other educated perspectives, so it sinks back down into the unconscious. The uniting symbol re-emerges later through a disaster. In Neumann's hero myth, however, the heroic ego values the jewel – it goes down into the unconscious to seek out the treasure and overcomes various obstacles that are in the way. The hero fights and defeats the dragon to find the symbol that reconciles the opposites.

Both myths start and finish in the same way. They begin with the development of a one-sided attitude, represented by Epimetheus' appointment to be king or by the creation myth from which the ego has emerged. They both end with a transformation. In Spitteler's story, this is represented by the caterpillar, or by the emergence of Messias as a new king who is also divine. In Neumann's work, the transformation myth follows the hero myth. But the intervening stages differ. Spitteler's account shows what happens if we think literally – the one-sided ego avoids the treasure because it doesn't understand it. Neumann's account shows what happens if we think symbolically – the psychologically heroic ego looks for the treasure and overcomes the inner obstacles to recover it.

The two accounts show alternative ways of dealing with the unconscious. One is to ignore or repress it and to project it into other people. The ego creates a stable and secure world for itself, but it is illusory. Projections help us avoid the responsibility of having to be psychological heroes or having to come to terms with the unconscious. As the story of *Prometheus and Epimetheus* shows, this approach is inadequate. It can lead to a disaster, which might appear in the life of the individual or aggregate to the level of society.

164   One-sidedness and analytical psychology

The other way of dealing with the unconscious is to seek out its contents and integrate them into conscious life. The task of this type of hero is to discover the psychic world, a concept that we shall examine in more depth in the next section on philosophy. We recognise that our view of events or fictional stories is to some degree mythological or symbolic; it has a subjective aspect that reflects our unconscious psyche. When the heroic ego withdraws archetypal projections and takes responsibility for them, it discovers the deeper parts of the psyche. This new understanding might include recognising the various unconscious assumptions and mythic perspectives that structure our conscious thoughts. These little treasures of knowledge are difficult to find (in hero myths the treasure is hidden), and they are mixed up with complexes and psychological defences (dragons guard the treasure). But when we gain each piece of extra knowledge, it changes our personality, transforming both our conscious and unconscious attitudes. We see ourselves and the world in a new way.

Neumann relates the hero myth to introversion and extraversion because, when people are working through it, they tend to do so in either the inner or outer worlds. But both are one-sided ways of relating to the world. The transformation myth is related to centroversion which is not merely the balance between extraversion and introversion but is an entirely new direction. Its purpose is to change our personality through the integration of the unconscious. As we go beyond the one-sidedness of the hero myth, we enter the realm of the transformation myth. There is still a need to be heroic, but its goal is no longer to defeat evil; the goal is self-transformation. Another key difference with this new form of heroism is that we no longer 'act out' the hero myth, we consciously choose to 'enact' it.

Acting out

The 'normal person ... acts out his psychic disturbances socially and politically, in the form of mass psychoses like wars and revolutions' (Jung 1916/1948, p. 272). When something is acted out, it drives our thought and behaviour unconsciously and, because it is outside conscious control, it can even take possession of us (Samuels *et al.* 1986, p. 8). One form this can take is to make another person, group, or society carry our villainous projections which we (or the heroes we project into) must then defeat. As this is unconscious, we do not recognise this as projection but see ourselves as the (heroic) defenders of what is right and just. We must overcome the others – who are dangerous, or ignorant, or incompetent, etc. – or persuade them to mend their ways. When the myth is acted out, the rightness of our one-sided, heroic standpoint is an incontrovertible truth. If those on the other side are also acting out a one-sided hero myth, it creates a polarised conflict that can escalate into violence or war.

We can see examples of acting out in the 9/11 attacks on the World Trade Center in 2001, the retaliatory invasion of Iraq in 2003, and the later rise of

Islamic terrorism. At the heart of the conflict are two opposing attitudes, each seeing themselves as having the moral high ground. Osama bin Laden had the most extreme view on the Muslim side. He 'had become a hero in much of the Islamic world, as much a myth as a man' (Zernike and Kaufman 2011). He justified the 9/11 attacks based on, what he saw as, the evil attitude of the United States. He pointed to events in 1982, in which the US supported Israel's invasion of Lebanon, which he saw as an unjust act:

> As I watched the destroyed towers in Lebanon, it occurred to me [to] punish the unjust the same way [and] to destroy towers in America so it could taste some of what we are tasting and to stop killing our children and women.
>
> (bin Laden 2004)

This perspective saw the US as terrorists and bin Laden as a hero – and one school named a library after him. The Imam who runs it described bin Laden as 'a hero for us all. He stood up to America and he won. He inspired the mission of the school' (Azhar 2014). Also, a parliamentary leader in a region of Pakistan paid tribute to him by saying: 'terrorists and fundamentalists have been given to us by foreigners ... Osama is a hero' (Kifayatullah 2011). However, other members of the same parliament saw bin Laden as a terrorist.

The roots of these attitudes go back to the time of the Crusades and before. The Crusades were 'organized by Western Christians in response to centuries of Muslim wars of expansion' (Doniger 2006, p. 271). There is a long history of conflict between Islam and Christianity, between East and West, and between different nations that have competed for political power and the control of territory and resources. In the quote above, bin Laden points to an event in the Palestinian conflict as the inspiration for the attack on the World Trade Center. But the roots of his pro-Muslim, anti-American, and anti-Christian attitude go back centuries.

The conflict between the West and the Middle East worsened in the late twentieth century because of a change of attitudes at a collective unconscious level. There are elaborate sets of projections in the relationships between societies, including the historical conflict between the US and the former Soviet Union. Before the fall of the Berlin Wall in 1989, the Jungian analyst Jerome Bernstein predicted that the end of the Cold War would lead to the rise of terrorism from the Middle East (Bernstein 1989). He based this view on the US' collective need to sustain their projections. If the USSR could no longer carry them, someone else would have to.

The 9/11 attack on the twin towers was the acting out of the hero myth by a section of the Islamic community. There is, however, a symbiosis with the acting out of the hero myth on the Western side. We can see evidence of this in the invasion of Iraq. In 2002, the US president at the time named Iraq, along with North Korea and Iran, as part of the Axis of Evil (Bush 2002). Also, the British prime minister repeatedly expressed the view that Iraq was 'a regime whose mind is in fact evil' (Blair 2003). They both framed the invasion of Iraq as a matter of good defeating evil. They positioned the West and its leaders as the heroes who needed to destroy the evil villains. As with all projections, there is some evidence to support the description of the Iraqi regime as evil, because Saddam Hussein was a brutal and repressive dictator. However, before the Second Gulf War, his ability to do damage to others was limited by sanctions, no-fly zones, and UN weapons inspections. Also, Iraq was not involved in 9/11, nor did they have weapons of mass destruction. The decision to invade Iraq had its roots in psychology, in the acting out of the Western hero's need to defeat evil in the world.

If we act out a myth collectively, it does not mean the problem comprises only psychological projection. There are indeed real international dangers that we need to deal with, such as the potential for nuclear terrorism. The difficulty caused by the hero myth, when acted out, is that it is a one-sided attitude that limits and distorts judgment. It can lead to actions that do not solve the problem but make things worse.

Enactment

If we enact the hero myth, we make it conscious and use it deliberately (Samuels *et al.* 1986, pp. 52–53). It then no longer drives us unwittingly, but we can see when it is of value and how to use it. As Neumann has shown, the hero myth's best contribution is psychological, in confronting our unconscious projections, and in pursuing the work of transforming our psyche. Being conscious of the hero myth in our own lives, and our projections, allows us to make better judgments – individually and collectively. We can then deal better with other people in the world who might be acting in destructive ways through the acting out of their hero myths. The use of political power or violence then becomes more limited, focused, and productive. As the example of Nelson Mandela shows, the goal is no longer to inflict a defeat but to make opposing parties come to the negotiating table.

Even when we enact the hero myth and seek reconciliation, it may be necessary in some extreme cases to inflict defeat. For example, Daesh (also known as ISIS) were not willing to negotiate under any circumstances, so the protection of Iraq and other countries required their elimination. The difference between acting out and enactment is not the action, but the degree of self-awareness and the motivation. When we act out the hero myth, we have very little self-awareness and our primary goal is for good to triumph over evil. When we enact the hero myth, our primary goal is to transform our attitude, relationships, and culture. By overcoming the tendency to repress evil in ourselves and project it into others, we are able to deal better with the actual evil in others, as far as it exists. The highest goal is always a transformation of attitude, in oneself, or in culture, or between people and groups who conflict.

Philosophy

Another way of coming to terms with the unconscious and overcoming one-sidedness is to adopt a new philosophy, particularly a new epistemology – that is, how we know what is real. In *Psychological Types*, Jung refers to his epistemology as *esse in anima* – which translated literally means 'being in the soul'. Jung presents it as a third thing between the two conflicting philosophical standpoints of nominalism and realism (Jung 1921, pp. 45–52). The former sees reality as being primarily in the mind, the latter as being in the world. However, Jung does not adequately explain what *esse in anima* means and it has caused much confusion, not only throughout his life but also through to the present day. We can see this in how different correspondents or commentators have portrayed his attitude towards the existence of God. Jung was accused of extreme opposites, of being an atheist (Jung 1933, p. 123) and having a blind faith that God exists (Dawkins 2006, p. 50). Many Jungian academics have a more nuanced view through drawing a distinction between image and object, between the god-image and God, but even here there are multiple views. John Dourley – a Jungian analyst, priest, and professor of religion – sees Jung as asserting there is only a god-image and no God (Dourley 2001, p. 2). Roderick Main, a professor of Jungian Studies who specialises in religion, sees the distinction between the god-image and God as being moot (Main 2007, p. 35). Victor White, a priest and collaborator of Jung, saw psychological and theological terms as having 'different [meanings but] referable to the selfsame phenomenon' (White 1952, p. 190). And Ann Ulanov – a Jungian analyst and professor of psychiatry and religion – sees the god-image being the mediator between us and God (Ulanov 2008, p. 319).

Jung overestimated the clarity of his writing because he regarded his description of his epistemology in *Psychological Types* as being clear to anyone who read it carefully (Jung 1933, p. 123). He had recognised there was some confusion during a series of lectures and tried to clarify it by adding some supplementary notes to lecture 16 (Jung 1925, p. 134). However, his clarification used the words *image* and *object*, which add to the confusion even more. The words imply, incorrectly, that his philosophy is dualistic – that there is an image and a corresponding object. For example, there is an actual table in the room and a picture of that table in our minds. This dualistic interpretation is problematic and has attracted criticism for philosophical reasons (Brooke 1991). But the suggestion that Jung's philosophy is dualistic is also problematic because it contradicts some of his other writings.

One reason that the words image and object mislead is that Jung associates his epistemology with the philosophy of Immanuel Kant. The phrase 'image and object' corresponds with Kant's phenomena (which we can see or experience) and noumena (which we cannot). Many philosophers understand Kant as suggesting there is a one-to-one correspondence between phenomena and noumena, such as the example of a table in the world and the picture of a table in our mind. However, the philosopher Roger Scruton argues that this is a misreading of Kant because noumena are negative borderline concepts. That is, phenomena and noumena are two different domains that overlap but can have very different contents (Scruton 1982, pp. 50ff). As the analogy of being a prisoner in a room illustrates, the phenomenal world is the one that we can see and experience. The noumenal world is outside the room and we can only look at the walls, which are the 'negative borderline concepts'. There can be many phenomena (things inside the room) for which there are no corresponding noumena (things outside the room). Similarly, there can be many noumena for which there are no corresponding phenomena. The only place where there is a one-to-one correspondence is on the wall itself, on the border between the two domains. Jung's philosophy is more in line with Scruton's interpretation of Kant than the more common view.

Jung takes his argument a step further than Kant, however. In *Psychological Types*, the psyche is not merely an observer of reality; it has an active role in creating it – 'the psyche creates reality every day' (Jung 1921, p. 52). That is, by interacting with the external world, we are co-creating the world that we experience. There is some support for this idea in quantum physics, which Jung explored in his collaboration with Wolfgang Pauli (Pauli and Jung 2001). There is also support in recent experiments that show the act of observing a particle can change the properties the particle had before it was observed (Manning *et al.* 2015). That is, there appears to be evidence of a strange relationship between the psyche and the material world.

The colour green

One of Jung's better illustrations of his epistemology was the colour green (Jung 1928, p. 218). Colour does not have an independent existence in the external world; there is only a wavelength. Nor does it exist solely in our minds, for there is an external reality that prompts most of us to see the same green in everyday objects. It is a combination of the two. Our mind–body system of perception interacts with the wavelength of light to produce the phenomenon of green (see Figure 11.3). Not everyone sees the colour in the same way, and some forms of colour blindness cannot see green at all. Even when we can see it, the intensity can vary according to where in our field of vision it is, due to the variation of receptor cones in different parts of the eye (Hagstrom *et al.* 1998). Our interaction with the world to co-construct the colour green is unconscious. We see the colour without knowing how the colour is produced. In a similar way, the processes in Jung's epistemology are unconscious. Our knowledge of things is based on an archetypal foundation (Papadopoulos 2006, pp. 31–38).

Jung's philosophy is very similar to William James' late-developed philosophy of radical empiricism (Kotsch 2000). James suggested that reality arises from interactions and from the interactions between interactions (James 1912). We can see this matrix of interactions in, for example, the flag of Dominica. It is shown in Figure 11.4 in shades of grey, but it normally has a green background with a black, white, and yellow cross, and a multicoloured emblem. There is no receptor in the eye for yellow. We perceive the colour yellow from the

One-sidedness and analytical psychology   169

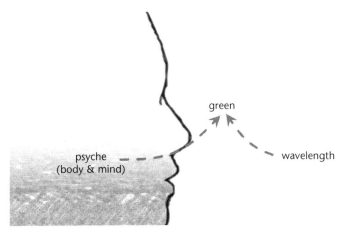

Figure 11.3 The colour green in *esse in anima*.

interaction of the wavelengths with our red and green receptor cones. We recognise the flag of Dominica because of the juxtaposition – the spatial interactions – of yellow and other colours within a rectangular space. This matrix of interactions creates the perceived reality that is the Dominican flag.

Esse in anima is a matrix of such interactions. At the very root are interactions of psyche and the external world, but there are many interactions built on top of those basic foundations, within the domain of *esse in anima*. These other interactions are also real. They are analogous to a hologram, which appears between the beams of light that originate from two sources. The sources interfere with each other to produce a three-dimensional pattern or image. Another analogy might be the image that appears when you open the two arms of a hand fan. One wing of the fan is the perceiving individual, referred to as *esse in intellectu*. The other wing is the reality that is external to the individual, referred to as *esse in re*. The two edges of the fan do not form part of the picture itself;

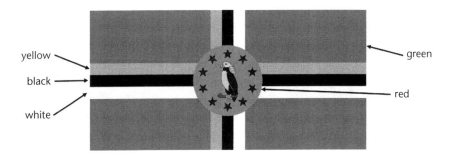

Figure 11.4 The flag of Dominica.

170 One-sidedness and analytical psychology

there is an overall pattern of images in the network of fibres or fabric between them. All reality that we experience is co-created in the interactions between the external world and the perceiving part of the psyche, just as images form between the two sources of the hologram or wings of the hand fan.

Creating reality

We can see the active role of the psyche in creating reality in various optical illusions, such as the image of the checkerboard in Figure 11.5 (Adelson 1995). The wavelengths emitted by the squares marked A and B are identical. However, one is a black square on the board, and the other is white.

The image on the right shows the wavelengths are the same by superimposing two vertical lines, which also emit the same wavelength. The reason we see two identical squares as being opposite colours is that our psyche is involved in creating them. The process of creating reality combines (a) the external wavelengths and context, with (b) our internal attitude, knowledge, and expectations, to construct (c) the image of the checkerboard that we see. Through a process of apperception (Jung 1921, p. 412) we understand what we see in terms of what we already know. As we are familiar with chessboards, we recognise this image as a board with black and white squares. We construct a reality in which square A is dark and square B is light. Otherwise, the image makes no sense. In the external world of matter, there is no actual checkerboard object; there are only dots on the screen or page. In our internal world, this is not a hallucination, because there is something real that creates the same reaction in all of us. The checkerboard is neither pure imagination nor pure matter. It is the result of the interaction between the two. It is a psychic reality that exists in the domain of *esse in anima*.

This same principle applies not only to the objects we see but also to our view of ourselves, and to our opinions of other people, groups, and cultures. For example, when we look at a political leader, we construct their character and motivations between the interactions of our attitudes – conscious and

Figure 11.5 The checkershadow.

unconscious – and what we see of their behaviour. The same is true when we look at people who align themselves with different political standpoints, national identities, or religious outlooks. We co-construct our view of them between our attitude and their behaviour. Other people may see them do different things and have different perspectives, so they might come to very different conclusions about their character and intentions.

An example of the same person representing a different reality for different people is Robert Mugabe. Amongst the many different collective attitudes towards him, there are two central themes – a Western perspective and an African one. To the West, he was a brutal and repressive dictator. To many Africans, he was a hero who fought colonialism. In 2017, the Malawian president described him as 'the only remaining hero of African nationalism, the struggle for independence. He is the last man standing' (Huni 2017).

Neither of these perspectives is objective; both are co-constructed but involving very different collective attitudes. Each creates the reality of Mugabe's character through the interaction of his behaviour and the collective Western or African psyche (see Figure 11.6). For one side, he tramples over the values that the West expect national leaders to uphold. For the other, he epitomises the African fight against colonialism. When Mugabe appropriated land from white farmers in the year 2000, the British saw it as an illegal act. What many Zimbabweans saw, however, was that the British had reneged on an agreement to return the land to black ownership and Mugabe was enforcing that agreement. Each side viewed the same act differently because of their different attitudes.

The reality of other people that we see is a combination of their personalities and our own. Therefore, how we view them tells us something about ourselves and, most usefully, something about our unconscious attitudes. In *esse in anima*, these attitudes are not merely filters that select or abstract some forms of information and disregard others. They are actively involved in creating the reality that we see and experience. The world we see reflects who we are. We can change the world we see by changing ourselves. And when we change ourselves, we can see the world more as it is, rather than as we project it to be. But the world is always a co-construction.

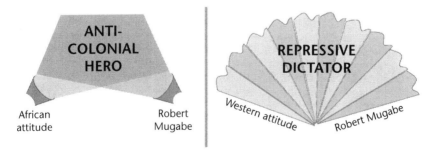

Figure 11.6 Creating the reality of others' personalities.

References

Adelson, E.H. (1995). 'Checkershadow illusion'. Massachusetts Institute of Technology. Online at: http://persci.mit.edu/gallery/checkershadow, accessed 9-Feb-18.

Azhar, M. (2014). 'The school that says Osama bin Laden was a hero'. British Broadcasting Corporation. Online at: www.bbc.co.uk/news/magazine-30005278, accessed 8-Feb-18.

Becker, K.L. (2001). *Unlikely Companions: C.G. Jung on the Spiritual Exercises of Ignatius of Loyola*. Leominster: Gracewing.

Beebe, J. (2006). 'Psychological types'. In *The Handbook of Jungian Psychology*, edited by Renos Papadopoulos. Hove: Routledge.

Beebe, J. (2017). *Energies and Patterns in Psychological Type: The Reservoir of Consciousness*. Abingdon: Routledge.

Bernstein, J.S. (1989). *Power and Politics*. Boston, MA: Shambhala.

bin Laden, O. (2004). 'God knows it did not cross our minds to attack the towers'. *The Guardian*. Online at: www.theguardian.com/world/2004/oct/30/alqaida.september11, accessed 8-Feb-18.

Blair, A. (2003). 'Tony Blair's speech on the Iraq crisis in the House of Commons'. *The Guardian*. Online at: www.theguardian.com/politics/2003/mar/18/foreignpolicy.iraq1, accessed 8-Feb-18.

Brooke, R. (1991). *Jung and Phenomenology*. Pittsburgh, PA: Trivium Publications, 2009.

Brown, J.M., Hannigan, T.P. (2006). 'An empirical test of Carl Jung's collective unconscious (archetypal) memory'. *Journal of Border Educational Research* 5(Fall): 114–28.

Bush, G.W. (2002). 'State of the union'. *The Washington Post*. Online at: www.washingtonpost.com/wp-srv/onpolitics/transcripts/sou012902.htm, accessed 8-Feb-18.

Campbell, J. (1949). *The Hero with a Thousand Faces.* London: Fontana, 1993.

Corlett, E.S., Millner, N.B. (1993). *Navigating Midlife: Using Typology as a Guide*. Palo Alto, CA: CPP Books.

Dawkins, R. (2006). *The God Delusion*. London: Bantam Press.

Doniger, W. (ed.) (2006). *Britannica Encyclopedia of World Religions*. Chicago, IL: Encyclopædia Britannica.

Dourley, J.P. (2001). 'Revisioning incarnation: Jung on the relativity of God'. International Association of Jungian Studies. Online at: www.jungianstudies.org/publications/papers/dourleyjp1.pdf, accessed 30-Jul-09.

Edinger, E.F. (1992). *Ego and Archetype.* Boston, MA: Shambhala.

Edinger, E.F. (2002). *Science of the Soul: A Jungian Perspective*. Toronto, ON: Inner City Books.

Grant, C. (1998). *Myths We Live By*. Ottawa, ON: University of Ottawa Press.

Hagstrom, S.A., Neitz, J., Neitz, M. (1998). 'Variations in cone populations for red-green color vision examined by analysis of mRNA'. *Neuroreport* 22(9): 1963–67.

Huni, M. (2017). 'Zimbabwe: "president an African hero"'. *The Herald*. Online at: http://allafrica.com/stories/201709220815.html, accessed 9-Feb-18.

James, W. (1912). *Essays in Radical Empiricism*. Mineola, NY: Dover Publications, 2003.

Jung, C.G. (1911–12/1952). *CW5*.

Jung, C.G. (1916/1948). 'General aspects of dream psychology'. In *CW8*.

Jung, C.G. (1917/1926/1943). 'On the psychology of the unconscious'. In *CW7*.

Jung, C.G. (1921). *CW6*.

Jung, C.G. (1923). 'Letter to Oskar A. H. Schmitz, 26 May 1923'. In *Letters 1*.
Jung, C.G. (1925). *Analytical Psychology: Notes of the Seminar Given in 1925 by C.G. Jung*. Princeton, NJ: Bollingen Paperbacks, 1989.
Jung, C.G. (1927/1931). 'Mind and earth'. In *CW10*.
Jung, C.G. (1928). 'The relations between the ego and the unconscious'. In *CW7*.
Jung, C.G. (1928–30). *Dream Analysis: Notes of the Seminar Given in 1928–1930 by C.G. Jung*. London: Routledge, 1984.
Jung, C.G. (1928/1931a). 'Analytical psychology and *Weltanschauung*'. In *CW8*.
Jung, C.G. (1928/1931b). 'The spiritual problem of modern man'. In *CW10*.
Jung, C.G. (1930/1950). 'Psychology and literature'. In *CW15*.
Jung, C.G. (1932). 'Letter to Mr N., 5 July 1932'. In *Letters 1*.
Jung, C.G. (1933). 'Letter to Paul Maag, 1 June 1933'. In *Letters 1*.
Jung, C.G. (1935). 'Letter to Pastor Ernst Jahn, 7 September 1935'. In *Letters 1*.
Jung, C.G. (1936a). 'Individual dream symbolism in relation to alchemy'. In *CW12*.
Jung, C.G. (1936b). 'Yoga and the West'. In *CW11*.
Jung, C.G. (1938–40). 'Modern psychology'. Quoted in *The Psychology of Kundalini Yoga*, edited by Sonu Shamdasani. Princeton, NJ: Bollingen Paperbacks, 1996.
Jung, C.G. (1938/1940). 'Psychology and religion'. In *CW11*.
Jung, C.G. (1939/1954). 'Psychological commentary on "The Tibetan Book of the Great Liberation"'. In *CW11*.
Jung, C.G. (1940). 'The psychology of the child archetype'. In *CW9i*.
Jung, C.G. (1945/1948). 'On the nature of dreams'. In *CW8*.
Jung, C.G. (1950). 'Letter to Sibylle Birkhäuser-Oeri, 13 July 1950'. In *Letters 1*.
Jung, C.G. (1954). 'Foreword'. In Neumann 1954.
Jung, C.G. (1955–56). *CW14*.
Jung, C.G. (1957). 'The Houston films'. In *C.G. Jung Speaking*. Princeton, NJ: Bollingen Paperbacks, 1977.
Jung, C.G. (1963). *Memories, Dreams, Reflections*. London: Harper Collins, 1995.
Jung, C.G., Neumann, E. (2015). *Analytical Psychology in Exile: The Correspondence of C.G. Jung and Erich Neumann*, edited and introduced by Martin Liebscher. Princeton, NJ: Princeton University Press.
Kifayatullah, M. (2011). 'JUI-F shocked over Osama bin Laden's killing'. *The International News*. Online at: www.thenews.com.pk/archive/print/298870, accessed 8-Feb-18.
Kotsch, W.E. (2000). 'Jung's mediatory science as a psychology beyond objectivism'. *Journal of Analytical Psychology* 45(2): 217–44.
Lucas, G. (2004). 'The making of Star Wars'. *Star Wars Trilogy*, DVD bonus material. Los Angeles, CA: Twentieth Century Fox.
Main, R. (2007). *Revelations of Chance, Synchronicity as Spiritual Experience*. Albany, NY: State University of New York Press.
Manning, A.G., Khakimov, R.I., Dall, R.G., Truscott, A.G. (2015). 'Wheeler's delayed-choice gedanken experiment with a single atom'. *Nature Physics* 11: 539–42.
Miller, J.C. (2004). *The Transcendent Function*. Albany, NY: State University of New York Press.
Myers, S. (2009). 'The cryptomnesic origins of Jung's dream of the multi-storeyed house'. *Journal of Analytical Psychology* 54(4): 513–31.
Myers, S. (2017). *Mythology for Christians: An Investigation and Empirical Test of C.G. Jung's Proposal that Protestant Theologians and Adherents Should Think of God as a*

Mythologem. Colchester: University of Essex Research Repository. Online at: http://repository.essex.ac.uk/20065/1/mythology%20for%20christians%20-%20author%20final.pdf, accessed 13-Mar-18.

Nardi, D. (2017). *Jung on Yoga: Insights and Exercises to Awaken with the Chakras*. Los Angeles, CA: Radiance House.

Neumann, E. (1954). *The Origins and History of Consciousness*. Princeton, NJ: Bollingen Paperbacks, 1970.

Papadopoulos, R.K. (2006). 'Jung's epistemology and methodology'. In *The Handbook of Jungian Psychology*, edited by Renos Papadopoulos. Hove: Routledge.

Pauli, W., Jung, C.G. (2001). *Atom and Archetype: The Pauli-Jung Letters 1932–1958*. London: Routledge.

Pew Research (2011). 'Global Christianity – a report on the size and distribution of the world's Christian population'. Pew Research Center. Online at: www.pewforum.org/2011/12/19/global-christianity-exec/, accessed 24-Feb-18.

Popper, K.R. (1963a). *The Myth of the Framework*. London: Routledge, 1996.

Popper, K.R. (1963b). *Conjectures and Refutations*. London: Routledge, 2002.

Rosen, D.H., Smith, S.M., Huston, H.L., Gonzalez, G. (1991). 'Empirical study of associations between symbols and their meanings: evidence of collective unconscious (archetypal) memory'. *Journal of Analytical Psychology* 36(2): 211–28.

Roy, M. (2004). 'Religious archetype as cultural complex'. In *The Cultural Complex: Contemporary Jungian Perspectives on Psyche and Society*, edited by Thomas Singer and Samuel L. Kimbles. Hove: Brunner-Routledge.

Samuels, A., Shorter, B., Plaut, F. (1986). *A Critical Dictionary of Jungian Analysis*. Hove: Routledge.

Scruton, R. (1982). 'Kant'. In *German Philosophers*. Oxford: Oxford University Press, 1997.

Segal, R.A. (1999). *Theorizing about Myth*. Boston, MA: University of Massachusetts Press.

Spoto, A. (1989). *Jung's Typology in Perspective,* revised edition. Wilmette, IL: Chiron Publications, 1995.

Thury, E.M, Devinney, M.K. (2005). *Introduction to Mythology*. Oxford: Oxford University Press.

Ulanov, A.B. (2008). 'Jung and religion: the opposing self'. In *The Cambridge Companion to Jung*, edited by Polly Young-Eisendrath and Terence Dawson. Cambridge: Cambridge University Press.

Velmans, M., Schneider, S. (eds.) (2007). *The Blackwell Companion to Consciousness*. Oxford: Blackwell Publishers.

Vogler, C. (1992). *The Writer's Journey: Mythic Structure for Storytellers and Screenwriters*. Sydney, NSW: Image Book Company.

von Franz, M.L. (1977). Filmed interview. In M. Whitney, M. Whitney (1983). *Matter of Heart (DVD),* a Michael Whitney-Mark Whitney Production, sponsored by C.G. Jung Institute of Los Angeles. New York: Kino International, 2001.

White, V. (1952). *God and the Unconscious*. Dallas, TX: Spring Publications, 1982.

Zernike, K., Kaufman, M.T. (2011). 'The most wanted face of terrorism'. *The New York Times*. Online at: www.nytimes.com/2011/05/02/world/02osama-bin-laden-obituary.html, accessed 8-Feb-18.

Chapter 12

The future of reconciliation

So far, we have taken a one-sided attitude to the subject of typology and individuation. The 'governing principle' of the attitude in this book has been Jung's claim that most readers have overlooked the gravamen of *Psychological Types*. This gravamen is the problem of one-sidedness and its solution, which is based on the transcendent function. Jung wanted the book to be the means by which the lay reader could make use of his process for transformation. Although his theory has indeed reached a wide audience, now in the guise of Myers-Briggs typology, that audience has not been exposed to the all-important 'transformation' part of it.

Jung's theory in *Psychological Types* and other works is concerned with 'becoming'. Although he acknowledges the biology and experiences that have shaped us thus far, he focuses on who we can be, on realising our unique potential. He sees Western culture as an obstacle to that development because it puts too much emphasis on collective psychology and not enough on the individual. Superficially, it may appear to be the other way around, but when we analyse our apparent individuality it shows itself to be collective. Typology can be an example – of collectivity masquerading as individuality – if we make it the dominant feature of our personal identity. The aim of Myers-Briggs typology is to 'expect specific personality differences in particular people' (Myers 1980, p. 1). It looks past the uniqueness of the individual to find the common psychology. Although that has value in the overall scheme of things, Jung developed his theory of individuation to show how we develop from common psychology towards the unique individual.

Individuation is a dialectical process in which the individual is formed between the opposites rather than identifying with one of them. Jung does not advocate the abandonment of collectivity, for that would lead to individualism rather than individuation. The primary difference between the two is that individualism goes entirely its own way whereas individuation retains a healthy respect for societal norms (Jung 1921, p. 449).

The unconscious

Jung's theory draws particular attention to an attitude that is sorely neglected in Western culture – the recognition of the role of the unconscious in everything we think and do. As we have seen throughout the book – from the example of Capulet to the discussion of philosophy – the unconscious has a dramatic impact on the reality that we experience, even to the point of influencing life-or-death decisions.

In early stages of psychological development, the ego believes it is the main authority in the personality. Through individuation, we come to realise there is much more to the self. As consciousness expands (that is, we become aware of more content) the power that the ego believes it has diminishes in favour of the self. We start out by thinking that 'I' am in control of my personality but, as awareness increases, we realise that there are much more powerful forces in the unconscious over which the ego has very little influence. It is a paradox that as consciousness increases it seems to become less powerful. One aspect of individuation is recognising and coming to terms with that paradox.

We can illustrate this by returning to Jung's military analogy of the ego commander. A neophyte leader of a large military organisation might assume that the army is at the disposal of the commander. When the most senior officer determines what needs to be done and issues commands, the theory of command-and-control says that those instructions are followed. But the commander soon learns that this army is not as well-organised and disciplined as it first seemed. The more the commander learns, the more it seems the organisation has a mind of its own and there are distinct factions that are working against each other. The transactional leadership style of issuing decrees and expecting those orders to be followed does not work. As the commander's awareness of the army organisation increases, the ability to do things seems to diminish. The leadership task becomes one of coming to terms with reality, with the disorganised nature of the army that is led. For the army to become a formidable fighting force, there are many internal divisions that need to be reckoned with. That is, the more the commander learns about the army, the less powerful the position of commander seems to be.

Applying this metaphor to ourselves, individuation involves an expansion of consciousness by increasing awareness of previously unconscious contents. But this greater awareness also leads to a diminution of the ego's power – or rather, its perceived power, because it never did have much power; it only thought it did. Without any awareness of the unconscious, it is easy to delude ourselves that we are in control of our personalities. But as we become more aware of the unconscious psyche, we begin to realise the extent of its influence over what we see, feel, think, or do.

Individuation also leads us to recognise the strength of the link between our personal development and that of society. Our internal dialectic – or lack of it – is reflected in the external dialectic. The less we know about our own unconscious psyche, the more we project it into the outer world and see other people and groups in distorted terms. This leads to conflict between societies through the aggregation of attitudes, the projective identification of leaders, and the acting out of the hero myth. They start to believe the heroic projections we place

The future of reconciliation 177

on them and they take an even more one-sided approach on the domestic and international stages.

The more we recognise the conflict as being within ourselves, the better we are able to deal with any actual conflict there may be in the world. This can in some instances lead to more conflict, at a conscious level. By learning to engage in an inner dialectic, we can recover the lost art of disagreement that not only develops ourselves but encourages more constructive debates in society – 'a sane and normal society is one in which people habitually disagree [though] agreement is equally important' (Jung 1964, pp. 46–47). A constructive interaction between ourselves and people who disagree can enhance the dialogue between our own conscious and unconscious, and vice versa. This in turn will lead to less unconscious conflict that is aggregated at a societal level. If at the relationship level we all repress our conflicts in order to preserve harmony, they aggregate and build up at a collective level to create conflict between groups or societies. If we express and work out our conflicts at a relationship level, there is less unconscious compensation at the collective level.

Individuation may therefore lead to more conflict in some cases – though of a more productive kind – as we observe an increasing number of opposites and draw attention to them in order to engage in a dialectic. Ignoring opposites, and treating them as if they were the same, is reverting to stage one of the axiom of Maria ('one becomes two, two becomes three, and out of the third comes the one as the fourth'). To reach stage four we have to first recognise and acknowledge the opposites and understand how they conflict.

Three schisms

In the present book we have highlighted some areas of difference between Carl Gustav Jung and Isabel Briggs Myers, most notably that Jung's focus was primarily on the transformation of attitude and Myers' focus was on the description of it. Myers-Briggs typology is widely viewed as closely aligned to Jung's theory with only minor differences. However, as demonstrated by Jung's various objections described in Chapter 1, there is a deep theoretical schism between his version of the theory and the popular reception of it. That schism, which has been overlooked by all except a small number of people for nearly a century, is primarily due to seeing type as being both the source and destiny of the personality, rather than as a stepping stone on the way – something to become and then something to leave behind as part of our history. The schism is also due to differences of language. Analytical psychology describes the inner process of development using the terminology of symbols and dreams. For many in wider society, that terminology has little significance because culture tends to disregard symbols as being insubstantial.

The task of this book has been to draw attention to the theoretical schism and particularly to Jung's original aspirations for his typological theory. In doing so, it has used the language of psychological functions; Jung's four functions and a

178 The future of reconciliation

symbol have been reframed as five functions. From the point of view of analytical psychology, this may seem a minor, unnecessary, and perhaps unwanted terminological change. The fifth function – the transcendent function – was always there; it was wrapped up with the concept of the symbol. But from the point of view of Myers-Briggs typology, this is a radical change because it increases the number of functions from four to five and reframes the theory. It is radical because Myers-Briggs typology does not see the symbol as anything substantial; only the psychological functions are real. But this change helps to bring the two theories a step nearer because Jung points to the symbol – the character of Messias who becomes the divine boy king – and says it represents a function and an attitude (Jung 1921, p. 271). All three – symbol, function, and attitude – are closely linked.

> This symbol appears to be intimately connected with the opposition between the psychological types and functions, and is obviously an attempt to find a solution in the form of a renewal of the general attitude … It expresses a transformation of attitude by means of which a new potential, a new manifestation of life, a new fruitfulness, is created.
>
> (Jung 1921, p. 193)

In addition to the theoretical differences, there are two other schisms that need to be considered. One is between the two main communities of users of Jungian ideas – Myers-Briggs typology and Jungian individuation. They comprise mostly different groups of people, each with their own conferences and journals. Historically, these communities have focused primarily on different applications. Myers-Briggs typology has been concerned with career choice, team building, leadership development, etc., and Jungian analysts have been focused on the psychotherapeutic needs of clients. However, in recent decades those boundaries have started to erode. For example, the *MBTI Step III* questionnaire is being used in psychotherapeutic applications, and Jungian analysts and academics are becoming increasingly involved in mainstream topics such as politics and leadership (e.g. Kiehl *et al.* 2016).

These two communities are themselves a pair of opposites. They share the theoretical foundation of Jungian psychology, but they have very different standpoints where the opposite might seem to be other to their own. For example, Myers-Briggs typology is popular, collective, and used in commercial applications. This may seem an anathema to Jungian analysts who pursue individuation. On the other hand, it may seem an anathema to users of Myers-Briggs typology if we view a type as a form of one-sidedness that needs to be overcome and transcended.

The other schism is between mainstream psychology and both sets of users of Jungian-derived theories – though the reasons for rejecting Myers-Briggs typology and Jungian individuation are different. For analytical psychology, the criticisms are directed primarily at Jung's personality and prejudices. For example,

The future of reconciliation   179

he had extra-marital affairs, expressed elitist views about other cultures, and tried to analyse the difference between races in the 1930s at a time when such differences were being exploited by German National Socialism. The most serious criticism is that Jung was anti-Semitic. In response to such accusations, I'm not going to defend Jung. Although in many ways he was a pioneering genius, he was also a product of his time and he had many human flaws. But the validity or otherwise of each accusation does not negate the validity of some of his radical insights into the workings of the human psyche. Many 'great' characters in history had significant failings. However, we shouldn't ignore Jung's failings either. To get the best value from his psychology, we need to act like old-fashioned gold prospectors. We sit on the river bank, panning the flow of ideas for the golden nuggets that may have value for our development. We discard the mud and the fool's gold.

Criticisms of the MBTI questionnaire

There are also criticisms of the *MBTI* questionnaire that keep recurring in academic psychology and mainstream media (e.g. Burnett 2013; Grant 2013; Zurcher 2014). These criticisms have very little to do with the *MBTI* instrument itself, which is supported by a substantial body of psychometric research undertaken by the publishers (e.g. Myers and McCaulley 1985) and in thousands of PhDs and other research studies held by the Center for the Applications of Psychological Type (CAPT 2018). If we look at these criticisms from the perspective of Jungian individuation, most of them relate to the popular interpretation of the theory and not the psychometric instrument.

One early and influential critic is Pittenger (1993) who raises a number of points. He claims the types are stereotypes, which chimes with Jung's description of types as being 'Galtonesque family portraits' (Jung 1921, p. 405). Also, Pittenger notes that 'there is no evidence of bimodal distributions for the MBTI' (Pittenger 1993) which is contrary to the expected result when classifying people in two groups. However, Jung's view was that there is a third group in the middle that is the largest (Jung 1921, pp. 515–16). This is more in line with the platykurtic (near normal) distribution that usually appears in typological data.

Pittenger criticises the reliability of the *MBTI* because it is not high enough for inborn, life-long traits – but, again, this was not Jung's interpretation. Although extraversion/introversion may have an innate aspect (Jung 1921, p. 376), and there might also be an original disposition for the functions (von Franz 1971/1986, p. 13), type changes or becomes a part of our history as a result of the transcendent function. Also, as type is associated with the persona, it can sometimes change if our circumstances change.

Pittenger also points out that poor reliability is a consequence of having strict cut-off points between the types. However, Jung used spatial metaphors that do not involve setting boundaries between two domains – such as 'four points of the compass' (Jung 1931, p. 541), or 'a trigonometric net [or] crystallographic

180   The future of reconciliation

axial system' (Jung 1936, p. 555), or 'points for orientation' (Jung 1957, p. 304). These do not describe geographical regions with clearly-defined boundaries. They are frameworks or landmarks – static reference points that help identify our unique location.

There have been rebuttals of these various criticisms constructed from a Myers-Briggs perspective (e.g. Rutledge 2013). Rather than reject such criticism, it may be more effectively dealt with by recognising there is some validity in the arguments. In many cases, integrating those aspects that are valid into Myers-Briggs theory could be done by reverting to Jung's original interpretation of typology.

Diversified theories

There is a further complication that adds to these three schisms (theoretical interpretations, two communities, and mainstream vs Jungian psychology). The two main communities who make direct use of Jungian theories have themselves diversified into a number of different streams. Within the field of Jungian analysis, typology is not a universally used tool. This is partly due to a divergence of clinical theory which, whilst not based on typology, has contributed to a diversity of attitudes amongst practising Jungian analysts. In the 1980s, Samuels named three distinct therapeutic schools in clinical analytical psychology – developmental, archetypal, and classical. The difference between them was how they saw, and the priorities they gave to, the definition of archetypal, the concept of self, and the development of personality (Samuels 1985, p. 15). These schools changed by the end of the twentieth century, with the archetypal school disappearing as a separate clinical entity, and the addition of two new schools. Jungian fundamentalism is an extreme version of the classical school, and the psychoanalytic school merges Jung's theory with Freud's (Samuels 1998).

Jungian analysts have debated a variety of topics related to typology, such as whether types are fixed or can change, if it is possible to transcend the opposites, and differing post-Jungian adaptations of the theory (Samuels 1985, pp. 84–88). Such debates tend to position typology as a discrete theory that is concerned with the structure of consciousness, and not as addressing the central goal of analytical psychology, which is integrating consciousness and the unconscious. There have been occasional works by Jungian analysts that relate typology to the process of individuation, most notably by von Franz (1971/1986), Meier (1995), and Beebe (2006). There are few Jungian analysts who try to bridge the two domains, but John Beebe is one of them. He keeps an active involvement in conferences, publications, workshops, etc. on both sides. As discussed in Chapter 11 of the present book, Beebe has also constructed a model that works within the constraints of Myers-Briggs theory to raise awareness of archetypes and thereby integrate some contents from the unconscious.

In the world of Myers-Briggs typology there has also been a diversity of theory and application. For example, David Keirsey and Marilyn Bates related

The future of reconciliation 181

it to classic temperament (Keirsey and Bates 1978), a perspective developed further by Linda Berens. More work by John Beebe (2017) and Carol Pearson (1986) has raised the awareness of specific lists of archetypes. Authors and researchers such as Lenore Thomson (1998) and Dario Nardi (2011) have related typology to brain functioning. Corlett and Millner (1993) have highlighted the significance of changes that take place in midlife – though, as discussed in Chapter 11, they portray the changes as confined within one's type and not as transforming the personality to transcend type. And there have been various portrayals of typology based on: four preferences; whole type; eight function-attitudes; systems thinking; integration with other theoretical models; the management of opposites; and others. There are some models that use typology without sticking to the constraints of the Myers-Briggs framework, such as the Singer-Loomis Inventory of Personality (SLIP). And there have been attempts to draw attention to the role of the transcendent function in typology such as Groesbeck (1978), Spoto (1989), Bennet (2010), and Johnston (2011). Nevertheless, Myers-Briggs theory now dominates the popular application of Jung's ideas and it has also influenced the thinking of many Jungian analysts.

Bridging the gaps

It is beyond the scope of the present book and its author to identify how these various schisms can be overcome. The role of this book has been to highlight the theoretical schism and some of its causes. It is up to the two communities to determine if and how bridges can be built between these various domains. There have been some efforts to bridge the gaps, such as the involvement of some people in both sets of conferences and the creation of the online journal *Personality Type in Depth* (Shumate and Hunziker 2010). However, the argument of the present book is that we need to recognise the depth of the theoretical schism first so we can bridge it fully. We can't resolve the differences by reverting to stage one of the axiom of Maria. We have to progress to stages three and four.

If we try to reshape the theory of Jungian individuation to fit within the constraints of Myers-Briggs typology, there will always be a division with those who are more focused on becoming. More significantly, we will also lose sight of Jung's message of transformation that potentially has the power to address some of the contemporary problems of one-sidedness in Western culture. On the other hand, if we view Myers-Briggs typology as a satellite theory to Jungian individuation, society will again miss out on a powerful message to overcome many of its conflicts. The advantage of the contemporary interpretation of typology is that it succeeds where Jung tried and failed. It presents Jungian theory in a way that the layperson can understand and use in a practical way. The presentation and the content of the message are equally important to its ultimate value.

Individual development

The gravamen of *Psychological Types* makes a strong connection between a wide range of cultural conflicts and the task of the individual in coming to terms with their own unconscious psyche. The level at which change must take place is the single individual. The path to cultural transformation is paved with personal transformations. Becoming a type is associated with stage two of the axiom of Maria. The axiom of Maria not only describes the reconciliation of particular opposites, but it is also a theme in the stages of life. Jung suggests that the transition from stage two to stage three tends to occur around the age of 35 to 40 (Jung 1930–31, p. 391).

The two main periods of adulthood, before and after midlife, align with the two movements of *separatio* and *coniunctio.* In the *separatio* of the first half of life, we develop from the unconsciousness of childhood to the one-sidedness and collectivity of young adulthood. During midlife, we come face to face with the opposite side of our personality. We then reconcile opposites and begin to develop our individuality – that is, we pursue the task of individuation. In terms of the jigsaw metaphor, in the first half of life we tend to pay attention to the edge pieces. In the second half, we turn our attention to that dark, shadowy pile in the middle.

Different paths

The axiom of Maria as a life theme is only an ideal pattern of development. Individual lives can vary significantly, and there can be other patterns. In his essay 'The stages of life', Jung suggests that the path taken by 'the great majority of people [is to] get stuck in the first stages' (Jung 1925, p. 197). That is, Jung observes that most people in the West become one-sided and stay that way throughout life. Hall and Young-Eisendrath observe that 'only some adults continue to develop after they reach maturity' (Hall and Young-Eisendrath 1991, p. 31). They attribute this to the relative absence of the neuroticism that can act as a spur for greater self-knowledge and individuation. Aggregated across society, this lack of further development reinforces the one-sidedness of Western culture, which in turn encourages those in later life to remain one-sided.

Another route after midlife is to have a complete change of lifestyle and become one-sided in the opposite direction, perhaps by changing career or swapping roles in a marital relationship (Jung 1930–31, p. 398). Or we might actively resist any hint of individuation, try to keep the one-sidedness of our youth, and become more entrenched or extreme in our attitudes (ibid., pp. 395–96). There are also some people who individuate, but these are a minority.

It is unlikely that Isabel Briggs Myers read or noticed Jung's observation about most people getting stuck in the first stages of development. She and her collaborator Mary McCaulley believed that most people would become

The future of reconciliation   183

one-sided in the first half of life, and then moderate their one-sidedness in the second half. They expected this to be reflected by *MBTI* data showing a moderation of preference scores in the second half of life:

> Type theory assumes that in midlife people normally gain more respect for hitherto neglected third and fourth functions and therefore develop them further. One effect might be to ... move scores toward the midpoint ... The data ... support the opposite hypothesis – that with maturity people report their preferences with greater consistency.
>
> (Myers and McCaulley 1985, p. 239)

They were disappointed to find the *MBTI* data contradicted their prediction. They explained the unexpected results by suggesting people become more comfortable with their preferences in later life. However, the data fits with Jung's prediction, that in Western culture most people do not individuate but tend to remain one-sided. This would mean that one-sidedness scores would tend to stay the same or increase in later life, which is what happens in the *MBTI* data.

I examined this question as part of my PhD research by producing a measure of typological one-sidedness based on a different questionnaire. This produced a similar result to the research by Myers and McCaulley. The average of all the data suggests that one-sidedness tends to increase throughout life. More complex statistical analysis provides further evidence to support Jung's observations about there being some diversity of paths after midlife – minorities that increase their one-sidedness, or flip roles, or individuate. The 'standard deviation' of the one-sidedness score provides a measure of how widely spread the scores are. If Jung's observations are correct, then around the time of midlife we would expect to see the spread of scores start to increase, and for that spread to keep increasing through later life. When the degree of spread is calculated for the one-sidedness score in my PhD data, as Figure 12.1 shows, it does indeed increase from midlife through to later life. However, there is a puzzling change for those after the age of 60.

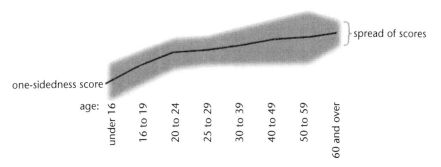

Figure 12.1 How Western one-sidedness spreads out in later life.

184 The future of reconciliation

What these graphs suggest is that, up until the age of thirty-something, on average we become increasingly one-sided. That trend continues during and after midlife but after that the scores tend to spread out. Some people become much more one-sided and others start to individuate, even though the overall average one-sidedness continues to increase. In much later life, which coincides with retirement, something different happens – we tend to converge back to an increasingly one-sided approach. Apart from that anomaly, the data supports Jung's various assertions about psychological development in the West.

Type as a stepping stone

In Chapter 1, we saw that Jung compared identifying with a type to identifying with a corpse (Shamdasani 2003, p. 87). This was probably based on his view that the types are stereotypes (Jung 1921, p. 405) and that typological functions serve a social purpose and suppress individuality (ibid., p. 440). However, Jung also argued that identifying with a type can be 'a necessary transitional stage on the way to individuation' (ibid.). This is not a contradiction because identifying with a type is associated with stage two of the axiom of Maria. In early adulthood, becoming a type can help us to differentiate (*separatio*) a conscious attitude. But at the next stage (*coniunctio*) identifying with a type can be an obstacle to individuation.

When we progress to stages three and four we differentiate ourselves *from* the opposites, so we no longer identify with a type because a typological function no longer dominates our attitude. As illustrated by the story of *Prometheus and Epimetheus*, although the brothers remain in the land, neither of them are king. The place of dominance has been taken (in Jung's implied epilogue) by the character of Messias, who symbolises a new attitude that is furnished by the transcendent function. That means our type or types become a part of our history. This is illustrated by Jung's response, in a BBC interview in 1959, to a question that asked about his type. Jung replied using the past tense:

> I most certainly *was* characterized by thinking … and I *had* a great deal of intuition too. And I *had* a definite difficulty with feeling, and my relation to reality *was* not particularly brilliant.
>
> (Jung 1959, p. 435, emphasis added)

The benefit of identifying with a type at an early stage of development is that it pushes aside one aspect of our unconsciousness. It helps us to move from stage one to stage two in the axiom of Maria when seeking to develop the typological functions. However, when the time comes for further development at midlife, to move to stages three and four, identifying with a type can hold us back.

At midlife, the ideal scenario is that we confront the inferior function by withdrawing projections and giving it full parity of respect and seriousness. As a result, we begin to come to terms with the unconscious, and develop a new, more unique attitude from the reconciliation of opposites. In practice, as we have seen from the data, most people take a different course and remain attached to a one-sided attitude. They establish a clear identity early in life and then stay at that stage of development. In midlife, they take a peek at the opposite but do not pursue the full course of individuation.

The current interpretation of Myers-Briggs typology conveys a similar message. Although it encourages some development of the tertiary and inferior functions, it nevertheless promotes the idea that, in later life, we become a better version of our type. However, as the Jungian analyst Joseph Wheelwright put it, 'the most important thing about types is detyping' (Wheelwright 1982, p. 54). The aim is to give full parity to the inferior so that – as von Franz describes – the conscious structure collapses and something new comes up. This transforms the personality, making it more whole and individual.

This presents some challenges for users of Myers-Briggs typology. Many contemporary applications involve encouraging people to identify with a type. How can we make type a stepping stone from stage two of the axiom of Maria to stages three and four? How can we remove the anchor that keeps our development in a state of one-sidedness, and develop an approach that gives full parity to the typological opposites in our personal lives? How can we raise awareness of the unconscious and develop a constructive attitude towards it so that we face up to the opposites in ourselves rather than projecting them into other people, groups, and societies? And how can we use type to apply this development process to other forms of one-sidedness in society, in fields such as politics, religion, science, etc.?

The self as a black hole

The image on the front cover of this book shows a variety of coloured strands circumambulating a black hole. The four main colours are associated with the typological functions – sensation (green), intuition (yellow), thinking (blue), and feeling (red). As the strands fuse into white light they also get drawn into the black hole. Jung used the image of a black hole to illustrate the principle of individuation; it represents a powerful but unknown force at the centre of our psyche (Jung 1955, p. 258). Our instinct might be to avoid it, but coming to terms with it is necessary to increase consciousness and develop our individual potential. 'One does not become enlightened by imagining figures of light, but by making the darkness conscious. The latter procedure, however, is disagreeable and therefore not popular' (Jung 1945/1954, pp. 265–66).

If we embark on this journey, it does not mean that we disassociate from who we are or where we have come from. For example, if we have developed a particular skill or knowledge, then that expertise remains at our disposal and it can be of value to both ourselves and society. What changes is our attitude to that expertise. We recognise the difference between collective and individual psychology, and find a better balance between the two. We no longer see things

186   The future of reconciliation

in a one-sided way, but value the opposite. We let go of the attachments that we had previously clung to as defining us. As the Buddha is reputed to have said, 'it is not our preferences that cause problems, but our attachment to them' (Kornfield 1996, p. 35).

If we take Jung as an example, although he sought to overcome one-sidedness through pursuing his personal individuation and promoting it in others, he continued to specialise in the field of psychology and there were some things he was good at and others that he was not. What he developed towards was not an ideal human being, nor someone whom everyone could admire, but an individual self in which he made a unique contribution to culture and society. Jung's challenge to us is to not be subsumed by contemporary culture and collectivity, but to develop as unique individuals so we can enhance the collective culture by being able to step outside it. This task of creating culture is primarily a task for those who are in the second half of life:

> What I am saying here is not for the young ... but for the more mature ... whose consciousness has been widened by experience of life ... It is the privilege and the task of maturer people, who have passed the meridian of life, to create culture.
>
> (Jung 1927, p. 132)

The culture he refers to here is not traditional culture, or aesthetic appreciation, or what we conventionally regard as being civilised or mature. Here, culture refers to a greater wholeness and awareness of the unconscious.

The case study of Nietzsche

What wholeness means in practice is illustrated by Jung's critique of Nietzsche in *Psychological Types*. Nietzsche describes two impulses. One is the drive towards individuation, towards the creation of the unique individual who is distinct from collective psychology. This is the movement up the caduceus, the advancement of consciousness, and Nietzsche associates it with Apollo, the god who represents cultural interests, such as poetry, music, truth, etc. The other impulse is downwards, for the individual to be intoxicated by the appeal of collective instincts, and for individuality to be obliterated, which Nietzsche associates with Dionysus, the god of wine. For Jung, these two impulses – Apollonian and Dionysian – are themselves a pair of opposites that need reconciliation. Although we advance up the caduceus, we also need to keep a secure connection down into the unconscious. This is represented in the caduceus by the staff that goes from any point where the snakes cross back down to the bottom.

Jung makes two criticisms of Nietzsche. A minor criticism, towards the end of chapter III in *Psychological Types*, is that Nietzsche projects his typology into the Greek gods. He portrays the Apollonian with intuitive characteristics and the Dionysian more in terms of sensation. This 'must be characteristic of his own personal psychology' (Jung 1921, p. 146); it is a projection of his own dominant and inferior typological functions. This criticism is not significant in Jung's critique of Nietzsche's presentation of the two impulses, because another type would project other functions into the two gods.

The main criticism is that, although Nietzsche recognises the Apollonian and Dionysian impulses as opposites, his solution is too aesthetic and positive. Nietzsche's (initial) standpoint implies that the instincts of civilised people have aesthetic qualities. Jung dismisses this assumption as a mistake, due to a 'profound lack of psychological knowledge' (Jung 1921, p. 140). A civilised and aesthetic conscious attitude is akin to one side of a see-saw rising high into the air. As a result, the other side descends even lower. The more civilised the attitude, the more the instincts are cut off, and the more primitive and dangerous they become.

This is another example (in addition to those considered earlier in the present book) where the nature of something is very different from what it appears to be. Earlier examples include the persona appearing to be individual but actually being collective, evil that seems to lie in others actually being in ourselves, or consciousness seeming to be the entirety of our personality but only being a small part. In this case, Nietzsche suggests the instincts of civilised people are more advanced and aesthetic than people who are less developed. However, Jung argues that an undeveloped culture is better connected with the instincts in the unconscious than a civilised culture, because the former is still at stage one of the axiom of Maria. Although there is an advancement in civilised one-sidedness, because it has moved to stage two, it also presents more of a danger. It is at stage two when we are most separated from the unconscious, because we repress instincts and displace them into other people or cultures. When aggregated across groups or societies, this creates all the problems of polarisation that lead to dangerous international conflicts.

This conundrum cannot be solved by producing aesthetic products, as Nietzsche's early work suggests. In Jung's view, the solution that will move us from stage two to stage three is a religious one. This does not refer to any particular tradition but to the need to reconnect – to *religare* – with the unconscious psyche, particularly the collective unconscious. Seeing this as a religious task can be problematic because many contemporary forms of religion are themselves one-sided – they are based on creeds and dogma. In Jung's view, this religious task is a journey of discovery into the darkness of our own soul.

Self-knowledge

Many of Jung's discussions conclude with some form of epistemological point about our knowledge of self and the world. For example, at the end of a lengthy letter about the nature of God, he summarises the key stages of Tantric yoga, and then suggests the highest level is only attained when we no longer see image and object as being identical (Jung 1955, p. 264). At the end of his magnum opus

188   The future of reconciliation

Mysterium Coniunctionis he finishes with a discussion of 'the self and the bounds of knowledge' (Jung 1955–56, p. 544). And in his lectures on Kundalini yoga, Jung argues that the benefit of yoga is not in the experience or conscious attainment but in raising awareness of the unconscious. He points to 'the great paradox' (Jung 1932, p. 64), that in consciousness we can be at one of the highest levels of development in yoga (*ājñā*) but the way we live is at the lowest level (*mūlādhāra*). He suggests we can see that principle at work by looking at life in India. What the system of yoga does for us is provide a perspective that is outside our own culture. It reminds us of the totality of the psyche, that 'our personal consciousness can indeed be located in … *ājñā*, but nonetheless our psychic situation as a whole is undoubtedly in *mūlādhāra*' (Jung 1932, p. 65, original italics).

Jung's typological theory is a methodology for transforming the personality; we develop our individuality through experiencing the conflict of opposites. No matter who we are, how much we have developed, or how much we have achieved in life, the unconscious always remains the dominant factor in our personality. It is so vast and so powerful that no amount of development can empty it. We are always the rider on the elephant (Haidt 2012, p. 54); the ego is never able to dismount and walk on its own. The most we can do is learn about the unconscious and allow ourselves to be transformed by the experience of coming to terms with it.

References

Beebe, J. (2006). 'Psychological types'. In *The Handbook of Jungian Psychology*, edited by Renos Papadopoulos. Hove: Routledge.

Beebe, J. (2017). *Energies and Patterns in Psychological Type: The Reservoir of Consciousness*. Abingdon: Routledge.

Bennet, A. (2010). *The Shadows of Type: Psychological Type Through Seven Levels of Development.* Morrisville, NC: Lulu Enterprises.

Burnett, D. (2013). 'Nothing personal: the questionable Myers-Briggs test'. *The Guardian.* Online at: www.theguardian.com/science/brain-flapping/2013/mar/19/myers-briggs-test-unscientific, accessed 24-Aug-15.

CAPT (2018). 'Mary and Isabel's library online'. Center for the Applications of Psychological Type. Online at: www.capt.org/milo/.

Corlett, E.S., Millner, N.B. (1993). *Navigating Midlife: Using Typology as a Guide*. Palo Alto, CA: CPP Books.

Grant, A. (2013). 'Goodbye to MBTI, the fad that won't die'. *Psychology Today.* Online at: www.psychologytoday.com/gb/blog/give-and-take/201309/goodbye-mbti-the-fad-won-t-die, accessed 24-Aug-15.

Groesbeck, C.J. (1978). 'Psychological types in the analysis of the transference'. *Journal of Analytical Psychology* 23(1): 23–53.

Haidt, J. (2012). *The Righteous Mind: Why Good People are Divided by Politics and Religion*. London: Penguin Books, Kindle Edition.

Hall, J.A., Young-Eisendrath, P. (1991). *Jung's Self Psychology: A Constructivist Perspective.* New York: The Guildford Press.

Johnston, J.G. (2011). *Jung's Compass of Psychological Types.* Perrysburg, OH: MSE Press, 2015.

Jung, C.G. (1921). *CW6.*

Jung, C.G. (1925). 'Marriage as a psychological relationship'. In *CW17.*

Jung, C.G. (1927). 'Woman in Europe'. In *CW10.*

Jung, C.G. (1930–31). 'The stages of life'. In *CW8.*

Jung, C.G. (1931). 'A psychological theory of types'. In *CW6.*

Jung, C.G. (1932). *The Psychology of Kundalini Yoga,* edited by Sonu Shamdasani. Princeton, NJ: Bollingen Paperbacks, 1996.

Jung, C.G. (1936). 'Psychological typology'. In *CW6.*

Jung, C.G. (1945/1954). 'The philosophical tree'. In *CW13.*

Jung, C.G. (1955). 'Letter to Pastor Walter Bernet, 13 June 1955'. In *Letters 2.*

Jung, C.G. (1955–56). *CW14.*

Jung, C.G. (1957). 'The Houston films'. In *C.G. Jung Speaking.* Princeton, NJ: Bollingen Paperbacks, 1977.

Jung, C.G. (1959). 'The "Face to Face" interview'. In *C.G. Jung Speaking.* Princeton, NJ: Bollingen Paperbacks, 1977.

Jung, C.G. (1964). *Man and His Symbols.* London: Picador, 1978.

Keirsey, D., Bates, M. (1978). *Please Understand Me: Character & Temperament Types.* Del Mar, CA: Prometheus Nemesis Books.

Kiehl, E., Samuels, A., Saban, M. (eds.) (2016). *Analysis and Activism: Social and Political Contributions of Jungian Psychology.* Abingdon: Routledge.

Kornfield, J. (1996). *Buddha's Little Instruction Book.* London: Rider.

Meier, C.A. (1995). *Personality: The Individuation Process in Light of C.G. Jung's Typology.* Einsiedeln: Daimon.

Myers, I.B. (1980). *Gifts Differing.* Palo Alto, CA: Davis Black, 1995.

Myers, I.B., McCaulley, M. (1985). *Manual: A Guide to the Development and Use of the Myers-Briggs Type Indicator.* Palo Alto, CA: Consulting Psychologists Press.

Nardi, D. (2011). *Neuroscience of Personality: Brain Savvy Insights for All Types of People.* Los Angeles, CA: Radiance House.

Pearson, C.S. (1986). *The Hero Within: Six Archetypes We Live By.* New York: HarperCollins, 1998.

Pittenger, D.J. (1993). 'Measuring the MBTI ... and coming up short'. *Journal of Career Planning and Employment* 54(1): 48–52.

Rutledge, H. (2013). 'The MBTI–my most valid tool'. Otto Kroeger Associates. Online at: http://oka-online.com/the-mbti-my-most-valid-tool/, accessed 9-Dec-16.

Samuels, A. (1985). *Jung and the Post-Jungians.* London: Routledge, 1986.

Samuels, A. (1998). 'Will the post-Jungians survive?'. In *Post-Jungians Today: Key Papers in Contemporary Analytical Psychology,* edited by Ann Casement. London: Routledge.

Shamdasani, S. (2003). *Jung and the Making of Modern Psychology: The Dream of a Science.* Cambridge: Cambridge University Press.

Shumate, C., Hunziker, M. (2010). 'About us'. *Personality Type in Depth.* Online at: http://typeindepth.com/personality-type-in-depth-about-us/, accessed 6-Apr-18.

Spoto, A. (1989). *Jung's Typology in Perspective,* revised edition. Wilmette, IL: Chiron Publications, 1995.

Thomson, L. (1998). *Personality Type: An Owner's Manual: A Practical Guide to Understanding Yourself and Others through Typology.* Boston, MA: Shambhala.

von Franz, M.L. (1971/1986). 'The inferior function'. In *Lectures on Jung's Typology*. Putnam, CT: Spring Publications, 2013.

Wheelwright, J.B. (1982). *St. George and the Dandelion*. San Francisco, CA: The CG Jung Institute of San Francisco.

Zurcher, A. (2014). 'Debunking the Myers-Briggs Personality Test'. British Broadcasting Corporation. Online at: www.bbc.co.uk/news/blogs-echochambers-28315137, accessed 24-Aug-15.

Appendix A

Prometheus and Epimetheus

This appendix provides a more detailed summary of Spitteler's epic poem *Prometheus and Epimetheus* (1881). The subheadings below do not appear in the original text but help clarify its structure.

Prometheus and Epimetheus

Appointment of the king (pp. 17–46)

Prometheus calls his brother Epimetheus to join him in being separate from society. They go and live away from other people, rejecting external customs, creating a barrier between themselves and others, and acting and speaking differently from everyone else. Their attitude evokes an ambivalent attitude from their neighbours, who have the feeling that the brothers lack something whilst also doing something to excess.

After 12 years, there are rumours that the Angel of the Lord will appoint a new king. The people of Earth will welcome this because they want something new. The Angel considers naming Prometheus as king, but there is a problem: Prometheus allies himself too closely with Soul. The Angel can see heaven on one side, and a dark shadow on the other. The Angel tells Prometheus that he might have to reject him, because of his relationship with Soul, and asks him to take the widely respected Conscience as his friend instead. Prometheus declines, and declares his allegiance to Soul, even though he has not actually met her. The Angel of the Lord scolds him for this decision.

Epimetheus realises that, by living apart from the people, he has made a mistake. He declares his allegiance to Conscience. The Angel of the Lord says that Prometheus rejected the offer to be king because of his arrogance and delusion. He chooses Epimetheus to be king, who initially declines the proposal because the office is too much for him. But the Angel persuades him to accept it and takes him to the king's castle in the people's land.

Epimetheus sees it as his role to gratify the people's desires. The people set up a camp by the castle and celebrate his appointment as king. Epimetheus feels humbled by the whole experience. Conscience becomes a vital part of his

192 Appendix A: *Prometheus and Epimetheus*

day-to-day life. In every situation, Epimetheus consults him about what to do, and Conscience guides him as to what is right and wrong.

Prometheus, however, is grumbling and sore. He leaves his home valley to climb the mountains. He becomes more withdrawn, violent, and fearful. Then the goddess Soul appears. Prometheus falls deeply in love with her, and they become betrothed. She promises to live with him for just one hour at some point in the future, for which, she says, all future generations will envy him.

As Soul is about to leave, Prometheus asks her to give him some words to keep. She tells him to kill the young puppies and lion cubs that he has at home because they will lead him astray. She also says that it is easy to see from hill to hill and asks whether the valleys matter.

Prometheus now feels uplifted, even though he can still hear the celebration of Epimetheus becoming king in the distance. He returns home and kills the puppies, apart from one that the mother pleads with him to spare. He then kills the lion cubs apart from one. However, the lion mother kills the last one, declares her hate for Prometheus, but will not kill him because of his betrothal to Soul.

Prometheus' suffering (pp. 47–112)

Epimetheus takes responsibility for the welfare of the people. He becomes a powerful and virtuous king who stops evil-doing and settles disputes. He marries Maya, and they have a happy, idealistic life.

Prometheus has a comfortable life, but his only friend is an earthworm. He dislikes what Epimetheus has become and prays that he would never become like his brother. The Angel of the Lord's wife, Doxa, objects to the prayer and demands that the Angel stops Prometheus' life from being so easy. Therefore, the Angel of the Lord sends a guide to take Prometheus on a journey that involves doing menial chores. The dog wants to go as well, but Prometheus turns him away and asks the lion instead, who refuses to go. However, both the dog and lion follow at a distance anyway.

On the journey, they go past King Epimetheus' castle. When the dog peers inside, he sees the king kiss his wife. The dog is unhappy at seeing other people's happiness. Prometheus speaks to his thoughts and asks them to give him some peace. But his thoughts mock him. They point out that he could have had Epimetheus' life. Prometheus is angry at his thoughts, and they scatter, but then slowly creep back to mock him some more. So, Prometheus prays to his Soul goddess. A maiden appears singing that we need to know both happiness and suffering. But he rejects it, saying there is a better and sadder song, which he refuses to sing now but may do in the future.

They arrive at an unloved land where Prometheus finds a low-paid building job. His new master criticises Prometheus for his lack of artistic ability and tells him to build a house with walls at a slant. Prometheus does so, and the house collapses. The master says this is because the walls still had right angles, so Prometheus builds it according to the new demands, and it collapses again.

Appendix A: *Prometheus and Epimetheus* 193

Friends of the master admire Prometheus' work, and he eventually becomes indispensable to the master.

The lion, who says he stands for inner sensitivity, falls sick and the Angel of the Lord decides to end Prometheus' strife. However, guided by an inner voice, Prometheus expects the Angel to repent of the suffering he has caused him. The lion becomes sicker, thinks his cubs are alive, and asks the dog to take him back to them. The cubs rise from the dead, the lion kisses them, and then the dog leads him back home where the lion dies. The dog lies down at the lion's grave. Prometheus calls him away, so the dog asks for an edifying tale. Prometheus tells a couple of stories, after which the dog also dies.

Prometheus, who is becoming ill and whose eyesight is starting to fail, visits a doctor who tells him to walk to the brook each day to get some fresh air. This has no effect. But one evening he meets Epimetheus who offers Prometheus a salve for his eyesight. Prometheus rejects it. Epimetheus then shows Prometheus all his mistakes. A voice rebukes Epimetheus, but Prometheus defends him because he is his brother.

The Pandora interlude (pp. 113–55)

God is sick. His daughter Pandora enters, having made a treasure that will assuage the suffering of mortals, which God blesses. A brook guides Pandora to earth so she can give the gift to civilisation. Pandora does not understand the differences between things, but she can absorb the general picture, and distinguish between sounds and smells. She hides the treasure under a walnut tree, and departs. Various creatures ask the treasure questions, and the branches of the tree ask it to sing. It sings a riddle in a strange language which has a beneficial impact on those who hear it, spreading goodwill and calming hateful feelings.

However, the sun is not happy with all this goodwill and notices that the tree is hiding something. When the tree does not tell the sun what is beneath its branches, the sun becomes angry and burns the tree. It then realises what the tree is hiding, and its value, and is humbled. The sun calls for a parade to take him down to earth to see the treasure.

As the sun is travelling down, a shepherd boy brings the treasure to the attention of seven peasants. Being wary of the unknown, they inspect it but then conclude that, if they take it to the king, they will get a reward. When the peasants go to the castle with the treasure, a sentry greets them and tells them to wait for the king by a statue of a man holding a jewel. Epimetheus arrives and, before seeing the peasants, gives an interpretation of the jewel in the statue. When the peasants show him their jewel, Epimetheus shows it to Conscience – who finds the treasure alarming and hides. As Epimetheus cannot get a decision from Conscience, he turns the peasants away, suggesting they take the jewel to the priests.

When the peasants show the treasure to the priests, they consult the Hilphal-Hophal, who grows angry and says, 'away with this shameful thing', describing

194　Appendix A: *Prometheus and Epimetheus*

it as blasphemous and carnal. The priests suggest they take the treasure to the teachers in the college.

When the peasants arrive at the college, they can hear at a distance a teacher talking in a class about a wonderful treasure. The children split into discussion groups, and the peasants show some of them the jewel. The children laugh at it, and the teachers reprove them for laughing. But when the teachers inspect the jewel themselves, they also start laughing, saying it has no value, nor soul, feeling, seriousness, or thought. They suggest the peasants visit the goldsmith to see if it has any value when melted down.

The peasants take the treasure to the goldsmith, who says it is worthless. He suggests seeing if they can get anything for it in the market. When they go to the market, the berries notice how valuable it is and expect people to congregate around it. But no one does. The peasants, being hungry, offer the treasure to someone in exchange for bread, but he gives them some food as a gift because, in his view, the jewel is worthless. The keeper of the market then scolds the peasants for trying to sell the 'obscene' jewel in his market. He covers it so that no one can see it.

The peasants start to make their way back home, and they meet the shepherd boy who had told them about the treasure. Some of the peasants want to beat him up, but others manage to prevent it. The peasants then throw the jewel away, at the side of the road. A guard sees that they have thrown litter away, and he makes them pick it up. They find a quieter place and throw it away again behind some bushes. As they walk away, they see a passing Jew search the bushes and then run off. A boy appears, crying and sobbing.

Searching for the treasure (pp. 156–68)

The Angel of the Lord visits Epimetheus, but the normality of life shocks him. He asks Epimetheus why there is no festival to celebrate the treasure and tells him to fetch it. Epimetheus realises his error and blames Conscience who, he remarks pointedly, the Angel of the Lord had given to him. Epimetheus says he told the peasants to take the treasure to the priests. The Angel asks Epimetheus where his soul was in his actions. Epimetheus again denies culpability and makes a defensive remark – that it was the Angel who took his soul away. The Angel orders Epimetheus to stand and wait, like a naughty child. When Epimetheus' wife sees his capitulation, her love for him turns to disgust.

The Angel tells the courtiers to fetch the priests. He demands the treasure from them and, when they cannot provide it, he scolds them. The priests say they sent the peasants to the teachers, so the Angel of the Lord tells the courtiers to fetch the teachers. When they come before the Angel, the teachers try to hide behind wise and intelligent phrases. The Angel rebukes them and tells the courtiers to summon the seven peasants. The Angel was feeling confused and numbed by all that he had discovered.

Appendix A: *Prometheus and Epimetheus* 195

When the peasants approach the Angel of the Lord, they tell their story. The Angel asks about the Jew who had searched the bushes, but nothing they said could identify who he was. Therefore, the Angel concludes that they have lost the treasure, and the only thing to do now is to forget about it. He laments this generation for their treatment of the jewel.

The Angel of the Lord tells a story about a man who has a dog that defends his property. When his first-born son tries to enter it, the dog kills him. Therefore, the man kills the dog, even though the dog had only done his duty. Once the dog is dead, the man's enemies are then able to attack and kill the rest of his family. The Angel of the Lord announces merciful judgments for those who lost the treasure.

Befriending the enemy (pp. 169–209)

Epimetheus is protecting the three sons of the Angel of the Lord: Mythos, Hiero, and Messias. The Angel falls sick and, ominously, a vulture appears. Expecting he will die soon, the Angel plans a wedding to hide his sickness and death from his enemy Behemoth, until he can crown his son Mythos as his successor. In the meantime, Behemoth is having a festival in honour of his only daughter, Ashtaroth. He notices the vulture and takes it as a sign that the Angel of the Lord is going to die. He promises to give Ashtaroth to anyone who can place the three children in his power so that he can steal the Angel of the Lord's crown.

A servant is clumsy at the end of the festival, and Behemoth asks him to explain his clumsiness. The servant composes himself and tells a story of Epimetheus sleeping with bees appearing from his mouth. He introduces himself as Leviathan, tells another story, and suggests these stories might teach them something. That is, they can deceive Epimetheus' people with a crude lie, such as creating a treaty of friendship between them. Behemoth offers a reward to Leviathan if he can win over the people of Earth as friends.

Leviathan predicts it will happen in two days. He uses three chairs and a stool to explain his plan. Like a hunter laying a trap, they will use bait to lure the people. They will also appeal to the people's conscience, using two totem poles or standards. One will have an imaginary bird to represent Behemoth's people. The other will have an imaginary whale to represent the people of Earth. If everyone points to these imaginary creatures earnestly, they will make them seem real.

They choose somewhere to raise up the poles with the imaginary creatures. They arrange to meet Epimetheus and his people. Behemoth's men arrive and start singing, and Leviathan sings a solo, which endears him to the people of Earth. Leviathan then invites Epimetheus' right-hand man to sing – the Captain of the Athenians. His singing is appalling, but Leviathan embraces him anyway, which makes the Captain feel affection for him.

The singing games continue, but then they all become hungry. The Captain's wife suggests that everyone fetch some food and share it, which they do. Then the sun becomes too hot, so the people of Behemoth suggest they all go back to their cool grove. Leviathan lauds the Captain's wife for the feast and gives her his chair of honour. In return, the Captain offers Leviathan his chair, and the two peoples exchange honorary places.

Behemoth then sends a stool to Leviathan, to remind him to begin the next stage of the plan. Leviathan stands on the stool and suggests they remove the borders between the two lands so that the bird can live close to the whale. Everyone welcomes this idea enthusiastically. Leviathan then proposes that they exchange delegations, with him leading one and the Captain the other.

Epimetheus consults Conscience, who encourages him to remove the borders. Epimetheus is initially reluctant because he says Behemoth is wicked. But when Leviathan shows him a picture of Behemoth, Epimetheus falls in love with him, so he changes his mind. The two kings meet, and they remove the boundaries between their countries.

Kidnapping the Children of God (pp. 210–42)

There is a short interlude that shows how alarming these developments are. Every day, in the centre of the earth, Prosperina goes to the father of all men, Adam, and tries to persuade him to come home. Adam refuses each time, so Prosperina accepts that she is powerless to do anything and returns. One day, Adam hears the far-off tumult and sends his son Atlas to investigate. When he reports back that Behemoth and Epimetheus have developed a close relationship, Adam then goes home.

Back in the land of the people of Earth, the relationship between Behemoth and Epimetheus rapidly develops. As they are watching various wonders, such as the rising of a blood-red moon, Behemoth asks Epimetheus to seal their bond of love by committing their offspring to each other. Epimetheus refuses because he has no power to hand over the Children of God. Behemoth storms off and Leviathan tells Epimetheus that he has wounded him deeply.

Epimetheus looks to Conscience for guidance, but spots him sneaking away. He chases after Conscience but cannot catch him. He must choose whether to follow Conscience or Leviathan because they are going in different directions. He decides to capitulate to Behemoth's wishes. He agrees with Leviathan to hand over the Children of God, but in a way that conceals his decision – through an arranged kidnap.

Leviathan goes to see if Behemoth will accept the proposal, to hand over the Children of God in a faked kidnap. Epimetheus and the Captain ride home where they find Conscience, cold and unhappy. Epimetheus' wife leaves home.

They implement the plan that hides Epimetheus' complicity. Behemoth sends his son Beelzebub to stay with Epimetheus for seven days. The day after he returns, Behemoth sends men to kidnap the Children of God – which they can do because Epimetheus puts up only token resistance.

Appendix A: *Prometheus and Epimetheus* 197

In another brief interlude, Laila, a sick and sorrowing goddess, appears on the horizon. Mantis, her daughter, appeals to her to end the grief for her son Oneiros. Laila says that a new threefold divinity has been born and sends Mantis to warn the Angel of the Lord about his children. But the Angel, being sick, mishears the message and imagines the children (his 'jewel') are safe.

Killing the Children of God (pp. 243–60)

As a reward for his achievements, Behemoth makes Leviathan a king over everyone in his country, including the princes of his land. Behemoth asks what they should do with the Children of God. Leviathan recommends killing them. That worries Behemoth, so he suggests killing one and keeping the other two as hostages, for protection. Leviathan agrees and kills Mythos.

Behemoth tells Leviathan to prepare defences against an inevitable attack from the race of men, following Mythos' death. Epimetheus and his men do indeed begin an attack, but Leviathan takes on a gentle and disarming manner. Rather than attacking him, they start asking Leviathan questions. He does not answer, but his demeanour means they continue to calm down. They then hear a voice that points out that nothing has changed in the world; it is still as before. They convince themselves that Mythos was a bad influence anyway, and they return home.

Given this reaction, Behemoth decides to kill another of the Children of God, and a similar thing happens. Leviathan kills Hiero, and men come to attack, though this time there are fewer of them. Through Leviathan's demeanour, they convince themselves that it is better to have one Child of God, not two.

Behemoth feels very satisfied with the way things have turned out. But his princes plot a rebellion because Behemoth has appointed Leviathan king over them. They plan to rescue the remaining Child of God, which will cause Leviathan and Behemoth to fall out. Their plan succeeds, and they take Messias back to the land of men. When Behemoth finds out that Messias has gone, he is furious and rages at Leviathan, who then promises to get the child back within three days. He summons an army, surrounds the men of Earth, and demands the return of the Child of God. Conscience will not let Epimetheus agree, but the people want to hand him over because they now see him as the source of their troubles.

Epimetheus must decide between protecting the Child of God or satisfying the people. He asks Conscience whether he should give up the Child of God, but Conscience runs away. Epimetheus chases after him, and servants catch him and bring him back. Epimetheus forces Conscience to answer, but he says yes and no at the same time.

Epimetheus sees no alternative but to resign as king, though there is no one else who can take over. Epimetheus sees a 'Jeremiah figure' who suggests a way out of the situation. If Epimetheus does not acquiesce to the demands of the people, they will kill him. But if he can give the divine child up with an

198   Appendix A: *Prometheus and Epimetheus*

assurance of his safety, then he will save everyone. Epimetheus goes and gets such an assurance from Leviathan, even though it is a sham. Once the child is handed over, Epimetheus knows that Leviathan will kill him.

The salvation of Messias (pp. 261–300)

The Angel of the Lord wakes and asks how things are. His friends hurry away to avoid answering. His wife (Doxa) tells him that two of his children are dead, and the third is about to suffer the same fate. The Angel expects that Epimetheus and some of the men of Earth would have died defending the Children of God. But he is shocked to learn that they are all still well. He grabs his sword and tries to leave, but he collapses because he is still sick.

The Angel regrets that he appointed Epimetheus as king. He muses that, if he had named Prometheus as king, his children would still be alive, and the kingdom would still be in possession of Pandora's jewel. Doxa departs to find Prometheus, to see if he can rescue the situation.

However, the people react mockingly to Doxa because she is seeking Prometheus, and the Athenians and a Lambkin lecture her. Doxa takes refuge in an unpleasant wayfarers chapel, which smells from the stench left by tramps. Epimetheus turns up, they exchange glances, and Doxa flees. She sees a signpost pointing towards Prometheus. On the way, she meets a beggar woman who treats Doxa with respect. She claims that she can instruct Prometheus to help, and then reveals herself as Soul. She calls Prometheus and starts to lead him away.

As they are leaving, the lion and the dog appear from their graves, no longer sad. All their little ones try to follow, but they keep slipping and cannot climb out of the pit. Prometheus greets them but then lets them slip back. As Prometheus leaves, the lion and dog return to the grave as well.

Prometheus now faces the future with fresh courage. He sees the procession that is leading the last Child of God to be handed over to Leviathan. Inspired by Soul, he approaches the procession claiming that he will help to tighten Messias' bonds. But he cuts them loose instead and starts to lead the Child of God away. Some men remonstrate with Prometheus that they will end up paying the price for his deed. He points out that, unlike the Child of God, they are not sacred. So, they back off. Other men complain that the invisible bird will be burned. Prometheus says, if that happens, he will raise up an invisible hedgehog in its place. So, they back off as well. Prometheus deals with everyone's objections. The Lambkin does not object. He is just angry and confused.

Prometheus finally leads the Child of God away to safety. Epimetheus has by now disappeared. Prometheus returns to the men to tell them to fight Behemoth rather than capitulate. But the enemy has also gone.

The Angel of the Lord recovers his health and fixes a day when men are to account for their actions. He acknowledges the injustice done to Prometheus and appoints him as king instead of Epimetheus. But Prometheus rejects the appointment, as well as other offers of reward, and he seeks solitude.

Appendix A: *Prometheus and Epimetheus* | 199

The Angel of the Lord goes to judgment day, is reunited with his son, and sees his dead children. He then sits on the throne in front of the people and snaps his sword. He says he will pardon them if they beg Doxa (his wife) for forgiveness for mocking and lecturing her. But she does not react well, forcing the Child of God to spit at the people, and kicking the Lambkin.

The Angel of the Lord commits the Child of God to the people's protection again, with a warning that their fate is inextricably bound to his. The people leave. The Angel of the Lord does not know who to appoint as king, saying: 'Perhaps, another day may bring us a solution of this problem'.

The reconciliation of the brothers (pp. 301–18)

From a distance, Prometheus sees the Child of God beckoning from a castle window, for him to go there to live. Prometheus replies that he must go and bury a friend and will then return. But he wanders away. Prometheus eventually finds himself in an evil valley, and his heart leads him to go deeper. A sunbeam confronts Prometheus, and then he has his moment of living with Soul.

Afterwards, on his way back, he falls asleep on a bench. A thought asks him what has become of his brother. Prometheus initially pushes the thought away, but then he goes in search of Epimetheus. As he goes down a steep passage, Prometheus discovers a woman reading a book. She tells him his quest is in vain and directs him to the lowest places of the earth. When Prometheus goes there, it is miserable, but he forces himself to go on.

Meanwhile, Epimetheus is lying in a wet pit and having a dream about being naked in front of the people. He tries to find a hiding place but is blocked by a snake and then a pig. He lies down to die, but the ground tells him he is not good enough to die there.

He then seems to be in another dream when Prometheus speaks to him. He regrets his past treatment of his brother, but Prometheus dismisses it as normal brotherly behaviour. Prometheus convinces Epimetheus this is not a dream. However, Epimetheus tells his brother to go away because he thinks Prometheus is becoming king and only there for revenge. Prometheus denies it and lifts him up, but Epimetheus again rebukes his brother, calling him a liar and expressing the wish to die.

Prometheus suggests that heaven and earth are nothing compared to being brothers. Epimetheus realises that Prometheus is serious about restoring their relationship. He confesses that he had abandoned Soul for Conscience. Prometheus reassures him that Soul would take Epimetheus back.

As they leave to find Soul, the Lambkin appears, uttering smug and noble sentiments. With Prometheus' permission, Epimetheus kills the Lambkin. Then Doxa, the wife of the Angel of the Lord, appears in front of Prometheus and asks him about Soul. The book concludes with the following dialogue between Doxa and Prometheus:

200 Appendix A: *Prometheus and Epimetheus*

'Tell me, why is it thou takest so much trouble for the sake of thy brother Epimetheus, who never did thee aught but ill, and hast stolen thy well-deserved reward before thy very eyes, and has mocked thee in the time of thy worst misfortune?'

And it happened by chance that while she was talking, a caterpillar fell from the leaves at the top of the world on to the path between them. And when it had recovered itself and got upon its legs, it fled hastily, with head erect, towards the ivy at the entrance-gate.

And Doxa involuntarily turned her head, following unconsciously the escape of the animal. And Prometheus, noticing the direction of her eyes, did likewise. But when after a little the caterpillar made good its retreat and disappeared amid the leaves, he lifted up his voice and answered, with a reverential inclination:

'Exalted Lady, this it is concerning which thou askedst me: "What is the Soul that has brought all this about, whom thou obeyest blindly in all things, and for whom thou hast willingly sacrificed the happiness and wellbeing of thy life?"

And the two questions question each other. What the one wishes, the other will not refuse.'

Having thus spoken, he humbly awaited her commands. But as she continued dumb, he bowed and departed thence, after a respectful salutation.

(Spitteler 1881, p. 318)

Reference

Spitteler, C. (1881). *Prometheus and Epimetheus*, trans. James F. Muirhead. London: Jarrolds Publishers.

Appendix B

Psychological Types

This appendix provides a summary, paraphrase, and interpretation of Jung's book *Psychological Types* (1921), with emphasis on how it reflects his view of the problem of one-sidedness and his solution. Each chapter is described using the headings and paragraph numbers from the book. There are occasional introductions or explanatory notes in italics.

The current edition of *Psychological Types* forms the basis of *Collected Works 6* (*CW6*) which consists of four forewords, an introduction, nine main chapters, two chapters that give reference information, and four appendices that are supplementary papers. The selected forewords reveal how Jung's frustration with readers made him disinclined to revise the book. The first Swiss foreword (Jung 1920) explains Jung's desire to make his theory relevant to laypeople because of its wide significance. The Argentine foreword (Jung 1934) admonishes readers for their misinterpretation of his text. In the seventh Swiss foreword (Jung 1937), he suggests he needs to revise the book, but there is no point in doing so if readers have not understood the basics of it. In the eighth Swiss foreword (Jung 1949), he says that there have been many small corrections, but otherwise it is still unaltered.

The first nine chapters contain the bulk of his theory, but they are not reader-friendly. They take the form of a literature review, examining in chronological order how earlier philosophers, psychologists, or poets dealt with the problem of one-sidedness or a related topic. Chapter I considers various classical and medieval writings. Jung then looks at ideas offered by Schiller (chapter II), Nietzsche (III), Jordan (IV), Spitteler (V), Gross (VI), Worringer (VII), James (VIII), and Ostwald (IX). Within those nine chapters, Jung weaves his understanding of the problem and his solution. He then adds some reference chapters, including descriptions of the most common forms of psychological one-sidedness (chapter X) and a set of definitions (chapter XI). There is also an introduction and an epilogue; he summarises some fundamental concepts and applies them to the conflict between Freud and Adler, their theories, and their followers. The four appendices are papers on typology written in 1913, 1923, 1931, and 1936.

202 Appendix B: *Psychological Types*

Introduction

(*Paragraphs* 1–7) Jung introduces typology with the notions of extraversion and introversion because they are the most apparent differences between people. He describes two other essential concepts – one-sidedness and compensation. They are relevant to typology because a type is one-sided, and one-sidedness leads to unconscious compensation. Jung then discusses some of the characteristic differences between extraversion and introversion. He links them to personal development by pointing out that they are mechanisms in the same person – which he likens to the diastolic and systolic alternation of a heartbeat. In ordinary life, the two mechanisms would naturally alternate. However, inner dispositions and outer contexts can sometimes encourage one to dominate. If that predominance becomes habitual, it produces a one-sided type. Extraversion and introversion are therefore two types of one-sidedness. Jung also introduces the four functions as other forms of intrapersonal opposites that can feature in one-sidedness and development.

I – The problem of types in the history of classical and medieval thought

In this chapter, Jung uses five historical examples from religion and philosophy to show how conflicts arise between one-sided viewpoints. The two sides are usually irreconcilable, and their one-sidedness is encouraged by both external factors (e.g. church tradition) and internal ones (e.g. individual psychology). Taking a one-sided approach can lead to compensation, i.e. the emergence of the opposite, to restore balance. This, in turn, can lead to the emergence of a reconciling third way, which is a move forwards in individual or cultural development. Jung gives some intrapersonal examples, such as the early church fathers Tertullian and Origen. They had to sacrifice their one-sided conscious standpoint to integrate their unconscious opposite. He discusses examples of collective attitudes, including theological and philosophical beliefs. Two common but opposing philosophies are nominalism (reality is in the mind) and realism (reality is in the world). Jung resolves this conflict with his own, third philosophy – esse in anima.

I Psychology in the classical age: The Gnostics, Tertullian, Origen

(8–12) The 'personal equation' is important to Jung's psychological theory, which is based on observation and experience. (*The term has its origins in astronomy, because each astronomer's measurements had a characteristic bias. The differences in measurements are reconciled by applying a personal equation to each of the astronomer's results*). It is therefore necessary to understand oneself, one's own personal equation, to understand other people, and to understand how one's

Appendix B: *Psychological Types*   203

own individuality is different from the collective. Jung introduces two other important concepts which he does not use until later chapters – participation mystique (unconscious identity with a collective group) and projection (seeing one's own psychological content in someone or something else).

(13–16) There is evidence of typological one-sidedness in the early church. Although the four classic temperaments have little relation to type, the three types in Gnostic philosophy – pneumatikoi, psychikoi, and hylikoi – correspond with thinking, feeling, and sensation. The psychological types of individual Christians meant they reacted to Gnosticism differently, which in turn led to different paths of spiritual development.

(17–27) Tertullian was an example of introverted thinking who had to sacrifice his intellect to integrate feeling. Origen was an extravert whose development involved sacrificing his ties to the world. These two examples show how the developmental process involves the reversal of the personality type of the individual. Jung dismisses the potential counter-argument that these reversals are due to the men finding their original, true types.

(28–30) There is a parallel between the Christian process of sacrifice, seen in these early examples, and psychological development. A person starts out with all the basic psychological functions. When we differentiate a one-sided attitude, this creates a deficiency in the other side. This later leads to compensation in which we must sacrifice the original one-sided attitude. Tertullian and Origen were examples of individuals going through that process of transformation from one-sidedness to integration. Gnosticism was an example of the unconscious breaking through into consciousness.

2 The theological disputes of the ancient church

(31–34) There are other examples of one-sided conflicts from the early church, such as the 'Arian heresy', or the 'Pelagian controversy'. The moral freedom of individuals developed as compensation to the stifling effect of the church's one-sidedness.

3 The problem of transubstantiation

(35–39) In a later phase of church development, there was a dispute about the doctrine of transubstantiation between Scotus Erigena and Radbertus. This involved the same psychological process – the development of one-sidedness, which then led to compensation – which may have been related to the differences between introverted and extraverted forms of thought.

4 Nominalism and realism

There has also been a conflict over many centuries between two philosophical standpoints. Although the subject of the conflict changes, the underlying process

204 Appendix B: *Psychological Types*

is the same. Initially there are one-sided views, then there may be compensation, then a third thing may emerge which represents a form of progress. The typology of individuals can reinforce the one-sidedness of the debates. Jung's philosophy of esse in anima, which forms part of his psychological theory, is a third thing that resolves the conflict between the two one-sided philosophical standpoints.

(40–51) Jung defines nominalism and realism as viewing reality primarily in internal words or in the external world. He views the two philosophies as related and inseparable, and he gives an example to illustrate how they relate: if a man covers his face, we do not know who he is; if we remove the cover, we recognise him. That is, 'recognition' is a complex concept that is constructed between the internal (perception) and external (the face). Another example is an electricity bill, which is based on the amount of energy used. This concept is not solely a physical thing, nor is it just a psychological perception. It is a third thing that is a combination of the two.

(52–55) There is a similar opposition between different typological standpoints. The introduction of typology to this discussion is not to categorise the types of the philosophers involved. It helps to classify the material not the individuals. There may, however, be associations between the observed material and the type of the philosopher.

(56–62) The phrase 'tertium non datur' means there is no third possibility between the two opposites. That is, it describes the state where the opposing and one-sided forms of argument have not yet been reconciled or integrated. Aristotle is an example of taking a moderate or realistic stance between two opposites; he recognised that we should not dismiss one or other side just because there may be problems in their argument. Grappling with opposites – such as idealism/realism, or spiritualism/materialism – is still a valid problem today, even when one or other side seems absurd.

(63–67) Jung's personal solution to the philosophical opposites is *esse in anima*, which stands between the philosophical opposites of *esse in intellectu* and *esse in re.* That is, all reality occurs in the psyche as the result of an interaction between the perceiving mind and external reality. This means, for example, that the concept of God is different in different people because, although the *esse in re* for God is the same for everyone, the *esse in intellectu* is different for each person.

(68–79) Having outlined his own 'third' solution to the problem of opposite philosophies, Jung then compares it with an attempt by one of the Scholastics to find a philosophical third way. Abelard found an intermediate position, between nominalism and realism, using the idea of *conceptualism*. Although Abelard's contribution was significant, because he sought a mediatory position, Jung muses that Abelard would have used Jung's philosophy of *esse in anima* had he known about it. The problem with Abelard's philosophical solution is that it is still one-sided. It is logical and intellectual, but it lacks concreteness, vitality, and immediacy. Jung's philosophy of *esse in anima* addresses this problem because

Appendix B: *Psychological Types* 205

it combines the opposites in a living psychological process. The reality we experience every day, of *esse in anima*, is constructed within the psyche under the influence of fantasy, which has its source in the unconscious.

(80–87) Our current era is one-sided because both Christianity and science have suppressed the fantasy that comes from the unconscious. Christianity offers stereotypical symbolic concepts instead. Science excludes fantasy altogether and thereby causes the psychological impoverishment of the individual. When the higher goal is for opposites to be united in a third or higher principle, the solution can only come from the creative fantasy of the unconscious. Every great idea or thing that ever came into existence has its origins in fantasy. Nevertheless, the one-sided suppression of fantasy by Christianity and science was a necessary step in the development of culture, because fantasy needs the structure they give to be a force for creative growth.

(88–95) The psychologies of Freud and Adler are one-sided in several respects. They both value science and they both value a particular governing idea, though their ideas are different. Freud values sexuality and the repression of incompatible wish tendencies. Adler values ego-superiority. Freud's approach is extraverted, and Adler's introverted. Both theories reject the constructive role Jung has outlined for the imagination. We cannot gain the benefits of fantasy by their approach of simply analysing it. Fantasy is a key part of the constructive method that produces a synthesis between the opposites. We can see the inadequacy of Abelard's efforts to reconcile opposites intellectually, without fantasy, when we compare his approach with the Chinese philosophers Lao-tzu and Chuang-tzu, and the poet Schiller.

5 The holy communion controversy between Luther and Zwingli

(96–100) Jung gives one more example of a dispute that shows the difficulty of reconciling one-sided standpoints – a controversy over communion between Luther and Zwingli. Their one-sidedness emerged from the combination of church tradition and the psychologies of the individuals involved. Jung does not offer a solution here but uses the example to reinforce the main message of the chapter – that there are frequent, typical, and one-sided differences of viewpoint that stand in opposition to each other and need reconciliation.

II – Schiller's ideas on the type problem

The second chapter focuses much more on intrapersonal, typological opposites. Jung examines Schiller's self-analysis of his psychological functions, which are split between the superior and inferior functions. Jung takes the view that Schiller is introverted and has thinking as his dominant function with a significant presence of intuition. His two inferior functions are sensation and feeling, which are fused. In Myers-Briggs terminology, Schiller is an INTP (preferring

206 Appendix B: *Psychological Types*

introversion, intuition, thinking, and perception). Jung does not like Schiller's solution because it is too one-sided, too oriented towards his own type, and he tends to go backwards (wanting to restore stage one of the axiom of Maria) rather than going forwards and seeking a full resolution of separate and conflicting opposites. But there is another, more generic solution within his writings that Jung draws out.

I Letters on the aesthetic education of man

a The inferior and superior functions

(101–4) As far as Jung could tell, Schiller was the first person to engage in a major attempt to describe two opposing psychological mechanisms within the individual and to seek to reconcile them. However, Schiller was one-sided, being introverted. Schiller therefore portrays an extraverted function as having more inferior qualities.

(105–6) Schiller observes that, although modern culture has advanced, individuals are inferior to those of antiquity due to a contemporary ' "Amfortas" wound' – a split in the modern individual. Schiller attributes this to culture, which enforces a one-sided differentiation of functions for individuals, so they can serve society by providing a specialised service. The downside is that they neglect other aspects of their own psyche.

(107–14) From this Jung concludes that the state in antiquity was an advantage for individuals, because they were more whole, but a disadvantage for society, because culture was less developed. The modern advancement of collective culture, brought about primarily by Christianity, has reversed this. The differentiation of psychological functions serves society but is detrimental to the individual, because of the internal psychic split it creates. This split is a necessary stage in development. It creates a form of one-sided barbarism, which will not be noticed if the person's dominant function fits with society's needs. But there will eventually be compensation that tries to abolish the inner division. Schiller recognised the inner conflict, but his solution was to restore a prior mode of life. He overlooked the Christian doctrine of redemption. This may have been because Schiller saw Christianity as part of the problem, creating a one-sidedness, and did not realise it also pointed towards a potential solution.

(115–29) Coming to terms with the inferior function is like engaging in an internal civil war, which Schiller recognises in himself. Schiller and Rousseau (who was encouraged by the parallels between his inner struggle and the French revolution) both try to solve the conflict between individual needs and the demands of society. But neither Rousseau nor Schiller produce a satisfactory solution. What Rousseau claims as unity or wholeness of the individual is participation mystique – i.e. unconscious identity with the collective. He also does not realise that differentiation of the dominant function is injurious

Appendix B: *Psychological Types* 207

to the individual. Both men err by taking an idealistic view of the past psychological state. They therefore ignore the symbolism of Christianity that brings hope for future psychological development. Jung criticises Schiller's one-sided and illusory fantasies about ancient Greece and suggests he could have resolved his internal battle better if he had thought about his own poetic side more symbolically rather than literally. That is, his thoughts about Greek antiquity were not descriptions of history, but reflections of aspects of himself, of his current unconscious nature.

(130–35) A one-sided person with a differentiated function must come to terms with the opposite, which in typological terms is the inferior function. But the conversion of the inferior function into the superior one can only happen if the original superior function is sacrificed, and support is provided by a higher power. Although Schiller and Rousseau have made errors in their analysis, they have pointed to the need to reconcile opposites.

(136–51) When we accept there is a paradox, and the opposites face each other as conflicting aspects of oneself, it creates the conditions for the third thing to emerge that is the start of a new way. There are many ways we can experience this, some of which are related to type. For example, for Schiller it is an introverted path, and for Goethe it is an extraverted one. Also, unconscious compensation may be forced upon the individual, or it may feel like an experience of divinity.

b Concerning the basic instincts

(152–58) Jung takes a detailed look at Schiller's personal type dynamics and how it limits his judgment. The superior function (thinking) is abstract and universal, but the inferior ones (sensation and feeling) are undifferentiated, passive, and reactive. Schiller views sensation and feeling as interchangeable terms, evidence of a single, fused function. Schiller does not identify with them, they are foreign to him. These characteristics are due to the inferior nature of the functions. His limited view of the fused sensation and feeling functions means that he attributes the higher, universal qualities to thinking. In doing so, he is taking a blinkered and limited view. If a different function were dominant, then these characteristics (abstract, universal, passive, reactive, etc.) would be associated with other functions. By excluding the inferior functions from his identity, Schiller gives himself the impression that he is a united or whole person.

(159–66) Having a dominant function, such as thinking as evidenced in Schiller, makes us collective beings. This means that our thought and speech conform to the general expectations of someone with differentiated thinking. People think this is a good thing, because it has social advantages, but it damages individuality. Jung regards it as a form of barbarism. Another aspect of Schiller's type dynamics is that the superior and inferior functions sometimes swap places. He behaves very differently, and is no longer himself, because he uses the inferior function to extreme. Schiller realises that the conflict between the superior

208 Appendix B: *Psychological Types*

and inferior functions is 'unbridgeable', even though he also recognises that each function has some value to the other.

(167–71) The recognition of the value of each opposite takes the discussion in a new direction, towards a potential solution. Schiller sees the conflict between opposites as valuable and life-promoting. If we renounce the dominant function's claim to a universally valid standpoint, this leads to the differentiation of the individual from the collective and the creation of the unique individual. Jung suggests that there are only two ways to reconcile the opposites – with a rational compromise or using an irrational solution. He criticises Schiller for trying to resolve the opposites within himself rationally. But he also points to Schiller's discussion of the symbol as being an important, irrational means of reconciliation. Jung then outlines his own solution for the first time in the book – a mediating function that creates symbols through fantasy. He also suggests there is a psychological function that understands symbols, which he refers to as symbolic understanding.

(172–76) The act of playing can make a significant contribution to the emergence of the solution. When the repression of the inferior function ends, it results in a collision and equalisation between the opposites. A third factor is needed which has at least the same degree of seriousness as the two opposites. Play removes all seriousness and thereby creates a level playing field for all three – i.e. the superior, inferior, and mediatory functions. This works because, in play, the individual differentiates him/herself from both the opposites, which makes it possible to pay attention to the more unique attitude that is emerging from between them. If the individuality does not emerge between the opposites, it is torn apart and dissolved.

(177–85) What is missing from the argument so far is how the third thing becomes strong enough to overcome the divisive power of the opposites. For this to happen, the individual's differentiation must be based on the symbol (which has the power to canalise libido in a different direction). Neither the basic psychological functions nor anything else in consciousness can create the symbol, because they are one-sided, and the nature of consciousness is to discriminate between opposites, not reconcile. The symbol can only come from the creative fantasy of the unconscious – through a differentiation of the self from the opposites, mediating between them, and keeping them in balance when each one tries to take over again. This is the role of the transcendent function.

(186–98) Schiller's solution is biased towards his own type, introverted thinking. Jung has adapted Schiller's ideas to form his own conception of the symbol and transcendent function, one that can be applied more generally to any opposites between consciousness and the unconscious. The mediatory function causes the opposites to cancel each other out, producing a void that a symbol from the unconscious then fills. Jung justifies the generic application of Schiller's solution by drawing parallels with development in Eastern religions, and German theology and philosophy.

Appendix B: *Psychological Types* 209

(199–212) Jung then summarises Schiller's approach as demanding a detachment from the opposites even to the point of a complete emptying of consciousness. This might seem to be a collective religious way of thinking but, by allowing symbols to emerge and interpreting them subjectively (as part of oneself), it can be a step forward for individuality. Jung acknowledges that his interpretation goes beyond Schiller's conception, which was limited by his aesthetic attitude. This aspect of Schiller's one-sidedness meant that he was unable to show how the mediatory state comes about, and he could not overcome various other barriers. Nevertheless, Schiller's solution addresses some critical issues, including the philosophical debate about the difference between appearance and reality, and awareness of the problems of projection.

2 A discussion on naïve and sentimental poetry

(213–22) Schiller describes two types of poet – naive and sentimental. Jung sees a temptation to draw a parallel between these types and the attitude types, i.e. extraverts and introverts. But he dismisses it, because both introvert and extravert types can produce both naive and sentimental poems. Nevertheless, it is valid to look at the intrapersonal mechanisms involved. Naive poetry involves an unconscious identification with an external object – i.e. it is participation mystique. The sentimental poet idealises and fantasises, which is the opposite of identifying with the object. So, there are extraverted and introverted mechanisms involved, irrespective of the type of the poet. There are also parallels between Schiller's naive and sentimental types and the functions of sensation and intuition. Finally, although there are links between Schiller's types and the philosophical conflicts discussed in chapter I – idealism and realism – he concludes that Schiller's observations are of no further interest.

III – The Apollonian and the Dionysian

Jung's writings on Nietzsche are short, but he throws some complex concepts into the mix. The Apollonian impulse stands for the principle of individuation, the drive up the caduceus towards higher consciousness. The Dionysian stands for the opposite, it drags the individual down into unconsciousness. Nietzsche's work is valuable in showing that we need both in individuation because the unconscious needs to be integrated into consciousness and, as consciousness develops, it needs to keep a good connection with the unconscious.

However, Nietzsche also presents the Apollonian and Dionysian impulses in a biased way, projecting his typology into them. In an earlier paper (Jung 1913), he saw Nietzsche as portraying them in introverted and extraverted terms. In this chapter, Jung sees the bias as more associated with intuition and sensation. Other types would present the Apollonian and Dionysian instincts differently, projecting their dominant function into the former and their inferior function into the latter.

210 Appendix B: *Psychological Types*

(223–33) Nietzsche's work develops that of Schiller, Schopenhauer, Goethe, and other traditions. It is significantly different in that it more directly confronts the oppositions in his own psyche. For Nietzsche, development is bound up with the interplay between the Apollonian and Dionysian impulses. The Apollonian impulse, comparable to dreaming, is the principle of individuation (drive towards consciousness). The Dionysian impulse, comparable to intoxication, dissolves the individual into the collective instincts. It sinks into the unconscious, where individuality is obliterated. However, these are opposites that need to be reconciled in the overall process because we cannot increase consciousness without also integrating the unconscious. This reconciliation cannot be done solely through art or aesthetics, as Nietzsche initially seems to suggest. We must incorporate the barbarian side of the personality into the side that is more cultured. Jung illustrates this with the example of a railway bridge, which we cannot judge to be adequate just because it looks nice. Taking an aesthetic perspective is a defence against getting involved with the dark side of one's nature. Nietzsche eventually realises this, through his own Dionysian experience.

(234–42) Jung then turns the discussion away from the conflict between the Apollonian and Dionysian impulses to see what typological functions are involved in Nietzsche's portrayal of them. His description of the Dionysian impulse seems to be extraverted and associated with sensation, and he portrays the Apollonian impulse as introverted. But this association is too simple and imposes a fixed structure on Nietzsche's personality. There are unique characteristics that he ascribes to the two opposites which do not correspond to introversion or extraversion. His writings suggest there are four functions – the rational ones of thinking and feeling, and the aesthetic ones of intuition and sensation – leading to four function types in total. The emphasis in Nietzsche's writings offers us evidence for his personal psychology. Through his dominant function of intuition, Nietzsche gains insights into the Dionysian state of his unconscious.

IV – The type problem in human character

I General remarks on Jordan's types

(243–54) Jung introduces the work of Furneaux Jordan by describing it as 'small and rather odd'. Jordan is concerned primarily with two types – feeling and thinking – though he also says there is a third type. Jung credits Jordan with a sophisticated analysis but as making the mistake of conflating activity/inactivity with the functional opposites. Activity and passivity are irrespective of type. Jung relates this to his own error, in his previous paper, of associating introversion with thinking, and extraversion with feeling. Although they are separate, Jung initially made this mistake because, when we look at an introvert, it seems as if they are thinking, and extraverts are more expressive. What

Appendix B: *Psychological Types* 211

Jung likes in Jordan's work is his recognition of the significance of the two sides to each other in the same personality. For example, in extraverts the (inner) intellect predominates and in introverts the (outer) emotions predominate. In other words, the dominant function is not as in charge as it may seem. The opposite function is the one that rules the roost, though this can depend on the strength of consciousness. Jordan's analysis is based on intuition and therefore through the lens of his unconscious. He overlooks the living reality of the person and focuses on an intuitive reality, which other types may not understand. Jung makes a side point that Jordan's middle group comprises sensate and intuitive types.

2 Special description and criticism of Jordan's types

(255–74) Jung's main criticism of Jordan is that he describes the less impassioned (extravert) type as being 'active'. Jung quotes Jordan's description of the 'Introverted Woman' and claims the description is one-sided because it emphasises the outward expression of feeling without recognising the conscious inner life. Jung goes on to give a detailed analysis of the inner and outer life of introverted women and why Jordan misunderstands them. Jung makes similar criticisms of the description of the 'Extraverted Woman' and again analyses the characteristics of Jordan's one-sided discussion. He criticises the description of the 'Extraverted Man', as one-sided and a caricature, and the description of the 'Introverted Man' for being less thorough. Jung attributes this to Jordan lacking knowledge of his own shadow. Jung dismisses the rest of Jordan's book as having similarly inaccurate portrayals of historical characters. Nevertheless, he credits Jordan with being the first to give a 'relatively appropriate character sketch of the emotional types'.

V – The type problem in poetry

1 Introductory remarks on Spitteler's typology

(275–78) Jung cautions the reader against interpreting Spitteler's story by thinking of Prometheus (the 'forethinker') as standing for an introvert and Epimetheus (the 'afterthinker') as standing for an extravert. The two characters represent two sides of the same individual. Each has become one-sided and does not relate well to the other. Epimetheus has surrendered his life to the persona, living according to the collective demands and expectations that society has of him. Prometheus has surrendered to his soul, the demands of the unconscious, to the extent that he has lost his ability to relate to the outer world. There is a split within the individual, and this chapter explains how that split is resolved.

(279–81) Jung embarks on a little tangent to discuss whether the unconscious exists or not. At the time of writing he can make no definite claim (though he does so in later years), but he treats it as if it is real. Therefore, just as one thinks

212   Appendix B: *Psychological Types*

of consciousness as dealing with objects in the outer world, one could also consider the unconscious as dealing with objects in the inner world, such as archetypes. For a balanced and integrated individual, or someone who is slightly one-sided, the inner objects are not problematic. However, when the individual becomes very one-sided then these inner objects (projected into other people) can become daemonic, create intense ambivalent feelings, and worsen the polarisation between opposites.

(282–87) Because Epimetheus does not have a relationship with his brother, there is no (psychological) constraint on what he does. He has a one-sided orientation to the outer world that has lost its balancing soul. He is caught up in meeting the desires and expectations of the world, and unwittingly lives a collective myth that is self-assured and self-righteous. He has an advantage, inherent within an extraverted orientation, that by going along with a collective conscience he does what society expects him to do. This gives him protection against the dangers of the outer world in which he lives. Prometheus, however, has surrendered himself to his soul and has no defence against the dangers of the inner world. The two characters represent a battle between two tendencies within the same person, each trying to each get the ego on its side.

2 A comparison of Spitteler's with Goethe's Prometheus

(288–98) Jung compares the different portrayals of Prometheus in Goethe's and Spitteler's work, to show that Spitteler has a better solution to the problem of opposites. There are some differences that are not significant, such as Spitteler's Prometheus being one-sided and suffering, and Goethe's being more extraverted, less one-sided, and creative. The key difference is that, in Spitteler's story, there is compensation from the unconscious, which comes in the form of Pandora's jewel. She represents the soul and a link to the unconscious and divinity. The jewel has similarities to descriptions of the Buddha and it symbolises renewal and rebirth. Spitteler's story examines the emergence of the jewel and the negative response of various characters to it.

(299–309) The symbolic jewel is an attempt to heal the split in the psyche, and to unite the differentiated with the opposite, undifferentiated function. It produces a new attitude towards the world. But the significance of the jewel is lost on Epimetheus because, in his one-sidedness, he cannot understand it. His attitude is rational (not symbolic), he only has a social conscience, and he has no connection to soul. Prometheus is unable to do anything with the jewel because he has no connection with the people. Jung explores various similarities and differences between Goethe's and Spitteler's plots and characters. Goethe's Prometheus lives out his repressed material through his son. His solution to the divide between the brothers is for their son and daughter to fall in love, and for them to develop a degree of mutual understanding. This solution is superficial and inadequate in Jung's view; he is looking for something with a deeper truth.

Appendix B: *Psychological Types* 213

(310–12) In Spitteler's story, Pandora's jewel is a compensatory product from the unconscious. The brothers cannot do anything with it, so they do not integrate it into conscious life and it is lost. However, the libido must go somewhere, so what had been compensation now becomes an enantiodromia. It goes back into the unconscious and returns in a much more daemonic form, as a disaster that conscious life cannot ignore. Epimetheus, the blameless man of conscience, finds himself making a pact with evil. Eventually, things become so bad that Soul makes Prometheus come out of his solitude and, at the risk of his life, point out to men the error of their ways.

(313–17) The one-sided emphasis on differentiated functions is due in part to Christianity, which has lost sight of living religion – of relating to the divine in the unconscious – because of the failure to recognise symbols. Goethe does grasp the problem in *Faust* where, unlike his superficial and incomplete solution in *Prometheus* and *Pandora*, he realises that renewal of attitude is only possible if the original (one-sided) attitude is abandoned.

3 The significance of the uniting symbol

In this next section, Jung reviews why symbols are overlooked. He links the problem of one-sidedness to various religious themes. He argues that the conflict between opposites can only be resolved through a transformation of the individual's attitude. He examines some of the ways that Eastern religions and philosophies deal with symbols.

(318–19) Spitteler's Epimetheus, like Goethe's Faust, makes a pact with evil. This was a consequence of Epimetheus' one-sided focus on meeting collective demands. Collectivity overlooks what is new and unique because uniqueness depends on 'soul'. Epimetheus' downfall came from his inability to understand the symbol that pointed in a new direction.

(320–23) Symbols interweave good and evil, and poets who produce such symbols can help us understand what is happening in the collective unconscious. However, although those symbols may point to a revolt against collective morality, poets often only appreciate the aesthetics of their symbols without realising their true, cultural significance. This is in part because the deeper insights of the collective unconscious seem strange to most people, so they reject symbols because of their instinct for self-preservation.

(324–26) The solution to cultural conflict is often religious in nature, but the superficially mythological content of Spitteler's poem obscures that aspect of the solution. Goethe's Faust and Nietzsche's Zarathustra are better in this respect, because they engage with the meaning of the symbol and show understanding of the religious aspect of the problem. Although Spitteler does not treat Pandora's jewel in that way, his story holds a deeper truth and gives more insight into the nature of collective life. It shows that the symbol is closely related to the opposition between psychological types and functions. It is an attempt to find a solution through the renewal of the general attitude.

214 Appendix B: *Psychological Types*

a The Brahmanic conception of the problem of opposites

(327–30) In Hindu religion there are many types of opposite, such as desire and anger, love and hate, hunger and thirst, care and folly, and honour and disgrace. It is by becoming indifferent to opposites that we obtain eternal happiness – just as a charioteer looks down on the two wheels when driving a chariot. One learns to deny external opposites first (e.g. heat and cold) and then internal ones. Jung cites more examples of opposites – being and non-being, reality and irreality, formed and formless, mortal and immortal, stationary and moving, actual and transcendental, day and night, knowing and not knowing, and others. Brahman (the highest principle in Hinduism) is the union and dissolution of all opposites.

b The Brahmanic conception of the uniting symbol

(331–42) Brahman, which Jung describes as both the producer and the produced, is a certain psychological state. It is a multifaceted life force. It is a state of holding the tension of opposites. It withdraws attention from the opposites so that it is detached from both. Development does not consist of one side turning into its opposite, but in keeping an equilibrium, which leads to a union, and to the emergence of a new form of libido.

(343–47) Jung considers the meaning of a text that refers to someone becoming a monster when they know the two monsters of Brahman. This refers to a split in the psyche. The two monsters are the personification of the two sides. In typological terms, this can happen when someone is too identified with a psychological function or group of functions. There is a difference between having the conscious ability to use one side or the other, which is the highest culture, and being involuntarily one-sided, which is a sign of barbarism. The individual can become carried away by their own introversion or extraversion. This one-sidedness can be moderated if the collective culture does not reinforce it but encourages the individual to express their own natural tendency to counter it.

c The uniting symbol as the principle of dynamic regulation

(348–54) The earlier sections have shown how redemption emerges from between pairs of opposites. It can also be related to other concepts and gods in Hinduism – most notably *rta* (the principle of natural order in the universe) and Agni (the conveyor of sacrifices to the gods). These are not only religious principles, but also psychological ones that reveal the workings of the psyche.

(355–57) Jung suggests that libido is analogous to physical energy. It is governed by laws and goes through various transformations, as shown in fantasies and myths. An individual can reach optimum development only by following the laws of libido, treating it as a form of systole alternating with diastole. This does not mean we surrender to natural laws, such as instinct. We need to recognise moral opposites as being part of our own nature and allow ourselves to experience the internal conflict that such opposites create.

Appendix B: *Psychological Types* 215

d The uniting symbol in Chinese philosophy

(358–74) Jung traces some of the similarities between the Brahmanic idea of a middle way and the concept of reconciliation in a wide range of other sources. These include the Chinese philosophy of *tao*, Christian symbols, African myths, Japanese philosophy, and German opera. For example, Taoism's opposites are *yang* (warmth, light, maleness, heaven) and *yin* (cold, darkness, femaleness, earth). The Chinese division of the psyche into two souls (*shen* and *kwei*) is a psychological truth of two mutually antagonistic tendencies that are resolved by an irrational third, which is *tao*. The opposites can be reconciled by actively 'not doing' (which is different from doing nothing, or rationalistic 'doing').

4 The relativity of the symbol

a The worship of woman and the worship of the soul

(375–401) In Christianity, the worship of God is a key element of uniting the opposites. In Buddhism, the key element is self-development. In Spitteler and Goethe, it is the worship of the soul, symbolised by the worship of woman. This theme appears in Dante's *Divine Comedy* and Goethe's *Faust*, where the worship of woman transforms into the worship of soul. This spiritualisation of worship also appears in an early Christian work, *The Shepherd of Hermas*. Hermas' erotic love for a woman is repressed, which directs the libido into the soul-image thereby giving it life. The libido then reappears as a spiritual function and love for the church. This process is also represented by the symbol of the vessel, which appears in Gnosticism, pagan mythology, the early church fathers, and the legend of the Holy Grail. Spiritualisation involves holding libido, so it does not flow away and go to waste. The vessel is both a product of that containment and the container itself.

(402–6) There is an evolutionary argument for symbol formation. Jung tells the story of a bushman who went fishing, caught nothing and, on return home, strangled his son. He had been angry with himself but, because he identified fully with his son, had acted out his anger against himself by strangling his son. Symbol formation prevents such tragedies and enables greater freedom of choice.

b The relativity of the God-concept in Meister Eckhart

(407–18) Jung then shows that this process, of a symbol emerging from between opposites, appears in the theology of Meister Eckhart. He was rejected as heretical at the time but is beginning to become more accepted in the contemporary church. Man and God are functions of each other, and one's personal image of God is a symbolic expression, a third thing that emerges from the unconscious between the two (from between oneself and the objective God). God is a divine

216   Appendix B: *Psychological Types*

power in the unconscious that can appear in the outer world due to projection. There is therefore a need to recognise there is an aspect of God in oneself, and the experience of God is in the soul.

(419–25) In an undeveloped culture, individuals have several souls, which they project into the world. As culture develops, they merge to become a single soul, found in the psyche. The soul and God may be personified, but the fact of anthropomorphism is unimportant. What matters is that we recognise that God and the soul are closely related. This turning inwards creates an inner concentration of libido, towards the treasure that is in God's kingdom.

(426–29) Consciousness can miss the significance of symbols by treating them as being artistic, or as philosophical speculation, or as quasi-religious (to form a new sect), or as worthless. To gain meaning from a symbol, we must elaborate on it, or consciously realise it. This differentiates the individual and produces a new attitude based on the transcendent function. The libido sinks into the unconscious and re-emerges as something new. This is a continual process, as expressed in Goethe's metaphor of systole and diastole.

(430–33) Jung summarises the religious process as a combination of two movements – the differentiation from the unconscious and reconciliation with it. He reinforces this point, and the relativity of God, using extracts from the poetry of Silesius. This is the beginning of a religious new age, which is a natural consequence of the reformation. It has re-established a personal relation with God and led to the recognition that God is relative (i.e. one's image of God is subjective).

5 The nature of the uniting symbol in Spitteler

(434) Jung begins the last section of this chapter by summarising the main theme. Spitteler's poem illustrates how what was at first united then splits into opposites. Prometheus, serving the soul, sinks into the unconscious. This leaves society soulless and, because it does not recognise the saving jewel that appears, it eventually succumbs to evil. Only when Prometheus re-emerges with insight and understanding does society come to its senses. This expresses one of the tenets of Jung's cultural criticism – collectively, people tend to preserve the status quo, which (when taken to extreme) can potentially lead to disastrous consequences.

(435–42) The jewel was divine, a new god, or a new manifestation of life. Although society wants this type of rejuvenation, they reject the jewel because they are looking for a purely rational solution. The symbol is irrational, just as (in religious myths) the birth of god occurs in an irrational way. Jung quotes from Isaiah 11 to show that a religious saviour represents the union of opposites – the wolf and the lamb, leopard and kid, calf and lion, etc., all led by a child.

(443–49) Through the emergence of the symbol from the unconscious, libido becomes constructive, and the repressed functions come to life. This is what the hero myth stands for – descending into the unconscious and bringing those

Appendix B: *Psychological Types*   217

functions back into consciousness. This runs the risk of bringing up difficult, powerful, and destructive images, though the symbol can protect the individual and society from them. Immanuel, in the book of Isaiah, is an example of such a protective symbol. Many myths portray the destructive threat as a dragon, but Spitteler treats the problem as purely psychological. Another risk is that, when the enantiodromia occurs, there is merely a reversal – the dominant attitude is replaced by its opposite.

(450–60) In Spitteler's story, everyone in society finds the jewel distasteful, so it descends back into the unconscious, and the enantiodromia begins. Good turns into evil, and value turns into worthlessness. Normally, a Christian attitude holds back the animal side of the psyche, but now evil comes to the surface. Eventually, this leads to the union of opposites. If Epimetheus and the other attitudes had accepted the jewel, the opposites could have reconciled in a straightforward way. But the rejection of the jewel stirred up dangerous contents and meant that the uniting symbol then had to force itself on consciousness in a different form. That is, there is a new function and attitude, represented by the symbol of Messias who becomes king. Epimetheus could no longer be king because he had to resign, and Prometheus did not want the role. Jung summarises the chapter by quoting William Blake on the prolific and the devouring: 'Religion is an endeavour to reconcile the two' (Jung 1921, p. 272).

VI – The type problem in psychopathology

(461–64) In this chapter, Jung looks at Otto Gross' two types. Both Jung and Gross argue that the lessons from psychopathology can be carried over into normal psychology. Gross bases his types on the relative strength of the primary and secondary function – by which he is referring to cerebral cell processes, not Jung's typological functions. Gross' secondary function restricts the scope of what the primary function produces. In one type (later identified as the more introvert) the two functions are balanced, in the other (more extravert) the primary function is strong, and the secondary function is weak.

(465–83) Jung discusses the relative characteristics and dynamics of the two types, exploring the consequences of the primary and secondary functions having different relative strengths. What is needed, in Jung's view, is a greater balance – the 'shortening' of the secondary function in one type, and its 'prolongation' in the other. Jung notes that introversion and extraversion are not character traits, but mechanisms in everyone that can be switched on and off at will. A tendency for one or the other depends on both inborn traits and environmental influences, and it only appears when the predominance of one or other becomes habitual. Jung disagrees with Gross' model. There is no reason, in his view, why one should base a theory of types on the secondary function, as it depends primarily on the dominant function. The two orientations are interchangeable and, depending on context, can result in a temporary reversal of type.

218   Appendix B: *Psychological Types*

VII – The type problem in aesthetics

(484–92) This chapter looks at Worringer's two aesthetic forms – abstraction and empathy. Empathy is feeling oneself into the object in the outer world. Western culture tends to be primarily empathetic in its appreciation of art. Abstraction is the opposite, withdrawing an idea from the object. The two forms give rise to different aesthetic attitudes. An unconscious attitude precedes both. Before empathy, the world is seen as dead, so empathy breathes some life into it and injects it with feeling. Before abstraction, the world is seen as full of life and therefore threatening. To defend against the world, abstraction takes the animated life out of it, to produce an inert idea.

(493–98) The two attitudes correspond to extraversion and introversion, the former being a more Western/occidental approach and the latter more oriental, as seen, for example, in Buddhism. Empathy sees the world as benign so is confident in dealing with it. Abstraction sees it as hostile, and is more fearful, so it counters participation mystique. Both are based on forms of projection, and both are needed for the appreciation of art.

(499–504) In Jung's view, both mechanisms are rooted in self-alienation. Abstraction identifies with the idea or image, empathy identifies with the object. Both forms of identification are defences against one's impulses – which therefore mean self-alienation. Identifying with a function involves adaptation to collective demands and, encouraged by the notion that selflessness is a virtue, it is a way of alienating oneself and thereby avoiding one's inferior function. Self-alienation leads to the degeneration of the individual and a lack of connection between the ego and the unconscious. A differentiated function needs self-alienation to work efficiently, but integrating unconscious contents is vital for the development of humanity.

VIII – The type problem in modern philosophy

(505–41) In this chapter, Jung examines the two types in the pragmatic philosophy of William James – rationalist and empiricist – and compares them with Flournoy's two kinds of thinking. Jung notes that, although James values both types, his portrayals are biased. This one-sidedness gives some clues as to James' disposition. Jung deconstructs the various pairs of qualities that James associates with his two types, separating those associated with introversion and extraversion. These are not fixed traits, as the characteristics can often be observed in the opposite type. James' work is significant in showing a relationship between type and philosophical standpoint. However, James does not offer a solution to the problem of opposites.

IX – The type problem in biography

(542–55) This chapter looks at Ostwald's two types – classic and romantic. Ostwald relates romantics to the traditional sanguine and choleric temperaments,

Appendix B: *Psychological Types* 219

and classics to the phlegmatic and melancholic temperaments. In Jung's view, Ostwald's analysis – like the temperaments – is based on outward appearances and does not take account of what is going on within the individual. There is a relation between romantic and extraversion, and between classic and introversion. Ostwald argues that romantics mature at an earlier stage of development than classics, but Jung suggests this is only because the maturity of the introvert is more hidden. Both types can be mature but in different ways. Both types can be enthusiastic, but the outward manifestation of that enthusiasm is different. Jung notes Ostwald's claim that not everyone falls into one group or the other, but that great men usually fall into one or other of the types, and average people occupy the middle ground. The material is useful to Jung in compiling his list of types.

X – General description of the types

The final two chapters are more straightforward than the earlier nine and have a simpler structure. They contain supporting reference information. Chapter X describes the most common forms of psychological one-sidedness, and chapter XI is a set of definitions.

I Introduction

(556–61) Jung starts with an overview of introverted and extraverted types. Both are attitudes towards objects in the outer world, one withdrawing interest from them, the other investing interest in them. The differences are common but often go unnoticed unless the individual's personality is pronounced. There is probably a biological foundation to them, with introversion having evolved as a form of defence and extraversion to promote propagation. A child can be born with a disposition towards introversion or extraversion which might be falsified in the opposite direction under environmental pressure.

2 The extraverted type

(562) When discussing extraverted types, one needs to distinguish between the psychology of consciousness and the unconscious.

a The general attitude of consciousness

(563–67) Everyone orients themselves in relation to the outer world, withdrawing or investing interest. Extraversion is one of two mechanisms in the same individual, and a person becomes a type when they use one or other of the mechanisms habitually. For the extravert, outer or objective factors are the decisive ones. There is a difference between adjustment, which only takes account of the immediate conditions, and adaptation, which takes account of wider needs (both in the present and in the inner urge towards individuation).

220   Appendix B: *Psychological Types*

b The attitude of the unconscious

(568–74) The attitude of the unconscious compensates consciousness. In an extravert, it is introverted. Extraversion represses impulses, which can remain hidden so long as the one-sidedness is not extreme. But it can break through into consciousness in the form of a disaster (enantiodromia) that can destroy one's business, trigger a nervous breakdown, lead to drug or alcohol abuse, etc.

(575–76) In most cases, however, when the one-sidedness is moderate, the compensation from the unconscious can keep psychic equilibrium. The compensatory introversion has an inferior quality. For example, dominant extraverted feeling may build rapport with people, but sometimes make tactless remarks from the inferior thinking. There is a constant influx of the unconscious into consciousness in this way.

c The peculiarities of the basic psychological functions in the extraverted attitude

(577–619) Jung describes the characteristics of the four functions in an extraverted attitude, firstly as a mechanism in the individual, and then what happens when the use of that mechanism becomes habitual, i.e. the person becomes 'a type'. He describes two sides of each type, the conscious and unconscious.

3 The introverted type

a The general attitude of consciousness

(620–25) For an introverted attitude, inner, subjective factors are the decisive ones. An inferior and exaggerated extraversion compensates them. The withdrawal of interest from the outer world means that the introvert becomes more oriented by internal, subjective contents. This might seem to refer to one's own conscious ideas, but they are underpinned by the structures of the unconscious, including archetypes.

b The attitude of the unconscious

(626–27) Just as 'the object' plays too great a role in the conscious life of an extravert, it also plays too little a role in the life of the introvert. The unconscious compensates through an inferior form of extraversion, for example in broken relationships, finance problems, or reputational issues. At extreme, it can lead to an irrational fear of certain aspects of the world.

c The peculiarities of the basic psychological functions in the introverted attitude

(628–65) Jung then describes the introverted forms of the functions, in a similar structure to the discussion of extraversion. He describes them as mechanisms in the individual, then as types when the use of those mechanisms becomes habitual. Each description, again, examines the two sides of the personality, the manifestations of both consciousness and the unconscious.

4 The principal and auxiliary functions

(This is section 4 in the 1960 German edition, incorrectly marked as 'd' in the 1971 English version.)

(666–71) Jung describes the eight types as 'Galtonesque family portraits' – that is, they are stereotypes. He notes that closer investigation reveals an auxiliary function. Combining the two (dominant and auxiliary) produces 16 types. The unconscious functions are grouped in a corresponding pattern. The value of the auxiliary is that it acts as a stepping stone in development. Developing the inferior function straight out of the unconscious is usually doomed to fail because it is too great a violation of the conscious attitude. It is more practical for development to go via the auxiliary first.

XI – Definitions

(672–844) The definitions chapter occupies 80 pages but, as we discovered in Chapter 2 of the present book, it does not make easy reading because Jung makes extensive use of cross references. During the course of the present book, we have examined those concepts that are most relevant to the theme of one-sidedness, using various examples and metaphors. Therefore, there is no need for further discussion of the definitions here.

Epilogue

The epilogue implicitly addresses the conflicts between the theories of Freud and Adler, and between their followers.

(845–50) Individual philosophers have derived their philosophy from their personal psychological premises, and many people recognise and share their views. They attack standpoints that are different, without achieving anything, because they are unable to accept any point of view other than their own. They are prisoners of their types, seeing only their own psychology. They need to stop abusing their opponents. The two sides can understand each other only if they recognise the diversity of psychological premises. In a one-sided perspective, we only see the psychological theory that chimes with our own type.

(851–53) There is a uniformity of the psyche within the collective unconscious, as shown by the similarities of myths across diverse cultures. But, in consciousness, there can be considerable diversity if individual conscious attitudes are differentiated from the uniformity of the unconscious. Therefore, the focus needs to be shifted from the (reductive) explanation of where an attitude has come from to the (constructive) goal of individual differentiation.

222   Appendix B: *Psychological Types*

(854–57) To think that there is only one explanation in psychology is problematic. There is a plurality of theories that involve paradox and contradiction. Although there is a strong human need for convenient answers, we need to understand the world from opposing points of view. Through the cooperation between opposites, we will be able to construct a perspective that is a higher synthesis.

Appendices

A contribution to Psychological Types (1913)

(858–82) There are four papers in the appendices. The first is a lecture given in 1913. The content is significant from a historical point of view; it shows a stage of development in Jung's thinking. It also shows some of the sources Jung was drawing on, most of which became the subject of a chapter in *Psychological Types.*

Psychological Types (1923)

(883–95) The second paper is a lecture from 1923 that focuses on Jung's categories of one-sidedness. They are of value because, to use a criterion to understand other people, one needs a broad, objective framework. It needs to be used on oneself, first, to develop self-awareness. Otherwise, our judgment of others only reveals how our own psyche works. There are three broad categories – extraversion, introversion, and a third group in between, which is the largest.

(896–98) Type differentiation begins in childhood and can lead to conflict between people or symbiosis between marriage partners. It is usual for there to be an increase in psychological understanding in marriage relationships, but this is often through some form of conflict which both parties are prepared to face and overcome.

(899–912) Ideally, all four functions should be given equal value. In practice, there is usually one function that occupies the foreground. This produces a type, which is a form of one-sidedness that is compensated by unconscious functions that have the opposite orientation, or by dreams. Unconscious functions are outside the control of the will and fused with other elements of the psyche. This compensation is not a conflict, so long as the one-sidedness is not too great. If it is too one-sided, the conscious attitude needs to change, to overcome the interpersonal or intrapersonal opposition. But this can be difficult because consciousness already sees its own attitude as an ideal. This principle applies not only to psychological differences but also to general views of life and the world.

(913–14) The categories of one-sidedness in Jung's scheme do not focus on extraversion and introversion alone, for these orientations combine with the functions to produce eight function-attitudes. The list could be expanded further by breaking each type down into three subdivisions. For example, intuition could be intellectual, emotional, or sensory.

A psychological theory of types (1931)

(915–59) The third appendix is a lecture given in 1928 to a group of psychiatrists. It was published in 1931 and incorporated into *Modern Man in Search of a Soul* in 1933. It is primarily a retrospective summary of how he developed his theory of types, and an overview that is geared towards clinicians.

Psychological typology (1936)

(960–87) The final paper is another retrospective of the development of the theory, and an overview of the main types.

References

Jung, C.G. (1913). 'A contribution to psychological types'. In *CW6*.
Jung, C.G. (1920). 'Foreword to the first Swiss edition'. In *CW6*.
Jung, C.G. (1921). *CW6*.
Jung, C.G. (1934). 'Foreword to the Argentine edition'. In *CW6*.
Jung, C.G. (1937). 'Foreword to the seventh Swiss edition'. In *CW6*.
Jung, C.G. (1949). 'Foreword to the eighth Swiss edition'. In *CW6*.

Index

abstraction 7, 123–24, 145, 171; in *CW6* 207, 218

Adams, Gerry 33, 44

adaptation 22, 27, 116, 124; in *CW6* 218–19

adjustment 74; in *CW6* 219

Adler, Alfred *see* Freud, Sigmund

aesthetics 100, 186–87; in *CW6* 206, 209–10, 213, 218

aggregation, psychic 34, 37–40, 72, 83–88

Ahern, Bertie 33, 41

alchemy xxii, 40, 92–96, 106, 119–20, 132; myth of 161–62; *see also* axiom of Maria; caduceus; Zosimos

altered states of consciousness 151

ambiguity 17, 86, 93, 99, 128

amplification 157

analogies 9; alchemy xxii, 92, 98, 162; archaeology 76; army commander 24–27, 139, 176; barbershop quartet 73–74, 88; basketball 125–26; beating heart 21, 202, 216; beaver dam 37; boat xix–xx; Bollingen tower 104; building site excavation 117; cartography 8; caterpillar 6; cityscape 134–35; colour green 168–69; compass 81; computer image 23–24; criminal 114; elephant and rider 101; elevator rescue 126; frameworks 179–80; gorilla 125–26; hammer and anvil 27; hand fan 169; hologram 169; iceberg xx; jigsaw 111–14, 123, 182; keel 61; ladybird 49; landmarks 81; magnets 10; medical 83; Newton's third law 37; physical energy 56, 214; pinhole projector 132; prisoner in a room xix, 168; railway bridge 210; restaurant 74–75; scaffold 29; see-saw 187; stepping stone 29; strategy and tactics 25; tidal bore 82, 85, 87; undercurrents xx, 63

analytical psychology xxi; and one-sidedness 45, 150–71

antimony 94–95

antinomy 6

apartheid 51–52, 54–55, 70, 123, 140

Apollonian and Dionysian 186–87; in *CW6* 209–10

Aquinas, Thomas 100

archetypes xx, 22–23, 83, 109, 153–56; *see also* hero; parents; self

art 21, 44, 62, 93, 157; in *CW6* 210, 218; psychological vs visionary 62–63, 101–2

attitude xviii–xix, xxi, 15–23, 139–46; symbolic 104–5; in *CW6* 219–21; *see also* one-sidedness

auxiliary 24–25, 115, 118–19; in *CW6* 221

axiom of Maria 42–44, 122–36; flexibility of attitude 44–45, 139–47; life theme 181

barbarism 18, 28, 43, 152; in *CW6* 206–7, 210, 214

Beebe, John 118, 154, 156, 180–81

Behemoth 64–66, 69, 195–98

Bennet, Angelina 131

brain xix, 8, 101, 150, 181

Brexit 141–47

Briggs, Katharine Cook xvi, 4, 8

Buddhism 186; in *CW6* 212, 215, 218

caduceus 40–41, 92–93, 107, 122, 127, 186

Campbell, Joseph 158–59

Capulet 14–17, 20, 22, 25–28; motivations 99; projections 76–77, 79, 154

caterpillar 65–67, 163, 200

centroversion 118, 163–64
checkershadow 170
Chuckle Brothers 33, 36, 127
circumambulation 111, 185
civility xix, 62, 70, 186–87
classification 2–5
Clinton, Bill 108
Clinton, Hillary 86–87
collectivity 20, 23, 38–40, 72–73, 133,
    171; in Brexit 142–47; in *CW6* 206–14;
    typology as 3, 48, 80–81, 175, 178, 218;
    see also differentiation; groups;
    participation mystique; psychic
    epidemics; unconscious, collective
compensation 61–62, 66, 69, 157, 177; in
    CW6 202–7, 212–13, 220, 222
complexes 77, 83–87, 154, 164
concretism 58, 77, 87
coniunctio 106–16, 154, 163, 182–84
conscience 28, 63–70, 191–99; in *CW6*
    212–13
consciousness xix–xx; advancement 40,
    92–93; collective 72–73, 78; in *CW6*
    206; *see also* ego
culture xx; East vs West 152; Eastern
    128–29, 208, 213; Western 1–3, 18, 24,
    68, 141, 181–83; in *CW6* 218
CW6 see Psychological Types

dialectic xviii–xix, xxi, 27, 108–9, 117,
    131, 156, 158, 175–77
differentiation 2–3, 22, 62, 109–13,
    118–20, 123; in *CW6* 203, 206–8; *see
    also* culture; one-sidedness
Dionysian *see* Apollonian and Dionysian
disaster 2, 14, 56, 66–69, 107; in *CW6* 213
divinity 64–66, 100, 107, 163, 196–97; in
    CW6 212–16
dominant 25, 66, 117, 119, 154; in *CW6*
    205–7, 209, 211, 217
dreams 75–76, 132, 153, 156–58, 177,
    199; in *CW6* 210, 222

Eastwood, Clint 128–29
ego xix–xx, 25–27, 73, 76, 151, 157;
    development 117, 131–36; split with
    unconscious 34–35, 38, 69, 88, 115; in
    CW6 205, 212, 218; *see also* hero
ego-self axis xxi, 154–56
enactment 166
enantiodromia 66, 68–69, 157; in *CW6*
    213, 217

Epimetheus *see Prometheus and
    Epimetheus*
epistemology 60, 153, 187–88; *see also
    esse in anima*
esse in anima 153, 167–71; in *CW6* 202,
    204–5
evil *see* good vs evil
extraversion and introversion xix, 18,
    20–27, 60–66, 115, 118; in *CW6*
    202–14, 217–22

fantasy 44, 57, 126, 158; in *CW6* 205,
    208–9, 214; *see also* art, psychological
    vs visionary; myth
Farage, Nigel 141, 145
Faust 103, 213, 215
fMRI 101, 150
Freud, Anna 82–83
Freud, Sigmund xxii, 1, 61, 67, 133, 180;
    conflict with Alfred Adler 7, 18, 20, 29,
    60; in *CW6* 201, 205, 221
functions, typological 19–27, 81, 109–20,
    123–24, 154–56, 185; in *CW6* 202–14,
    218–22; *see also* auxiliary; dominant;
    inferior; tertiary; transcendent

Galton, Francis *see* stereotypes
Gandhi, Mahatma 51, 82
Goethe, Johann Wolfgang von 21, 67–68,
    103, 146; in *CW6* 207, 210–16
good vs evil 15, 28–29, 35–43, 128–129,
    162–65; in *CW6* 213
Good Friday Agreement 32–33, 35, 44,
    140
groups 18, 72, 79–89, 136; *see also*
    aggregation, psychic

hero 15, 154, 158–59, 162–66, 171; in
    CW6 216; *see also* archetypes
Hiero 64–65, 195, 197; *see also* Messias

identity 37, 50, 56, 136; based on type 3,
    29, 81, 184–85; in *CW6* 207, 218; *see
    also* participation mystique
Ignatius of Loyola 151
imagination *see* fantasy
imitation 78–79, 144
individuation xxi, 2–4, 24–27, 70, 81,
    115–20; vs individualism 175; in *CW6*
    209–10
inferior 24, 27, 106, 117–19, 154–56,
    184–85; in *CW6* 205–9, 218, 220–21

inflation 114
instinct *see* archetypes
introversion *see* extraversion and
 introversion
Iraq 164–66
Irish Republican Army (IRA) 9, 33–36,
 39, 41, 43
Islam 86, 93, 141, 165
isms 20, 37

James, William 18, 168; in *CW6* 201, 218
jewel, Pandora's 67–69, 107, 157, 163–64;
 in *CW6* 212–13, 216–17; *see also*
 Prometheus and Epimetheus, summary
journalism 84
Jungian analysis xxi, 74–75, 115, 157–58,
 178, 180–81

Kant, Immanuel 167–68

leadership 34, 38–40, 80, 82, 143; as
 heroic 23, 166; *see also* Freud,
 Sigmund, conflict with Alfred Adler;
 Mandela, Nelson; Mugabe, Robert;
 Trump, Donald
Leviathan *see* Behemoth
libido, canalisation 37, 56, 67; in *CW6*
 208, 213–16

McGuinness, Martin 33, 35–36, 38, 127;
 see also Chuckle Brothers
Mandela, Nelson 49–57, 129–34, 136,
 139–40
Maslow, Abraham 132
maturity 132–35, 182–83, 186, 219
Messias 66, 107, 116–17, 163, 178; *see*
 also Prometheus and Epimetheus,
 summary
metaphors *see* analogies
midlife 113, 117, 155, 181–85
Mugabe, Robert 49–51, 53–54, 133–34,
 171
Myers, Isabel Briggs xvi, xxiii, 4–5, 8–9,
 24
Myers-Briggs Type Indicator (MBTI) xxi,
 4–5, 8, 178–79, 183
Myers-Briggs typology xxi, 5–8, 11, 58,
 67, 175; criticisms 29, 179–80; *see also*
 ego, development; functions, typological
mysticism xxii, 5–6, 93, 95, 131–32
myth 6, 45, 157–66; in *CW6* 212–17, 221;
 see also art, psychological vs visionary

Mythos *see* Hiero

negative borderline concept 73, 167–68
Neumann, Erich 118, 162–64
neurosis 70, 84, 114, 182
Nietzsche, Friedrich 110, 186–87; in *CW6*
 201, 209–10, 213
normality 21, 37, 64, 157, 164, 177; in
 CW6 217; *see also* stages of life
numbers 130, 163
numinosity 55, 68–69, 102, 113

one-sidedness xviii, 1–11, 15–29, 49–51,
 150–71; in *CW6* 201–14, 218–22; *see*
 also attitude; differentiation
opponents 29, 41, 49–50, 53, 88, 108; in
 CW6 221
opposites 37, 60–62; tension of 36, 44, 66,
 116, 125–27, 184–85; *see also*
 differentiation; one-sidedness; type, as a
 problem

Paisley, Ian 32–33, 35–36, 38–39, 41, 43,
 127
Pandora *see* jewel, Pandora's
parents xx, 22, 77–78, 83–84, 153–54; *see*
 also archetypes
participation mystique 78–79, 87, 143–44;
 in *CW6* 203, 206, 209, 218
Pauli, Wolfgang 60, 96, 168
persona 20, 22, 116, 128, 179, 187; in
 CW6 211
philosophy *see* epistemology
play 41–42, 44, 157, 208
politics xviii–xix, 29, 80, 107–9, 136; *see*
 also Brexit; Iraq; Mandela, Nelson;
 Paisley, Ian; UNESCO
Popper, Karl 160–61
Principe, Lawrence 93–104, 162
projection 16, 37–40, 43, 77–80, 109–10,
 113–15; in *CW6* 203, 209
projective identification 23, 154, 176
Prometheus and Epimetheus 62–70,
 106–7, 115–16, 163; summary 64–65,
 191–200
pseudo-Democritus 95
psychic epidemics 83–88
psychoanalysis xxii, 8, 83; *see also* Freud,
 Sigmund
Psychological Types xxii, 2–11, 201–23;
 translations 2, 7, 63
psychotherapy *see* Jungian analysis

quantum physics 8, 168
quaternity 45, 119–20, 130

regression 41–42, 92, 125, 127, 132
religion 69–70, 152–53, 167, 187; in *CW6* 202, 208–9, 213–17; vs science 140–41, 160
repression xx, 17, 21, 42, 134, 187; in *CW6* 205, 208, 212, 215–16, 220; *see also* projection
retirement 124, 184

Schiller, Friedrich 31, 59, 61, 81, 106, 135; in *CW6* 201, 205–10
Schmid, Marie-Jeanne 4
Schmid-Guisan, Hans 116
Schopenhauer, Arthur 110, 210
Schwartz-Salant, Nathan 130
science 93–96, 159–61; in *CW6* 205; *see also* religion, vs science
Scruton, Roger 167–68
self xviii, 73, 112–13, 150, 185–86; archetypes; *see also* ego-self axis
self-correcting 68; *see also* compensation
self-knowledge 57, 58, 87, 166, 182, 187–88; in *CW6* 222
self-transformation 93–94, 130, 164
separatio 106–16, 123, 163, 182–84
shadow 39, 112, 116, 182; in *CW6* 211
social identity theory 79
socialisation 74
spine of the personality 154–56
Spitteler, Carl *see Prometheus and Epimetheus*
Spoto, Angelo 155–56, 181
Springboks 56, 127
stages of life 182–84
standpoint *see* attitude
Stein, Murray 106, 113, 123
stereotypes 80–81, 179, 184; in *CW6* 205, 221
sublimation 97, 133–34
suggestibility 79–80, 87
symbiosis 39, 165; in *CW6* 222

symbols 36, 48, 55–56, 104–5, 126–27; in *CW6* 212–17; *see also* dreams; jewel, Pandora's; libido, canalisation; Messias

tertiary 24, 155, 185
third way 108; in *CW6* 202, 204
transcendent 66, 88–89, 106–7, 118–19, 126–27; in *CW6* 208, 216–17; in politics 35–36, 48–56, 136; in typology 57–59, 150
transference 83–84; *see also* projection
treasure *see* jewel, Pandora's
triangulation 136
Trimble, David 9, 33–34, 36
Troubles, the 31–32, 39, 41
Trump, Donald 85–87
Truth and Reconciliation Commission (TRC) 54–55, 109
type 22; in Jung's work 3–4; as a problem 24–29; use by laypeople 1, 4, 7–8, 31, 181, 201; *see also* identity; Myers-Briggs typology

unconscious: collective xx, 22, 34, 38, 73–76, 116; in *CW6* 221; personal xx, 62, 73–76, 133; *see also* art, psychological vs visionary
UNESCO 82–83
United Kingdom Independence Party (UKIP) 141–42, 145–46

valency 144
viewpoint *see* attitude
von Franz, Marie-Louise 45, 118–19, 161–62, 180, 185

Weltanschauung 25–27, 45, 58, 112, 127, 160
Wheelwright, Joseph 185
worldview *see Weltanschauung*

yoga 151–52, 187–88

Zosimos 97–99, 102–4